POPULATION BOMBED!

Exploding the Link Between Overpopulation and Climate Change

POPULATION BOMBED!

Exploding the Link Between Overpopulation and Climate Change

Pierre Desrochers and Joanna Szurmak

GWPF

ISBN 978-0-9931190-3-3

Set in Minion.
Cover illustration by David Gifford.

Printed by Createspace.
Published by The Global Warming Policy Foundation.

Contents

List of Figures

List of Tables

About the authors

Pierre Desrochers is an Associate Professor of Geography at the University of Toronto. His main research interests are economic development, technical innovation, business-environment interface, and energy policy and food policy. He has published over 50 academic articles on these and other subjects in a wide range of academic disciplines. Desrochers has been the recipient of several awards for his work on environmental policy issues, including the 2017 Julian L. Simon Memorial Award (Competitive Enterprise Institute). He is the author of over 200 columns on a variety of subjects in major international media including the *Wall Street Journal* and *Le Monde*. He is the author of *The Locavore's Dilemma: In Praise of the 10,000-mile Diet*, arguably the broadest case made on behalf of the economic, social and environmental virtues of the modern agri-business and transportation industries. His website is at http://geog.utm.utoronto.ca/desrochers/.

Joanna Szurmak is a doctoral student at York University's Department of Science and Technology Studies. She is also a research services librarian at the University of Toronto Mississauga, where she works with the Psychology and Anthropology departments and the Robotics program. She holds graduate degrees in electrical engineering and information studies from the University of Toronto and has worked in research labs, the Canadian telecommunications industry, and other university libraries both in Canada and in the USA. Szurmak has published in engineering, information studies and interdisciplinary academic journals. Her website is at http://sites.utm.utoronto.ca/szurmak/.

Authors' note

This book was originally conceived as a policy paper whose scope was limited to what is now Chapter 2. Reading the recent literature on population control and climate change while simultaneously delving into the background of both debates, however, convinced us of the necessity for a broader and more in-depth treatment. The result, while as concise as we could make it, attempts to weave together the historical and present-day narratives into a coherent whole of evidence and commentary.

Some of the ideas in this book are developments of our earlier work. The first subsection in Chapter 4 is largely based on Desrochers and Shimizu (2016); Desrochers (2010) and Desrochers and Reed (2008). The section on coal gas residuals in the same chapter is based on Desrochers (2009). The consideration of the erosion scare in Section 5.3 is adapted from Desrochers and Hoffbauer (2009).

Our first thanks go to Benny Peiser, the director of the Global Warming Policy Foundation, who, when confronted with a much larger manuscript than he had bargained for, enthusiastically became our book publisher. The text also benefitted greatly from the editing skills and patience of Andrew Montford, both of which he possesses in epic proportions.

Over the years, we have read the work of several specialists and commentators and discussed the various topics covered in this book with a wide range of individuals. Most of these influences can be found in our bibliography. Our special thanks, however, extend to Robert L. Bradley Jr of the Institute for Energy Research whose historical scholarship and efforts to keep the legacy of the late Julian L. Simon alive deserve unqualified praise.

Summary

Background

Many scholars, writers, activists and policy-makers have linked growth in population to environmental degradation, especially catastrophic climate change. They argue that:

- A more numerous and increasingly affluent population creates a growing demand for resources of all kinds. This increased demand requires increased combustion of fossil fuels.
- Burning ever larger quantities of these fuels (coal, petroleum and natural gas) increases atmospheric carbon dioxide concentrations to levels said to cause catastrophic global warming.
- Because having fewer children is the best way for people to reduce their overall environmental impact, curbing population growth is the most effective way to prevent dangerous climate change.

In the words of business magnate Ted Turner:

> We have global warming because too many people are using too much stuff. If there were less [sic] people, they'd be using less stuff.

In the last few years, however, a number of writers and academics have documented significant improvements in human wellbeing, resource availability and the general state of our environment (see, for instance, Steven Pinker's *Enlightenment Now: The Case for Reason, Science, Humanism, and Progress* (2018c) and the Roslings' (2018) *Factfulness: Ten Reasons We're Wrong About the World and Why Things Are Better Than You Think*). Among other incontrovertible facts, these writers have shown that:

- people the world over live longer and healthier lives, and are wealthier and better educated than ever before;
- despite increased consumption, reserves of scarce and non-renewable resources such as petroleum are more abundant than they have ever been;

- in advanced economies, the air and water quality are better than they have been in centuries, while in many parts of the world, including many developing economies, the forest cover has expanded significantly over recent decades.

While eager to highlight positive trends, however, optimistic writers rarely argue systematically for the spontaneous market processes that made these trends possible.

Distinctive contribution

This book is an attempt to present a relatively concise case for the environmental benefits of economic development, population growth and the use of carbon fuels.

- It explains how, paradoxically, economic prosperity and a cleaner environment are the direct results of both population growth and humanity's increased use of fossil fuels. Today's positive outcomes would have been impossible without them.
- It argues that while the predicted catastrophic impacts of climate change remain still largely uncertain, and in need of open scholarly debate instead of rigid consensus, the ongoing campaigns to reduce or constrain the development of fossil fuel use in the absence of truly affordable and electric-grid-friendly alternatives guarantee several negative outcomes:
    - a large death toll in developing economies;
    - a growing number of economically vulnerable people being pushed into energy poverty in advanced economies;
    - an alarming trend of replacing products ultimately extracted from underground (for instance, synthetic products derived from fossil fuels) with resources that are produced *on* the ground (for instance, renewable but unsustainable products made from plants and animals), a process that can result in widespread damage to ecosystems.

The distinctive features of this book are:

- Its comprehensive historical coverage of:
    - the long-standing debate between people who fear the economic and environmental impacts of population growth and those who believe that, in the context of market economies, more people are more hands to work and more brains to innovate, not merely more mouths to feed;

  - how fossil-fuel-derived products alleviate environmental pressures by replacing resources extracted from the biosphere by resources extracted from below the ground.
- Its insight into why looking at human population growth as though it were similar to that of any other species (for instance, bacteria in a test tube full of food) is profoundly misleading and mistaken. In the book, we highlight that, unique among other species, modern humans transmit information and knowledge between individuals and through time, innovate by combining existing things in new ways, and engage in long-distance trade, thus achieving, to a degree, a decoupling from local limits.
- Its detailed discussion of why, even after two centuries of evidence refuting the pessimistic narrative on population growth, resource availability and environmental impact, that viewpoint still dominates academic and popular debates. The issues the book examines range from financial incentives among academics and activists to behavioural insights into why well-meaning people are unable to change their mind when confronted by contrary evidence.

Key arguments

The introduction shows how prominent individuals (including Hillary Clinton, Al Gore and Bill Gates) have linked climate change to population growth and called for population control policies.

Chapter 2 summarizes the key historical arguments for and against population growth and their links to environmental health, resource depletion, and economic development. Pessimists believe that:

- In a finite world, continued demographic and economic expansion is impossible.
- Everything else being equal, a reduced population will enjoy a higher standard of living.
- Decreasing returns will always apply to natural resource use. In a world where resources are finite, the cream will always be skimmed first and developing more remote mineral deposits or less fertile lands will become increasingly more expensive and more environmentally damaging.
- Technological innovation and synthetic products cannot do away with the need for natural resources. Manufactured substitutes, including fossil fuel based ones, such as plastics, cannot extend the Earth's finite capacity to supply the needs of human beings. Population control must be given priority: reducing humanity's drain on natural resources is the only way to avert catastrophe.

- Past successes in overcoming natural limits are irrelevant to present conditions. Every generation believes that a new global environmental catastrophe changes everything and warrants severe constraints on population and economic growth.

Optimists believe that:

- A larger population that engages in trade and the division of labor will create more prosperity, per person, than fewer people working alone. A larger, denser population creates economies of scale that make both resource use and human labor more efficient and productive.
- Human creativity delivers increasing returns. Human beings routinely come up with progressively less damaging ways of doing things that increase the efficiency of agriculture, resource extraction, industry, transportation and communications.
- Human standards of living are not completely constrained by local resources. Biological metaphors and ecological concepts such as carrying capacity do not apply to economic systems because of trade, innovation, and ongoing optimization of resource use.
- Past successes are grounds for optimism. Of the 7.6 billion people now alive, fewer live in abject poverty than ever before; nature is rebounding despite larger and wealthier populations.

Chapter 3 compares the predictions made by pessimists and optimists over the last two centuries. The evidence is clear: the pessimists have been repeatedly and decisively proven wrong, often sooner rather than later. In market economies people have became more numerous, healthier and wealthier while resources have become more abundant than ever. In advanced economies the environment is cleaner than it has been in centuries while in the most prosperous developing economies similar positive trends are beginning to emerge. The pessimists have only been proven right in the context of centrally planned communist and socialist economies where people have become poorer and the environment increasingly worse over time.

Chapter 4 explains how positive results were achieved spontaneously via market activities and humanity's increasing use of fossil fuels. The key processes behind these trends are:

- *Increased efficiency:* Creative individuals have every incentive to save resources by developing processes that generate more or better outputs using fewer inputs.
- *Resource creation:* When reserves of key resources start to run low, their prices increase. This automatically encourages people to use the resource

more efficiently, but also to look for more of it and to develop more efficient and plentiful substitutes.

- *Transformation of waste into valuable by-products:* Far from rewarding wasteful behaviour, such as polluting the environment, the profit motive has always encouraged people to create lucrative by-products out of waste materials.

These processes are discussed in detail through a number of historical developments, showcasing their key environmental benefit: the replacement of resources extracted from the surface of the planet (for instance, fuelwood, lumber, rubber trees, wool, indigo plants, whale oil, animal labor) by resources that ultimately originated from below (for instance, transportation and heating fuels; plastics; synthetic rubber, fabrics and dyes).

Chapter 5 demonstrates that the main pessimistic intellectual frameworks ('IPAT', ecological footprint and planetary boundaries) have significant conceptual flaws. Alleged negative future outcomes, along with extreme climate change scenarios, are built into their assumptions. Instead of objective actual evidence of environmental harm, they reiterate these assumptions in a circular fashion, playing the role of axioms or tautologies, not unbiased scientific practices. Furthermore, population control advocates take for granted both the unique benefits of fossils fuels and of large population numbers while downplaying or being blissfully unaware of the full costs and implications of their policy recommendations.

Chapter 6 is a reflection on why, after two centuries of repeating the same arguments and being proven wrong, population control activists and sustainable development theorists remain wedded to a demonstrably false worldview and are unwilling to address anything more than a simplistic caricature of their opponents' case. We use evidence from behavioural science, political science, sociology and economics to show how even demonstrably false worldviews become entrenched intellectual positions. We examine the self-preservation mechanisms behind the survival of the iron triangle, we delve into the consequences of confirmation bias and motivated scepticism, and we dissect disciplinary mindsets. In addition, we offer a discussion of the limits and promises of scientific research and publication, highlighting how all the cognitive practices and biases may shape, and in the end distort, a scientist's motivation to gather and disseminate knowledge, to the point of turning it into an elitist's yearning to control and condemn.

In our conclusion we reiterate our case for both population growth and fossil fuel-powered economic development as the only practical way, now and in the near future, to lift much of humanity out of poverty, to build resilience against any downsides of increased anthropogenic greenhouse gas emissions, and to make possible a sustained reduction of humanity's impact on its environment.

In the educator's reaction to this fundamental problem of economics, he is bound, indeed, to favor every wise measure for the conscious control of population. Students of population and the means of subsistence do not hesitate to tell us that the problem is becoming continuously more acute... [The educator] should not fail... to oppose the idea that restriction of population is sinful or anti-social. The development of constructive eugenic policies, negative or positive, does not lie within the province of education; but the educational ideal cannot be achieved in a society that has not learned to control its own numbers in view of the means available for maintaining its chosen standards of living.

Henry Wyman Holmes, 1924. 'The new social order as seen from the standpoint of education.[1]

Let's begin with the strange reflexive loop that historians of the environment have recently insisted upon: to speak of ecology now is to repeat almost word for word what was said in 1970, in 1950, or even in 1855 or in 1760 to protest against the damage inflicted on nature by industrialization. This theme has been looping back and forth since the very beginnings of the industrial revolution.

Bruno Latour, 2017. 'The Anthropocene and the destruction of the globe.[2]

The 'population problem' has a Phoenix-like existence: it rises from the ashes at least every generation and sometimes every decade or so. The prophecies are usually the same – namely, that human beings are populating the Earth in 'unprecedented numbers' and 'devouring' its resources like a locust plague.

Murray Bookchin, 1994. The population myth.[3]

1 Introduction

Gender equality consultant Suzanne Petroni observed nearly a decade ago that many people believed 'that linking population growth to the issue of climate change will help to place family planning back into the political realm as an urgent matter of national and environmental security.'[4] A few months before, physicist John Harte and his biologist wife Mary Ellen Harte had published a short book entitled *Cool the Earth, Save the Economy*, in which they argued that 'one of the underlying causes of global warming, as well as all other environmental problems that we face, is human overpopulation of our planet' because it fuels 'a growing global demand for energy, a demand met by an ever-increasing combustion of fossil fuels that, in turn, increase atmospheric carbon dioxide levels.' Anticipating accusations by critics that their stance was built upon an 'underlying dislike of people,' they insisted they cared 'enough about the unborn, the future generations' so as to not leave them a 'world devastated from overuse by too many people.'[5]

Not long afterwards, a 2009 entry in *Scientific American*'s 'Earth Talk' blog warned readers that 'human population growth is a major contributor to global warming, given that humans use fossil fuels to power their increasingly mechanized lifestyles' and that the unavoidable carbon dioxide emissions created as a result of this process 'trap warm air inside [the atmosphere] like a greenhouse.'[6] Quoting a report of the Global Population and Environment Program of the Sierra Club, the blogger added: 'Population, global warming and consumption patterns are inextricably linked in their collective global environmental impact' and that, as 'developing countries' contribution to global emissions grows, population size and growth rates will become significant factors in magnifying the impacts of global warming.' This argument was also endorsed by the Worldwatch Institute, according to which the 'overriding challenges facing our global civilization are to curtail climate change and slow population growth.'[7] At about the same time, Colorado State University philosopher Philip Cafaro began to publish a series of books and papers on the theme of overpopulation and climate change, arguing that 'improvements in energy and carbon efficiency have been overwhelmed by increases in population and economic output' and that just 'as population growth is an important cause of global climate change, ending population growth could play a big part in solving the problem.'[8]

Since then, the idea that effective attempts to address climate change must involve population control – and that population control in itself is insufficient if overall mass consumption keeps increasing[9] – has become a new form of what author Greg Easterbrook calls 'collapse anxiety,' which he defined as a 'widespread feeling that the prosperity [of the developed world] cannot really be enjoyed because the Western lifestyle may crash owing to economic breakdown, environmental damage, resource exhaustion…or some other imposed calamity.'[10] Citing a 2018 *New York Times* column[11] on how climate change impacts couples' decisions to have children, population control advocates at the British charity Population Matters viewed increased coverage of this subject as part of a 'growing discussion surrounding climate change, the impact our growing global population has on it and how family size can help mitigate its effects.'[12] In the United States, the founders of Conceivable Future feared the 'life-threatening environmental and health impacts intensified by greenhouse gas pollution' and described the climate crisis as a 'reproductive justice crisis.'[13] The website of Negative Population Growth warned that averting 'disastrous climate change and global warming' requires that we 'first address the problem of world population size and growth, and its impact on the size of the greenhouse gas emissions that cause global warming. That means that we need to address the population size and growth of each nation, which together make up the world total.'[14] Recently, feminist icon Gloria Steinem argued that 'what causes climate deprivation is population. If we had not been systematically forcing women to have children they don't want or can't care for over the 500 years of patriarchy, we wouldn't have the climate problems that we have.'[15]

In the most publicized academic contribution to the topic, Johns Hopkins University's philosopher Travis N. Rieder argued that children are an environmental externality that puts 'irreparable stress on the planet' in an age of 'competition for scarce resources, huge disparities of wealth and poverty, and unsustainable practices.' Taking as given some of the most extreme climate scenarios, Rieder was concerned that 'each new person we create exacerbates global resource shortages and the threat of catastrophic climate change.'[16] His policy recommendations include 'carrots for the poor and sticks for the rich:' incentives to reduce family size that range from covering the cost of birth control methods to a progressive and income-based carbon tax on children.[17]

In 2015 biologist and author of the 1968 best-seller *The Population Bomb* Paul Ehrlich, arguably the best-known scientist turned prophet of doom, and a man with a long-standing track record of blaming virtually all of humanity's problems on population growth, scolded Pope Francis for 'overlook[ing] a crucial incompatibility at the heart of the climate change problem: marrying shared and sustainable development with demographic growth,' a stance that required 'curbing over-consumption and humane transitioning to a much reduced and thus sustainable population.'[18] Even more consistent, however, is the Voluntary Human Extinction Movement (VHEMT), which has equated planetary health with not just limiting but eradicating human population;[19] it defines its mission as '[p]hasing out the human race by voluntarily ceasing to breed.'[20] This, in turn, 'will allow Earth's biosphere to return to good health. Crowded conditions and resource shortages will improve as we become less dense.'[21]

Population control as a means of confronting climate change has also gained considerable momentum among business leaders and the global governance elite. Among important movers and shakers, no one described this stance more concisely than business magnate Ted Turner in a 2008 interview: 'We have global warming because too many people are using too much stuff. If there were less [sic] people, they'd be using less stuff.'[22] The following year then American Secretary of State Hillary Clinton found it 'rather odd to talk about climate change and what we must do to stop and prevent the ill effects without talking about population and family planning.'[23] Speaking at the 2014 World Economic Forum meetings in Davos (Switzerland), former American Vice-President Al Gore observed 'how population growth has exacerbated climate change' and called for 'voluntary measures to lower birth-rates across the globe.'[24] Sharing the stage with Gore, Microsoft founder Bill Gates 'made a pitch for birth control as a way to reduce excess population that generates pollution, which in turn creates unusual weather events.'[25] In January 2018, John Podesta, chair of Hillary Clinton's 2016 presidential campaign, counselor to President Barack Obama and member of the UN secretary general's high-level panel on the post-2015 development agenda, along with Tim Wirth, a former US senator and past president of the United Nations Foundation with a long-standing interest and legislative track record on both climate change and population control issues, penned an opinion piece in the *Washington Post* titled 'Women's rights issues are climate change issues.'[26] Summarizing the work of academic researchers according to whom 'slowing population growth can enhance economic outcomes and reduce emissions simultaneously,'[27] Podesta and Wirth argued that 'forging a coalition between the environmental movement and the women's rights movement will not only fundamentally advance women's rights but also do a world of good for the planet, which is bearing an environmental burden because of population growth.'[28]

While the linkage between population growth and climate change is of relatively recent vintage (although, as will be discussed in Chapter 5, not as recent as many writers believe), the notion that more people to provide for can only result in environmental armageddon and that human actions are negatively impacting the climate have long dominated the thinking of numerous activists, scientists and policymakers (who have been repeatedly proven wrong by their intellectual opponents and later developments).[29]

To quote an aphorism of the mathematician and philosopher Alfred North Whitehead, at the nexus of economic development, population growth and environmental degradation, '[e]verything of importance has been said before by somebody who did not discover it.'[30]

Because we believe this history is crucial to our case we have structured our book as follows.

In Chapter 2 we will present the key arguments for and against population growth and economic development – endeavours that utilize the earth's resources – and their linkage to environmental health and depletion. We make a deliberate effort to illustrate that the same ideas about resources, development, environment and population have been reborn – or, perhaps, recycled – every generation, and that turning to population control as a means of addressing ongoing environmental woes has been the standard (knee-jerk) reaction. We then assess, in Chapter 3, the validity of past conflicting claims regarding the relationship between population growth, development, resource use and the state of the environment, illustrating that, time and again, later developments have supported the optimistic perspective.

In Chapter 4 we explain how a significantly larger human population came to enjoy a higher standard of living while improving the state of its environment. This counterintuitive outcome arose as a result of the globalization of human economic activities and its ever more minute division of labour, which in turn made possible a near endless stream of technological advances that delivered more efficient use of a broader range of materials and the development of valuable by-products out of polluting production residuals. These processes are further illustrated with more detailed case studies of past carbon fuel developments. By using these fuels increasingly more efficiently, humanity ascended the energy ladder into a world of steam power, mass electrification, advanced materials, high-speed travel and communications, sanitation, domestic refrigeration, and instant communications, in the process reducing both human pressures on biodiversity and polluting emissions.

In Chapter 5 we discuss the main intellectual frameworks now invoked by environmental pessimists. We illustrate that alleged negative (and typically future) outcomes are built into the assumptions of these frameworks rather than being supported by credible evidence. This is followed by a more detailed discussion of the old rhetoric and shortcomings of the recent literature on climate change and population growth. Our key argument is that present-day population control theorists and activists take for granted both the unique benefits of carbon-fueled economic development and large population numbers while downplaying or being blissfully unaware of the full costs and implications of their policy recommendations. They also invoke extreme and unlikely climate change scenarios to justify their stances. We assert that, far from ruining the planet, additional economic development, carbon fuel use and a lack of coercively imposed restraint on population growth are humanity's only proven paths to sustainable development.

In Chapter 6 we reflect on why it is that, after two centuries of repeating the same arguments and being proven wrong every generation, population control activists and, more recently, sustainable development theorists remain wedded to a failed paradigm and unwilling to address anything more than a simplistic caricature of their opponents' case.

Because the prosecution's case against population growth and carbon fuels is presented on a nearly daily basis, we feel that a balanced debate is more important than a balanced book. Our goal is to articulate a case for both population growth and carbon-fuel-powered economic development as the means to lift much of humanity out of poverty, to build resilience against any possible downside increased anthropogenic greenhouse gas emissions might have, and to make possible a sustained reduction of humanity's impact on the biosphere. The distinctive feature of our approach is its broad historical coverage, illustrating that much recent thinking is often nothing more than a repackaging of long-debunked arguments and lack of appreciation of the typical outcome of spontaneous market processes. Although it should go without saying, human beings long ago evolved unique survival strategies through which they stopped behaving and impacting the environment like other life forms. Instead, they channeled their unique ability to trade and to innovate in an increasingly globalized market economy, a process that resulted in both wealth creation and reduced environmental impact. Given the right incentives and freedom of choice in key matters such as reproduction, people have long proven they can achieve prosperity and happiness for themselves and their children while improving the state of their surroundings.

2 Conflicting perspectives on population growth, resources and the environment

2.1 Conflicting discourses

There have long been two main perspectives on the relationship between humans and nature.[31] One argues that we can and should reshape the natural world for our own benefit. The other is that humanity should live within natural limits and that failing to do so will result in considerable harm.[32] These conflicting visions were recently restated by the philosopher Alex Epstein in the context of fossil fuel use when he asked his readers whether our goal should be to maximize human flourishing or to minimize human impacts.[33]

Before we flesh out these perspectives, it is useful to introduce the specialist and popular names given to each of them. These names are not mere labels: they distil truths about the key ideas, assumptions and long-term orientations of these viewpoints. The ecological economics and environmental policy expert John S. Dryzek went as far as to call these perspectives 'discourses,'[34] which means they are coherent storylines in which agents and actors have relationships with each other, fulfill certain roles and play out behaviours described with a stable set of metaphors or rhetorical devices. Dryzek identified the population-limiting perspective championed by Rieder, Ehrlich, Gore and others as the *survivalism* discourse, which tells 'a story about the need to curb ever-growing human demands on the life-support capacities of natural systems.'[35]

Its counterpart is the *cornucopian* or *Promethean* discourse, in which it is said that 'Prometheans have unlimited confidence in the ability of humans and their technologies to overcome any problems – including environmental problems.'[36]

More recently, in his book on the work of two champions of these opposing visions – William Vogt and Norman Borlaug – science writer Charles C. Mann observed that:

> Both Borlaug and Vogt thought of themselves as environmentalists facing a planetary crisis... But that is where the similarity ends. To Borlaug, human ingenuity was the solution to our problems... Vogt's views were the opposite: the solution, he said, is to get smaller... The burden on Earth's ecosystems would be lighter.[37]

To Mann, the terms survivalism, Prometheanism and cornucopianism did not resonate as strongly as new terms he coined:

> I think of the adherents of these two perspectives as Wizards and Prophets – *Wizards* unveiling technological fixes, *Prophets* decrying the consequences of our heedlessness. Borlaug has become a model for the Wizards. Vogt was in many ways the founder of the modern-day Prophets.[38]

Having many terms from which to choose, we decided to settle on perhaps the most readily recognizable ones found in, among others, geographer Judith Rees' work:[39] *pessimists* to denote the survivalists, the Prophets, and the doomsayers,[40] and (market) *optimists* to describe the Prometheans, the cornucopians, the Wizards and the doomslayers. Rees elegantly defined her names for the two discourses as follows: 'While the pessimistic school concentrated on the limits inherent in a closed, fixed physical system, the optimists argued that the market system, purposeful technological innovation and social change would act together to solve all scarcity problems.'[41] At the core of each of these discourses were, and are, not just names, assumptions and facts, but deeply held values.[42]

Table 2.1 shows a summary of common names for the two discourses, along with published sources in which the rationale for using them is made more explicit.[43] Some terms, such as *resourceship* and *depletionism*, are in our opinion more accurate, but are confined to a small subset of specialist literature.

Historical overview

As the chemist and geographer Daniel B. Luten observed on the eve of the famous 1980 Julian Simon–Paul Ehrlich wager,[44] since the late 18th century 'the question of limits to growth and optimism and pessimism regarding the human prospect [has been] debated without consensus' while interest in the issue has 'waxed and waned more times than can be counted.'[45] The British economist Alfred Marshall commented more generally almost a century earlier that if the 'study of the growth of population is often spoken of as though it were a modern one,' it has 'in a more or less vague form... occupied the attention of thoughtful men in all ages of the world.'[46] This perspective was shared by economists

Table 2.1: Names for the two opposing discourses.

Pessimist discourse	Optimist discourse
Survivalism	Prometheanism, cornucopianism
Dryzek (2005) *The Politics of the Earth*	Dryzek (2005) *The Politics of the Earth*
Pessimism	Market optimism
Rees (1985) *Natural Resources*	Rees (1985) *Natural Resources*
	Rational optimism
	Robinson (2009) *The Case for Rational Optimism* Ridley (2010) *The Rational Optimist*
Depletionism	Resourceship
Furedi (2010) 'A depletionist view of history and humanity'	Bradley Jr (2007) 'Resourceship: an Austrian theory of mineral resources'
Prophet	Wizard
Mann (2018c) *The Wizard and the Prophet*	Mann (2018c) *The Wizard and the Prophet*
Doomsayer	Doomslayer
Moore and White (2016) *Fueling Freedom*	Moore and White (2016) *Fueling Freedom*

Source: Compiled by the authors. Full details of the publications can be found in the bibliography.

Harold J. Barnett and Chandler Morse, who wrote that 'Man's relationship to the natural environment, and nature's influence upon the course and quality of human life, are among the oldest topics of speculation of which we are aware. Myth, folktale, and fable; custom, institution, and law; philosophy, science and technology – all, as far back as records extend, attest to an abiding interest in these concerns.'[47]

In his 1949 discussion of the then 'current scare' of 'the race between population and food supply,' the American agricultural economist Merrill K. Bennett identified four periods of intense interest in these questions in the English-speaking world.[48] The first followed the publication of Thomas Robert Malthus' *An Essay on the Principle of Population* in 1798.[49] A century later, the industrial rise of Germany, its accompanying population growth and increased demand for resources coupled with temporary shortages and a high price for wheat, re-ignited old fears. The years leading to and the immediate aftermaths of the two World Wars similarly saw several commentators link geopolitical tensions and demographic and economic pressures. Needless to say, several individuals and organizations did their best to generate interest in the topic outside of these time periods by linking it to other policy concerns such as immigration,[50] eugenics, and environmental preservation.[51] In the end though, policy and popular concerns about overpopulation arguably reached a high point at the turn of the 1970s.[52] Table 2.2 shows influential books on both sides of the debate published in the English-speaking world during the decades leading to the 1970s.

In 1973, the sociologist Martha E. Gimenez wrote that it was fashionable 'to argue that excessive population growth stands in the way of economic growth and that underdeveloped countries should take measures to reduce their rates of natural increase.' Indeed, population growth then appeared to be 'THE major factor determining underdevelopment and population control...advocated as the most urgent and necessary step if development is to be eventually achieved' (capitalization in original text). In developed countries a range of 'pressing problems such as urban blight, crime, pollution, environmental deterioration, etc.' were similarly said to 'have greater possibilities of being satisfactorily solved [sic] if population growth were to be curtailed.'[53]

A Hobbesian ethos in the study of human population issues surfaced at the time, its language not just borrowing from long-standing historical, social and demographic debates, but drawing on new terminology from population biology and resource economics.[54] Along with other analysts, John S. Dryzek[55] correlated the emergence of this language with the following four events: the publication of biologist Garrett Hardin's 1968 essay 'The tragedy of the commons,'[56] the near-simultaneous appearance of Paul and Anne Ehrlich's *The Population Bomb*,[57] the 1972 publication of the Club of Rome's *The Limits to Growth*,[58] and the 1973 energy crisis, then widely blamed on a sudden 'oil embargo organized by the Organization for Petroleum Exporting Countries'[59] that further dramatized the doomsday prophesying about the bleak future of humanity. 'Combined with economic growth,' Dryzek argued, 'a population explosion was going to exhaust stocks of energy, cropland, clean water, minerals, and the assimilative capacity of the atmosphere and oceans.'[60]

These fears eventually receded as, without any significant societal and eco-

Table 2.2: Significant semi-popular English books on population growth, human welfare and environmental impact, 1933–1981.

Pessimists	**Optimists**
Burch and Pendell (1947) *Population Roads to Peace or War*	Zimmermann (1933) *World Resources and Industries*
Vogt (1948) *Road to Survival*	Mather (1944) *Enough and to Spare*
Osborn Jr (1948) *Our Plundered Planet*	Hanson (1949) *New Worlds Emerging*
Cook (1951) *Human Fertility*	De Castro (1946/1951) *The Geography of Hunger*
Brown (1954) *The Challenge of Man's Future*	Barnett and Morse (1963) *Scarcity and Growth*
Sax (1955) *Standing Room Only*	Maddox (1972) *The Doomsday Syndrome*
Paddock and Paddock (1967) *Famine 1975!*	Beckerman (1974) *In Defence of Economic Growth*
Ehrlich (1968) *The Population Bomb*	Clark (1975) *Population Growth*
Meadows *et al.* (1972) *Limits to Growth*	Kahn *et al.* (1976) *The Next 200 Years*
Editors of The Ecologist (1972) *Blueprint for Survival*	Simon (1981) *The Ultimate Resource*
Ward and Dubos (1972) *Only One Earth*	

Source: Compiled by the authors. Full details of the publications can be found in the bibliography. For other such books published in the 1950s, see Barnett and Morse (1963, pp. 30–33). For mentions and occasional discussions of additional 1960s and 1970s popular publications, see Welch and Miewald (1983). For a comprehensive list of free-market environmentalist books published between the 1970s and the early 2000s, see Appendix 1 in Jacques *et al.* (2008).

nomic change other than greater trade liberalization and deregulation in the energy sector, environmental collapse failed to materialize, fertility rates fell to or below replacement level in most parts of the developed world and freer markets, together with technological advances, simultaneously delivered higher standards of living, more abundant resources and environmental remediation.[61] Reactions against coercive policies such as compulsory sterilizations and abortions in less advanced economies, increasingly strident denunciations of the anti-immigration stance of prominent environmental organizations and concerns about a 'baby bust' in industrialized countries[62] further pushed the topic off the policy agenda. By the late 1980s global warming had superseded overpopulation as the dominant environmental concern of most environmental activists, scientists, policy makers and celebrities.[63]

Outline of the debate

Perhaps the most memorable summary of the population–resources debate is the economist Kenneth Boulding's 1955 rhymed encapsulation entitled *Man's March to 'The Summit'*.[64]

Man's March to 'The Summit'

A conservationist's lament
The world is finite, resources are scarce,
Things are bad and will be worse.
Coal is burned and gas exploded,
Forests cut and soils eroded.
Wells are dry and air's polluted,
Dust is blowing, trees uprooted,
Oil is going, ores depleted,
Drains receive what is excreted.
Land is sinking, seas are rising,
Man is far too enterprising.
Fire will rage with Man to fan it,
Soon we'll have a plundered planet.
People breed like fertile rabbits,
People have disgusting habits.

Moral:
The evolutionary plan
Went astray by evolving Man.

The technologist's reply
Man's potential is quite terrific,
You can't go back to the Neolithic.
The cream is there for us to skim it,
Knowledge is power, and the sky's the limit.
Every mouth has hands to feed it,
Food is found when people need it.
All we need is found in granite
Once we have the men to plan it.
Yeast and algae give us meat,
Soil is almost obsolete.
Men can grow to pastures greener
Till all the earth is Pasadena.

Moral:
Man's a nuisance, Man's a crackpot.
But only Man can hit the jackpot.

Kenneth Boulding, 1955

Another stark contrast is between the 'Major findings and conclusions' of the *Global 2000 Report to the President* produced at the request of the Carter administration and the rebuttal penned shortly thereafter by the free-market economist Julian Simon and futurist Herman Kahn. The authors of *Global 2000*, which was characterized by Dryzek as 'a gloomy report for a gloomy presidency,'[65] summarized their findings as follows:

> If present trends continue, the world in 2000 will be more crowded, more polluted, less stable ecologically, and more vulnerable to disruption than the world we live in now. Serious stresses involving population, resources, and environment are clearly visible ahead. Despite greater material output, the world's people will be poorer in many ways than they are today. For hundreds of millions of the desperately poor, the outlook for food and other necessities of life will be no better. For many it will be worse. Barring revolutionary advances in technology, life for most people on earth will be more precarious in 2000 than it is now – unless the nations of the world act decisively to alter current trends.[66]

Simon and Kahn rewrote this passage in light of their own analysis and conclusions:

> If present trends continue, the world in 2000 will be less crowded (though more populated), less polluted, more stable ecologically, and less vulnerable to resource-supply disruption than the world we live in now. Stresses involving population, resources, and environment will be less in the future than now... The world's people will be richer in most ways than they are today... The outlook for food and other necessities of life will be better... life for most people on earth will be less precarious economically than it is now.[67]

Of course, as Simon observed in another comment on *Global 2000*, he was 'not saying that all is well now' and did 'not promise that all will be rosy in the future.' Indeed, he readily acknowledged that '[c]hildren are hungry and sick; people live lives of physical and intellectual poverty, and lack of opportunity; some new pollution may indeed do us all in. What I am saying is that, for most or all of the relevant matters I have checked, the trends are positive rather than negative.' He further doubted 'that it does the troubled people of the world any good to say falsely that things are getting worse though they are really getting better. The believing hearer of such false bad news may simply despair, or later yield to cynicism about all social problems when he or she senses having been conned yet again. False bad news is a very real social pollution, and a dangerous one.'[68] In a free society, Simon argued, the 'most important aspect of the relevant historical experience is that humans use their imaginative and creative powers to change their situation when caught in a resource bind, and the final result is usually that we are left better off than before the problem arose.'[69]

What follows is a more detailed summary of the most relevant points made by contributors to this debate.

2.2 Pessimists

Historical perspective

Sociologist and demographer George Martine summed up the pessimistic perspective by arguing that, '[w]hatever one's starting point,' the 'threat to global environmental security posed by this vastly growing population simply cannot be dismissed. Practically any possible environmental challenge facing humankind today, from ozone depletion to waste disposal, is made more difficult by a larger population size.'[70] Declining fertility rates attributable to economic development, he argued, remain problematic for 'while it is clear that fertility decline is absolutely essential for sustainability in the long term, it is only the starting point for more effective measures addressing [growing] consumption.'[71] Douglas Ashmead, a Scottish business entrepreneur and *bon vivant* who enjoyed elite sports such as yachting, became an unlikely proponent of natural environmental limits and population control in 1997.[72] His short book *Standing Room Only* got right to the point:

> It seems abundantly clear that if we continue to ignore the population problem, the outcome could be cataclysmic for mankind – because if we leave things too long, it will simply be too late to rectify the consequences. In the animal kingdom, of which we are part, when populations reach resource limitations they experience a crash in numbers with the attendant horrors inescapably linked to such a fall. Better to take prudent steps now and be proven wrong than to take none and find out too late that we should have taken action earlier.[73]

Writers such as John S. Dryzek typically argue that analysis 'which anticipates misery, starvation, and death resulting from unconstrained human procreation and consumption, and that sees the main political challenge as ensuring some level of human survival at an adequate level of amenity is not new. It goes back to William Forster Lloyd (1794–1852) and, more famously, Thomas Malthus (1766–1834), widely reviled as the "dismal parson".'[74] In truth, however, these basic concerns are as old as civilization. For instance, in the Atrahasis epic, written nearly four millennia ago, Babylonian gods deem the earth too crowded and unleash plagues, famine, droughts and a gigantic flood to address the problem, thus making it 'perhaps the earliest extant account of human overpopulation and the earliest interpretation of catastrophes as a response to overpopulation.'[75] Confucius (551–479 BC) and some of his followers argued that excessive population growth may reduce output per worker, lower standards of living and create strife.[76] Some ancient Indian writings similarly showed 'profound appreciation of the problems of food and populations'[77] while Plato (427–347 BC) warned that 'exceed[ing] the limit of necessity' and the 'unlimited accumulation of wealth' would trigger expansionary wars, especially in light of the populace's fondness for meat, which would result in struggles over pastureland. Interestingly, his solution was a vegetarian diet.[78] Writing half a millennium later, the Carthaginian Christian theologian Tertullian observed that:

> [What] most frequently meets our view (and occasions complaint), is our teeming population: our numbers are burdensome to the world, which can hardly supply us from its natural elements; our wants grow more and more keen, and our complaints more bitter in all mouths, while Nature fails in affording us her usual sustenance. In very deed, pestilence, and famine, and wars, and earthquakes have to be regarded as a remedy for nations, as the means of pruning the luxuriance of the human race...[79]

Over a century and a half later, another important figure in the early Church, Saint Jerome, commented that 'the world is...full, and the population is too large for the soil,'[80] a problem he believed best addressed through the creation of monasteries.

The first true population catastrophist theorist is generally acknowledged to be the Italian Giovanni Botero (1540–1617) who, two centuries before another lapsed Catholic cleric, Giammaria Ortes (1713–1790) and the better-known Malthus, argued that human population would increase to the maximum extent permitted by human fertility, that the means of subsistence wouldn't keep up, and that the unavoidable result would be poverty, starvation, war, diseases and population crashes.[81] For his part, Malthus is best remembered for arguing in the first edition of his essay that, in a world where food production grows arithmetically and population – when unrestrained – grows geometrically, mass want and population crashes are unavoidable.[82]

According to Dryzek's analysis of the four horsemen of survivalism, biologist Garrett Hardin and the authors associated with the Club of Rome 1972 report made additions to the discourse that were more significant than merely modernizing the metaphors of the pessimistic perspective. Thus while Hardin combined the earlier ideas of William Forster Lloyd with a standard resource economics analysis already employed since the 1950s, he also had 'the good sense to give the analysis a catchy name, publish in the large-circulation journal *Science*, refrain from graphs and algebra, and put it out just as the widespread perception of environmental crisis hit for the first time.'[83] Additionally, Hardin made the idea of the ecological crisis personal by translating hitherto private acts of human consumption, choice, and even procreation into ethical decisions affecting the entire earth, and the future of the human race. Dryzek captured it succinctly: 'So each decision maker... is facing essentially the same decision: private benefit and the public interests point in opposite directions. Hardin made a connection to childbearing decisions: if the world is a commons, each additional child adds stress to the commons, even though calculations of private interest determine that the child should be conceived, born, and raised.'[84] In this manner, Hardin's argument solidified both the environmental and the population debate agendas of the 1970s around the big-picture ideas that environmental limits were real, and that individual level 'concern about the environment was not just desirable, but also necessary.'[85]

The 1972 *The Limits to Growth* study, sponsored by the Club of Rome, accomplished a different epistemic feat. The initial founders and backers of the Club were industrialists and academics 'keen to show that industrialism itself might be unsustainable.'[86] They commissioned a team of computer modeling specialists, albeit with a business background, to run:

> simulations over a hundred years or more into the future of predicted pathways of key aggregates, which interacted with one another through a host of interrelated variables. The key aggregates were resources, population, industrial output, food supply, and pollution. (Critics quickly pointed out the absence of technology and prices.) All variables were measured at the global level. The predictions varied somewhat depending on assumptions... but given postulated limits to resource availability, agricultural productivity, and the capacity of the ecosphere to assimilate pollution, some limit was generally hit within a hundred years, leading to the collapse of industrial society and its population. The policy prescription was obvious: humanity needed to change its profligate ways if it was to avoid the apocalypse of overshoot and collapse.[87]

The genius of *The Limits to Growth* report was not its outcome, articulated by many over the centuries, but its novel method of conferring the trappings of objectivity and infallibility to the time-honoured belief in humanity's inevitable suicide. MIT modellers wrote the code and programmed the day's supercomputers that then generated the results based on machine calculations. This process could be described as independent from human passions and subjective judgements, relying instead on 'the calm authority symbolized by a computer and the experts who could run it.'[88]

The late 1970s through the 1990s saw a number of ideological and scholarly developments of the pessimist discourse. Arguably the main theme was the definition and refinement of global limits. While Paul and Anne Ehrlich kept writing, Lester Brown, the founder of the Worldwatch Institute, started publishing *State of the World* reports in 1984 to track how the world's systems, such as croplands, fisheries, grasslands and forests, were dealing with resource depletion.[89] Brown's novel contribution was the specific definition of the ecological limit his organization was tracking: 'the photosynthetic energy these systems can make available for human use... The challenge is to use photosynthetic energy more efficiently.'[90]

In academia, researchers such as Nicholas Georgescu-Roegen and Herman Daly started laying the foundation for the field of ecological economics.[91] In contrast to the earlier environmental and resource economics, ecological economics 'treats the environment not as an adjunct to the human economy, nor as a mere medium through which some human actions harm or benefit other humans. Instead, ecosystems are conceptualized as the fundamental entities within which human economic systems are embedded.'[92] As such, they are thought to have definite limits: 'Ecological economics treats natural systems as finite... [E]conomic growth sooner or later must encounter the environment's carrying capacity.'[93] Daly theorized about the economic steady state – without increasing inputs, outputs and growth – an idea originally put forward by the classical economist John Stuart Mill over a century earlier.[94] Georgescu-Roegen posited that real scarcity is that of low-entropy systems and materials exemplified by highly organized structures such as fossil fuels. Human interference and exploitation of these systems disordered them and increased their entropy, forever shifting the state of the universe. Increased human population meant more human exploitation, hence more unproductive randomness.

Since many theorists within the pessimist discourse had backgrounds in biology, their prescriptions rarely included much appreciation for spontaneously evolved market processes. Indeed, most veered towards some forms of authoritarianism – for example top-down planning and coercive schemas – for, if one believed like Hardin that 'freedom in the commons brings ruin to all,'[95] then curtailing personal freedoms, including the freedom to reproduce, was nothing short of an absolute necessity. Indeed, in his classic *On Liberty*, John Stuart Mill justified state intervention by arguing that 'in a country either over-peopled, or threatened with being so, to produce children, beyond a very small number, with the effect of reducing the reward of labour by their competition, is a serious offense against all who live by the remuneration of their labour.'[96] This mindset has prevailed ever since among pessimists such as economist Robert Heilbroner and political scientist William Ophuls who emphasized the necessity of putting an elite class of experts in charge of centrally managing scarce resources through the use of tools such as permits and quotas. Even Lester Brown, usually a proponent of individual and grassroots action, called for a stronger United Nations to force the hand of local governments whenever they appeared insufficiently resolute on population control issues.[97] The big battles – and they were perceived as such – of pessimist survivalism were to be fought by the experts, not the masses.

Hardin, the Ehrlichs, the Meadows, Ward, Brown, Daly and other theorists and academics were not operating in an institutional vacuum. In the period after World War II, population control activists re-purposed or created a number of national and international non-governmental organizations (NGOs) to spread and implement their message.[98] These efforts, however, built on a prior legacy. As economist Jacqueline Kasun and others have documented, eugenicists, whose movement had been discredited by Nazism, regrouped, 'renaming their organizations, forming new ones, and, above all, burrowing into the councils of power.'[99] By the early 1960s, she argued, their movement had re-emerged as, for example, the Campaign to Check the Population Explosion, and managed to 'capture the imagination of the mass media' and in this way influence public policy.[100] The progressive journalist Allan Chase similarly observed over four decades ago:

> The postwar population explosion hysteria initiated by Guy Irving Burch and Elmer Pendell in 1945, injected by Burch and Vogt into the body of Fairfield Osborn's benignly intentioned books on natural conservation, and carried to full intellectual fruition by the Paddocks, Ehrlich and Hardin, succeeded far beyond the wildest hopes of the oldtime eugenicists who started it all. Out of it came not only mass movements, such as Zero Population Growth, Inc., with chapters of active members in many American cities, but also new causes for older conservationist societies, such as the venerable Sierra Club.[101]

Up until the mid-1960s, American population control programs, both at home and abroad, were largely funded and implemented by private organizations such as the Population Council and Planned Parenthood that were themselves primarily funded by private foundations, such as Ford, Rockefeller, and Milbank. At that point in time, however, population control activists had managed to gather enough political support to get the US Congress to appropriate much larger sums for both domestic and international initiatives, some spent through USAID, but others funnelled through arms-length organizations and agencies such as the UN Fund for Population Activities (UNFPA). Numerous other governments throughout the world also supported these and other bureaucracies and funded NGOs that promoted and/or implemented population control policies through a variety of means.[102] Among individuals who stood out in this transition are American President Lyndon B Johnson who, arguably more than any other, enticed the government of Indira Gandhi to implement coercive population control measures in India, and Robert McNamara who, upon being appointed President of the World Bank, made 'loans to Third World countries contingent upon their governments' submission to population control, with yearly sterilization quotas set by World Bank experts.'[103]

We now turn to a more detailed overview of the main overpopulation arguments put forward by pessimistic writers.

Key arguments

Pessimists have long argued that, if not checked by voluntary or coercive means, a population tends to outgrow its limited supply of food and natural resources, resulting in famine and societal collapse. Writers in this tradition have typically invoked some version of the following arguments:

Continued growth in a finite system is unsustainable

> In a finite world, continued demographic and economic expansion is impossible.

In the early sixteenth century, Niccolo Machiavelli observed that 'when every province of the world so teems with inhabitants that they can neither subsist where they are nor remove elsewhere, every region being equally crowded and over-peopled,' and when 'human craft and wickedness have reached their highest pitch,' the world would purge itself through floods, plagues, and famines so that men, 'becoming few and contrite, may amend their lives and live with more convenience.'[104]

Nearly two centuries and a half later, Danish cleric Otto Diederich Lütken similarly commented that:

> Since the circumference of the globe is given and does not expand with the increased number of its inhabitants, and as travel to other planets thought to be inhabitable has not yet been invented; since the earth's fertility cannot be extended beyond a given point, and since human nature will presumably remain unchanged, so that a given number will hereafter require the same quantity of the fruits of the earth for their support as now, and as their rations cannot be arbitrarily reduced, it follows that the proposition 'that the world's inhabitants will be happier, the greater their number' cannot be maintained, for as soon as the number exceeds that which our planet with all its wealth of land and water can support, they must needs starve one another out, not to mention other necessarily attendant inconveniences, to with, a lack of the other comforts of life, wool, flax, timber, fuel, and so on. But the wise Creator who commanded men in the beginning to be fruitful and multiply, did not intend, since He set

> limits to their habitation and sustenance, that multiplication should continue without limit.[105]

In 1886, the former Methodist minister and birth control activist Joseph Symes wrote that, 'no matter how large the country', in the absence of deliberate efforts to the contrary 'the land will be over-stocked with people,' the food supply 'too scanty' and 'even standing room will soon be wanting.' What was true of any country was 'equally true of the world at large, the raft to which we cling in the boundless ocean of space.'[106] A generation later, the eugenicist Edward Isaacson argued that 'the time must come when the countries which now export food will be filled up to the point where they will need all they produce for themselves, and can no longer supply the over-populated countries at any price.'[107] Although emigration had acted as a safety valve in the past, this could only be done 'so long as there is a place for it; but what then?'[108] His solution, echoing John Stuart Mill, was a steady state of economic development in which 'population must be kept down to the numbers which [over-populated countries'] land with the best management can support.'[109]

In 1971, Paul R. Ehrlich and future Director of the White House Office of Science and Technology Policy John Holdren argued that as a 'population of organisms grows in a finite environment, sooner or later it will encounter a resource limit.' This environmental carrying capacity, they added, 'applies to bacteria on a culture dish, to fruit flies in a jar of agar, and to buffalo on a prairie. It must also apply to man on this finite planet.'[110] Soon afterwards, the economist Kenneth Boulding observed that 'Anyone who believes exponential growth can go on forever in a finite world is either a madman or an economist.'[111] Boulding, of course, is perhaps best remembered by environmental activists for popularizing the 'Spaceship Earth' metaphor, which he interpreted as implying that not only economic growth can have negative impacts on the environment, but must of necessity do so – and probably more so in the future.[112]

Today, activists at Negative Population Growth deride the notion of 'perpetual growth' as a solution to social and economic problems as a 'mathematical absurdity on a finite planet' on which there 'must be limits.' In their opinion, '[s]cience is demonstrating that human population and consumption in the United States and the world are already too large and are destroying the natural systems that support us.' 'We must not simply stop population growth,' they conclude, 'we must turn it around.'[113]

Everything else being equal, a reduced population will enjoy a higher standard of living.

> In a world where resources are finite, the biggest slices of pie get cut at

> the least-crowded tables; the more mouths to feed, the less food for each mouth.

While he admitted that the inhabitants of a country 'depopulated by violent causes' such as wars would 'probably live in severe want,' Malthus suggested that population reduction without destruction of the capital stock (say, the aftermath of an epidemic disease) would benefit the remaining inhabitants as they could 'cultivate principally the more fertile parts of their territory' and not have to cultivate more marginal lands.[114]

A decade ago, the economist Gregory Clark similarly observed that in England '1.5 million people died prematurely in 1349. In return 6 generations got to live very well with little further excess deaths. And then 1.5 million people got to live longer as the plague weakened its grip in the sixteenth century, and the population returned to its earlier level. The unlucky generation of 1349 was counterbalanced by the lucky generations of 1540–1620. God smiled on the English when he delivered the plague!'[115]

Writing in 1879, Edward Henry Stanley, the fifteenth Earl of Derby and a prominent British public officer and politician, commented somewhat more moderately that 'it is better to have thirty-five millions of human beings leading useful and intelligent lives, rather than forty millions struggling painfully for a bare subsistence.'[116]

In 1948 ornithologist and population control activist William Vogt observed in his *Road to Survival* – the biggest environmental best-seller of all time until the publication of Rachel Carson's *Silent Spring* in 1962 – that 'drastic measures are inescapable' in light of worldwide environmental destruction. 'Above all else,' he wrote, 'we must reorganize our thinking,' especially 'all thought of living unto ourselves' for, in a 'direct, physical sense,' humanity forms 'an earth-company, and the lot of the Indiana farmer can no longer be isolated from that of the Bantu.' As he saw it, an 'eroding hillside in Mexico or Yugoslavia affects the living standard and probability of survival of the American people. Irresponsible breeding makes amelioration of the conditions of the Greek – or the Italians or Indians or Chinese – difficult, if not impossible; it imposes a drain on the world's wealth...when this wealth might be used to improve living standards and survival chances for less people.'[117]

A common variation on this theme was expressed five decades ago by Paul Ehrlich who conceded that, in the unlikely case his radical population reduction stance was wrong but the policies it inspired proved successful, 'people will still be better fed, better housed and happier.'[118] A few years later, the chairman of Republican President Richard Nixon's Commission on Population Growth and the American Future, John D. Rockefeller III, would report:

> After two years of concentrated effort, we have concluded that, in the long run, no substantial benefits will result from further growth of the Nation's population, rather that the gradual stabilization of our population through voluntary means would contribute significantly to the Nation's ability to solve its problems. We have looked for, and have not found, any convincing economic argument for continued population growth. The health of our country does not depend on it, nor does the vitality of business nor the welfare of the average person.[119]

Writing in 1976, prominent University of Wisconsin climatologist Reid A. Bryson said he 'was convinced that there is very little in the way of human ill, ecosystem degradation, resource shortage, social stress, and international instability that would not be relieved markedly by having fewer people on earth than there are currently.'[120] Echoing countless writers before him on the topic of 'extra mouths to feed,' Douglas Ashmead later commented [original emphasis]:

> This year, an *extra* 100 million babies will be born into the world: in other words, 275,000 extra mouths today, tomorrow, the day after that... Human numbers are spiralling out of control... And each addition needs food, clothing, and shelter. Only humans reproduce this way; the animal kingdom has more sense. While our numbers have doubled over the last 40 years, the number of animals in the wild has reduced by a factor of 4... We now vastly outnumber all other significant mammals, and we are probably the only unendangered species – assuming, of course, that we do not destroy ourselves... One hundred million extra mouths is equivalent to ten Calcuttas; think ten more Calcuttas each and every year.[121]

In his 'Final thoughts,' Ashmead argued for the primacy of population control among other policy options:

> So over-population is hardly the only problem. It is, however, relevant, specific and one that mankind can solve. To this extent it is unique and if it is not dealt with, many other global concerns could become even more massively insoluble and overwhelming than they are at present. If you want to reduce the threat of global warming, pollution of the great oceans or the cutting down of our forests, you cannot ignore their origin. Yes, rising economic expectation and activity has to be addressed, but so too has the question of population numbers – and this issue above all must be placed center-stage.[122]

Today, as in the past, media, academic and business celebrities add their voices to the radical population-control chorus. Prominent broadcaster David Attenborough has thus 'never seen a problem that wouldn't be easier to solve with fewer people, or harder, and ultimately impossible, with more.'[123] Primatologist Jane Goodall expressed the belief that 'population growth... underlies just about every single one of the problems that we've inflicted on the planet.'[124] Another prominent British environmentalist, Jonathon Porritt, is getting increasingly frustrated by the fact that most people 'just don't understand how every single one of their hopes and aspirations for the future of humankind are rendered entirely null and void by the inability/refusal of humankind to address the challenge of restricting further population growth.'[125] Even head of computational science at Microsoft Research (Cambridge, UK) Stephen Emmott stated that 'cleverness and inventiveness are now the sources of all the global problems we face today – and those problems are only going to intensify as our numbers continue to grow.'[126]

Decreasing returns to investment in natural resources result in lower standards of living.

> In a world where resources are finite, the cream will always be skimmed first. Extracting or producing valuable resources out of less concentrated and/or more remote ores or less fertile lands will become increasingly difficult, expensive and more environmentally damaging over time.

Because valuable natural resources such as land suitable for agriculture and mineral resources come in different grades and are found in more or less convenient locations, pessimistic writers have long made the case for unavoidable decreasing (or diminishing) returns to economic effort over time, the result being retardation and the eventual termination of economic growth.[127] This perspective is usually traced back to the second edition of Malthus' *Essay,* where he argued that making less productive parts of the landscape fit for agricultural production would require more time and labour than was previously necessary. As a result, the 'additions that could yearly be made to the former average produce must be gradually and regularly diminishing.'[128] This argument was endorsed by John Stuart Mill in his *Principles of Political Economy*:

> A greater number of people cannot, in any given state of civilization, be collectively so well provided for as a smaller. The niggardliness of nature, not the injustice of society, is the cause of the penalty attached to overpopulation. An unjust distribution of wealth does not aggravate the evil, but, at most, causes it to be somewhat earlier felt. It is in vain to say that all mouths which the increase of mankind calls into existence bring with them hands. The new mouths require as much food as the old ones, and the hands do not produce as much.[129]

Looking back at the writings of Mill and other classical economists, the historical demographer Edward A. Wrigley later explained why such a stance seemed logical in a pre-carbon-fuels economy:

> Any pre-industrial economy was obliged to accept certain limits to growth set by the fact that the land was almost the sole source not only of food but of the great bulk of the raw materials used in manufacture. Since land was in fixed supply, production could only be expanded by obtaining larger and larger outputs from each existing acre of farmland or by breaking in inferior land, but at some stage it seemed unavoidable that diminishing returns would take hold, making further expansion progressively more difficult and costly. All pre-industrial economies were therefore by definition subject to a form of negative feedback, unable to engender changes capable of securing rising real incomes for the mass of the population. As growth progressed, the obstacles to further growth grew ever more pressing. It was their appreciation of these constraints which led the classical economists to make use of the concept of the stationary state as a device to epitomize the nature of the limits to growth, and to disbelieve in the possibility of a radical and permanent upward movement in real wages.[130]

In 1951 Robert Carter Cook, a prominent American geneticist, demographer, and eugenicist, commented that the 'world's growing population will force the use of marginal lands, which in general are extremely expensive to exploit. More and more human energy will have to be devoted to the basic problem of producing food, and the standard of living, instead of going up, will remain at subsistence level in the areas where it now stands at that, while the wealthier areas will find their standards of living declining.' He added that '[s]ince Malthus's day, the problem has actually become more acute rather than less acute.'[131] Four decades later demographer John Bongaarts re-iterated this point:

> Agricultural expansion, however, will be costly, especially if global food production has to rise twofold or even threefold to accommodate the demand for better diets from several billion more people. The land now used for agriculture is generally of better quality than unused, potentially cultivable land. Similarly, existing irrigation systems have been built on the most favorable sites. And water is increasingly in short supply in many countries as the competition for that resource among households, industry and agriculture intensifies. Consequently, each new increase in food production is becoming more expensive to obtain. This is especially true if one considers environmental costs not reflected in the price of agricultural products.[132]

Needless to say, the argument has also long been applied to carbon fuels. In 1865 the economist William Stanley Jevons suggested in his classic *The Coal Question* that, over time, the price of this resource would become 'much higher than the highest price now paid for the finest kinds of coal' because the most 'cheaply and easily accessible' fields and seams would always be developed first.[133] A century and a half later, a study headed by Tad Patzek, then chairman of the Department of Petroleum and Geosystems Engineering at the University of Texas at Austin, announced imminent peak coal production because 'the world will finish off the coal that is easy to reach and high-quality – the coal that produces a large amount of energy per ton... What remains will often be of lower quality, and progressively harder to dig up and bring to where it is used.'[134]

In 1969 Paul Ehrlich and John Holdren claimed that '[t]oday the frontiers are gone, and the evidence is mounting that technology cannot hold the law of diminishing returns at bay much longer.' This was especially true with the 'rapacious depletion of our fossil fuels' then already forcing producers 'to consider more expensive mining techniques to gain access to lower-grade deposits.'[135] In the wake of the oil shock of 1973, Ehrlich and his wife Anne blamed rapidly rising oil prices on the fact that '[m]ost of the easily accessible sources of fossil fuels and mineral resources are long gone, and the rising prices reflect the necessity to dig deeper, travel farther, and refine lower-grade ore in order to obtain them.'[136] Indeed, 'a genuine world shortage of pumpable petroleum appear[ed] certain by the turn of the century if demand continue[d] to grow as it did in the 1960s.'[137] Economist Robert Heibroner similarly warned at the time about 'the prospect of a ceiling on industrial production, imposed by an inability to overcome the rapidly diminishing returns of a natural world that is being mined more voraciously each year.'[138]

Undaunted by the failure of his past forecasts, Paul Ehrlich again claimed in 2015 that '[h]uman beings are smart and pick the low-hanging fruit first: they farm the richest soils first, drink the cleanest and closest water first, and tap the shallowest pools of oil first. They exploit the resources that are cheapest and that generally result in the least environmental impact first.'[139] The result is that as 'more people consume more resources, humanity is left with poorer quality, more expensive resources, the exploitation of which causes more harm.'[140]

Technological innovation and synthetic products cannot be substituted for natural capital

> Technological developments, including the development of synthetic products, cannot stretch the earth's finite capacity to provide sufficient resources to human beings. They might even make things worse by laying the foundations for a greater environmental catastrophe. Population control must be given priority.[141]

Writing in 1948, conservationist and long-time president of the New York Zoological Society Henry Fairfield Osborn Jr insisted that 'technologists may outdo themselves in the creation of artificial substitutes for natural subsistence, and new areas, such as those in tropical or subtropical regions, may be adapted to human use, but even such recourses or developments cannot be expected to offset the present terrific attack upon the natural life-giving elements of the earth.'[142] In Osborn's words, the 'grand and ultimate illusion would be that man could provide a substitute for the elemental workings of nature.'[143] For instance, 'chemical fertilizers alone [could never] be thought of as substitutes for the natural processes that account for the fertility of the earth,' for in the long run 'life cannot be supported... by artificial processes.'[144]

William Vogt similarly considered agricultural mechanization 'of dubious value to the land, as it is more purely extractive than older methods' for one did 'not find a manure pile outside the tractor shed'; it brought lesser quality land under cultivation; it was too dependent on rapidly dwindling petroleum reserves; and it triggered a drift away from rural to urban areas, thereby reducing 'the effectiveness of the self-contained rural population as an economic shock absorber' during future recessions.[145]

The economist Robert Heilbroner wrote in 1974 that while in theory 'no insurmountable barrier to growth need arise from resource exhaustion for millennia to come' as humanity learned to exploit ever poorer resource deposits, this belief assumed both the development of new technologies and, 'more important yet... that the ecological side effects of extracting and processing the necessary vast quantities of rock or sea water would not be so deleterious as to rule out the new extraction technologies because of their environmental impact,' a problem he believed significant. Even worse, the massive amounts of energy required to achieve this result might in itself be incompatible with 'environmental safety.'[146]

In the prologue to his 1968 *Population Bomb*, Paul Ehrlich famously announced that '[t]he battle to feed all of humanity is over. In the 1970s the world will undergo famines – hundreds of millions of people are going to starve to death in spite of any crash programs embarked upon now.'[147] The following year he and John Holdren made a detailed case for population control over technological change as a possible way out of looming disaster. Beliefs in innovative solutions, they argued, 'misjudge the present severity of the situation, the disparate time scales on which technological progress and population growth operate, and the vast complexity of the problems beyond mere food production posed by population pressures.'[148] Even under the most optimistic assumptions 'technology is likely to remain inadequate until such time as the population growth rate is drastically reduced' because 'no effort to expand the carrying capacity of the earth can keep pace with unbridled population growth' and 'all the technology man can bring to bear will not fend off the misery to come.'[149]

Interestingly, in another piece published a year later, Ehrlich and Holdren discussed the first stages of what would later be known as South Asia's 'Green Revolution': the introduction of shorter and higher-yielding varieties of wheat and rice grown with additional use of irrigation water, fertilizers and pesticides. Ehrlich and Holdren suggested that cultivating 'the new varieties creates enlarged monocultures of plants with essentially unknown levels of resistance to disaster,' that 'one of the prices that is paid for higher yield is a higher risk of widespread catastrophe' and that 'these crops may ultimately contribute to the defeat of other environment-related panaceas.'[150] In the end, the 'contention of certain well-fed journalists that the 'Green Revolution' will keep food production ahead of population growth over the next few decades is patent nonsense – food production has hardly begun to catch up.'[151] Looking back on Ehrlich's predictions in 2003, journalist Gregg Easterbrook observed that 'India went from harvesting eleven million tons of wheat in the early 1960s to harvesting sixty million tons by the late 1990s, becoming self-sufficient in food production.'[152] Revisiting the topic nearly forty-five years after his original comments, Ehrlich acknowledged having underestimated the 'speed with which many poor-world farmers rapidly adopted the green revolution technology, avoiding massive die-offs from famine,' but that the result had been to 'lead... us into today's agricultural cul-de-sac that shows signs of leading to even greater misery.'[153]

Ehrlich and Holdren's pessimism never knew any bounds. In 1980 they denounced the belief that improving living standards sustainably 'could be realized without the services derived from largely unmanaged bio-geophysical processes.' As they saw things:

> Today such processes regulate climate and the availability of water, screen out harmful radiation from the sun, maintain soil fertility and the chemical quality of air and water, control most potential crop pests and agents and vectors of human disease, and maintain a library of genetic information uniquely useful for the protection of existing food crops and the development of new ones, the development of new drugs and vaccines, the development of new industrial materials, and the understanding of life itself. The intricacy and the immensity of these processes preclude replacing them or their services with technological substitutes on any interesting time scale.[154]

In 2008 the Ehrlichs stated once more that there 'is no technological change we can make that will permit growth in either human numbers or material affluence to continue to expand. In the face of this, the neglect of the intertwined issues of population and consumption is stunning.'[155]

Past successes in overcoming natural limits are irrelevant to present conditions.

> Historical successes in overcoming resource scarcity through long-distance trade, technological advances and substitutions are irrelevant because of new and drastically changed circumstances.

In a chapter devoted to the 'Opinions of Previous Writers' who had 'prematurely apprehended' a British coal shortage, Jevons dismissed the notion that any useful lesson could be learned from past mistaken forecasts. By 1865, he argued, better data on coal availability and rapidly rising consumption clearly pointed to a new reality.[156] At the turn of the twentieth century, Alfred Marshall absolved Malthus for not foreseeing 'the great developments of steam transport by land and by sea, which have enabled Englishmen of the present generation to obtain the products of the richest lands of the earth at comparatively small cost,'[157] for 'unless the checks on the growth of population in force at the end of the nineteenth century are on the whole increased... it will be impossible for the habits of comfort prevailing in Western Europe to spread themselves over the whole world and maintain themselves for many hundred years.'[158]

Similar thoughts on Malthus were written half a century later by two other prominent American pessimists, Robert Carter Cook and the geochemist and eugenicist Harrison Brown. As Cook put it, Malthus 'lived at the threshold of an age in which a profound revolution in the physical circumstances of Western life was to occur' in terms of new modes of transportation, the opening of new territories and scientific advances.[159] Unfortunately, 'the nineteenth-century refutation of the population crisis is still a part of most contemporary belief' and the 'man in the street sees no compelling reason to be apprehensive that the science which has served him so handsomely thus far will fail him in the future.' This perspective, however, was completely mistaken. Indeed, 'such a paradise is strictly for fools' and 'is not one which those who look straight at the fact can believe.' As Cook put it, the 'scientists who have made the closest study of the population problem believe it the least. In 1950 a panel of a dozen population experts, after on-the-scene checks of some of the world's most serious danger points, confirmed Malthus. The proposed 'cures' show no prospect of providing for those wants.'[160] For his part, Brown similarly excused the deficiencies of Malthus' extrapolation into the future as they:

> suffered not from lack of proper reasoning, but from lack of sufficient knowledge of the potentialities of technological development. He was in no position to foresee the enormous influence of the railroad and the steamship upon European populations. He was in no position to foresee that greatly increased numbers of Englishmen would be fed with Australian meat, Canadian wheat, butter from New Zealand, and sugar from the West Indies. He lacked sufficient knowledge to estimate correctly the effect of industrialization upon agricultural production. Further, he could not have foreseen the extent to which the changed way of life in an industrial age would result in drastically declining birthrates coupled with decreasing mortality. In short, the scientific knowledge of his time was too

> meager to permit his drawing valid quantitative conclusions, no matter how sound his reasoning was.[161]

In 1923 another distinguished American scientist and eugenicist, Edward Murray East, put forward the idea in his influential book *Mankind at the Crossroads* that the 'facts of population growth and the facts of agricultural economics point... severally to the definite conclusion that the world confronts the fulfillment of the Malthusian prediction here and now. Man stands to-day at the parting of the ways, with the choice of controlling his own destiny or of being tossed about until the end of time by the blind forces of the environment in which he finds himself.'[162]

There was no comfort in looking at past developments, he argued, as the 'present age is totally unlike any previous age' with inventions like the telephone, the telegraph, the steamboat, the locomotive and the motor-car, and thus with 'the modern opportunity either for personal migration or for exchange of goods.' Thanks to these advances, he wrote, 'the world as a whole is more of a single entity than were some of the smaller kingdoms of Europe in the fifteenth century,' and 'the pros and cons of fifty years ago are as obsolete as the spinning-wheel.'[163]

The problem, as he saw it, was that recent progress was for the most part attributable to the opening of new lands to modern agricultural production technologies, but that in short order decreasing returns in agricultural production would mean that '[f]ood exportation from the younger countries will sink rapidly, as it did in the United States during the decades before the [First World] war, so rapidly that overpopulated countries will have the greatest difficulty in adjusting themselves to the change.'[164]

A generation later, William Vogt argued that past beliefs in progress or admonitions to be fruitful and multiply could provide no useful guidance for the postwar era. Dominant ideas evolved twenty centuries ago, while 'magnificent in their days,' had now become 'millstones about [human] necks' and would most certainly turn out to be 'idiotic in an overpeopled, atomic age, with much of the world a shamble.'[165] Two decades later, in *The Population Bomb*, Paul Ehrlich wrote that '[n]othing could be more misleading to our children than our present affluent society. They will inherit a totally different world, a world in which the standards, politics, and economics of the past decade are dead.'[166]

In 2011 consultants at McKinsey admitted that '[o]ver the past century, progressively cheaper resources have underpinned global economic growth' and that although 'demand for resources such as energy, food, water, and materials grew, this was offset by expanded supply and increases in the productivity with which supply was used.' Today, however, this 'relatively benign picture has now changed' because the 'unprecedented pace and scale of economic development in emerging markets means demand for resources is surging, and prices for most resources have risen since the turn of the century.' As a result, '[r]esource price inflation – and volatility – could increase as new supplies of some resources become more expensive to extract, resource prices become more linked, and environmental spillover effects impact crop yields and the availability of water. These trends could fuel protectionism and political unrest.'[167]

Prescription

Coercive population control policy has a long history. In ancient times, many societies promoted or regulated contraception, abortion, infanticide, senicide and emigration.[168] Indeed, Aristotle (384–322 BC) justified abortion and exposing children to the elements because of fears that population growth could outstrip local resources.[169] Historically, many individuals also opposed famine relief, on the grounds it would only make a bad situation worse in the long run and prevent necessary social change, and also immigration, as it would allegedly lower the living conditions of the native population. The practical results of Malthusian thinking, as Catholic economist Charles Stanton Devas argued at the turn of the twentieth century, had 'been a grave discouragement to all works of social reform and humane legislation, which appeared as foolish sentiment defeating its kind aims by encouraging population.'[170] In the words of another critic, nineteenth century French mutualist theorist Pierre-Joseph Proudhon, Malthusianism was from its beginning 'the theory of political murder; of murder from motives of philanthropy and for love of God.' While its supporters 'act in good faith and from the best intentions in the world' and 'ask nothing better than to make the human race happy,' they 'cannot conceive how, without some sort of an organization of homicide, a balance between population and production can exist.'[171]

On a theoretical level, Malthus distinguished 'positive checks', which increase mortality, such as disease, malnutrition, starvation, and war, and 'preventive checks', which lower fertility, examples being voluntary restraints, such as abstinence and delayed marriage, or coercive restrictions such as forced sterilization against people deemed defective or less desirable.[172] Since the end of World War II some pessimists have urged policymakers to let nature run its course in the case of the former and (an admittedly much larger number) to devise various approaches to promote the latter. For instance, in 1948 William Vogt considered public health measures inadvisable and even argued that the 'flank attack on the tsetse fly with DDT or some other insecticide' carried out by 'ecologically ignorant sanitarians, entomologists, and medical men'[173] was going to make things worse because there was no 'kindness in keeping people from dying of malaria so that they could die more slowly of starvation.'[174] (Interestingly, this argument resulted in some serious soul-searching at the International Health Division of the Rockefeller Foundation that year.[175]) A few years later, Archibald V. Hill, then President of the British Association for the Advancement of Science, asked publicly '[i]f men were certain that the present overpopulation trends would eventually engulf them, would they be right in withholding such things as insecticides, fertilizers, and anti-malarial and anti-tuberculosis drugs?... If men bred like rabbits should they be allowed to die like rabbits?'[176]

Novelist and philosopher Aldous Huxley laid out the same logic in his 1958 essay *Brave New World Revisited*:

> [W]e go to a tropical island and with the aid of DDT we stamp out malaria and, in two or three years, save hundreds of thousands of lives. This is obviously good. But the hundreds of thousands of human beings thus saved, and the millions whom they beget and bring to birth, cannot be adequately clothed, housed, educated or even fed out of the island's available resources. Quick death by malaria has been abolished; but life made miserable by undernourishment and over-crowding is now the rule, and slow death by outright starvation threatens ever greater numbers.[177]

In his famous 'ethic' essay in which the limited capacity lifeboats are rich nations and swimmers are poor nations, Garrett Hardin similarly made a case against helping the poor in the name of preventing future catastrophic outcomes.[178]

Whether based on incentives or coercion, policy instruments to promote preventive checks were justified in the name of apprehended societal and environmental collapse, fears that individuals transfer too large a part of the costs of their children onto society rather than 'internalizing' them,[179] and on the claim that many people who desire to practice birth control do not have access to adequate means to do so. Measures of this type took many forms. Those promoted by Paul Ehrlich included mandatory sterilization, temporary infertility (imposed through mandatory pills or drugging of the public drinking water supply), parenting permits, severe restrictions on immigration, triage (in which a small number of survivors would be selected from a mass of doomed individuals), tying food aid to strict population control measures, public funding of new birth control techniques, tax disincentives for childbirth and luxury taxes on layettes, cribs, diapers, diaper services and expensive toys. He further recommended the rebuilding of city centers, curbing suburban sprawl, overhauling transportation networks, new efficiency standards for buildings and appliances, survivalism-inspired techniques from gardening and foraging for food to storing water, and purchasing more durable clothing.[180]

Ehrlich believed that in order to save tomorrow '[w]e must use our political power to push other countries into programs which combine agricultural development and population control.'[181]

While many pessimists stopped short of advocating drastic and coercive solutions *à la Ehrlich*, most agreed on the modus operandi: top-down and centrally managed action by governments and technocratic elites, with the only nod to the larger public taking the form of having been properly educated on the topic and helping to spread the word. In a typical passage, Douglas Ashmead commented:

> To achieve a reduction, or even a standstill, in numbers will involve the use of persuasion, and this will depend on sophisticated means of communication. Fortunately, these are available. The subject of population numbers is generally taboo. Politicians – in democratic countries at least – are not going to ally themselves with such a sensitive subject if it will lose them votes. Anyway, the time-span of parliaments is too short to deal with a problem of this magnitude. ...So the major cause of global warming – the number of humans in the world – is not being tackled with the degree of commitment or urgency that is necessary.[182]
>
> ...
>
> We must achieve the objective of making anxiety about over -population one of the central planks of government. From that will come solutions. You, the reader, must take up the cudgels. You can make governments in the developed world sit up and take notice. Only you, the voter, can persuade your politicians that the problem discussed in this short book is of great moment.[183]

As John Dryzek observed: 'Elites...can choose to oversee the transition to a stationary state through coordinated global action. 'Populations,' be they national, global, or class-specific, have no agency; they are only acted upon, as aggregates to be monitored through statistics and controlled by government policy. At most, their component individuals can only follow their short-sighted desires...'[184] In short, only the experts have agency in the pessimist scenario; the citizens are part of a mob, bound to act irrationally. Given that there is a fundamental conflict over scarce resources of the commons and the masses' propensity to breed, only a strict control over individual decisions, and a strict hierarchy of those who can grant permission or deny it, can forestall the tragedy of civilizational collapse. Consequently, when it came to seeking implementation of their agenda, pessimists 'have for the most part sought the ear of the powerful rather than the mobilization of any broader public',[185] which they typically scorned and saw as an obstacle to be controlled, not a viable partner.

Since the role of experts was assured in a pessimist scenario, their analyses and prescriptions, particularly in the 1970s, were often presented as unavoidable because they were derived through the use of computer models, embodiments of objectivity and scientific rigour. Emotion, however, particularly despair at human profligacy accompanied by the simultaneous horror at the impending apocalypse, were never far from the invocations of mechanical objectivity. 'If the computer represented the rationalistic, calculating side of survivalist discourse, it coexists uneasily with quasi-religious images of doom and redemption. The earthly paradise of a stationary state is attainable – but only if we recognize our sin, and change our ways.'[186]

Whatever their specific policy recommendations, however, population control activists in the end had to concur with William Vogt who, seven decades ago, argued that the road to survival must be built on two foundations:

- that renewable resources be used to produce as much wealth as possible on a sustained-yield basis – in other words, wise use to support as high a living standard as possible was desirable, but they shouldn't be exhausted as there could be no artificial substitutes;
- that demand be adjusted to 'natural' supply, either by accepting less per capita (lowering living standards) or reducing population.[187]

To their credit, Paul and Anne Ehrlich acknowledged this reality when they commented that '[i]n fact, humanity has already overshot earth's carrying capacity by a simple measure: no nation is supporting its present population on a sustainable flow of renewable resources.'[188]

2.3 Optimists

Historical perspective

Historically, most political rulers considered a growing population beneficial. To quote French military engineer Sébastien Le Prestre de Vauban (1633–1707): 'For the grandeur of kings is measured by the number of their subjects; therein consists their welfare, their happiness, their wealth, their power, their fortune, & every consideration that they have in the world.'[189]

Frederick the Great of Prussia (1712–1786) believed that 'the number of the population constitutes the wealth of the State.' Several thinkers linked the quality of political institutions and population numbers. The philosopher David Hume (1711–1776) thus observed that, everything else being equal, it was natural to expect that 'wherever there are most happiness and virtue, and the wisest institutions, there will also be most people.'[190]

Jean-Jacques Rousseau (1712–1778) similarly held that 'the Government under which the citizens increase and multiply the most is infallibly the best.'[191]

Apart from political and military considerations, several past analysts further suggested that a growing population was beneficial to economic welfare as more people not only meant more mouths to feed, but also more arms to work and more brains to think of new solutions. Such optimists were found across the political spectrum. Writing in 1771, the French economist Nicholas Baudeau argued that the 'productiveness of nature and the industriousness of man are without known limits' because production 'can increase indefinitely' and as a result 'population numbers and well-being can go on advancing together.'[192] Baudeau, usually associated with the physiocratic school of economic thought, shared this belief with later members of the otherwise antagonistic Marxist, institutionalist, neoclassical, and Austrian schools of economics.[193]

Whatever their school of thought, however, optimistic writers agreed on the fundamental belief that, far from being constrained by environmental limits, valuable resources could become less scarce over time, provided that innovative solutions were developed and capital (manufactured and human) accumulated. New ways of dealing with pollution and health problems would similarly be devised. In such a context, populations would grow almost indefinitely as a result of better nutrition, sanitation, medical care, and improved overall standards of living. For instance, Malthus's 1798 original essay was published in part as response to such thoughts expressed by the English political philosopher William Godwin (1756–1836) in his 1793 *Enquiry Concerning Political Justice, and its Influence on General Virtue and Happiness*. Malthus expressed scepticism not only regarding Godwin's idea that if society could be reorganized, constraints on population growth could be eased, but also with respect to the modality of this reorganization, which involved redistribution of resources and transcendence of private property. What is interesting in the original framing of the Godwin–Malthus debate is that the pro-population growth narrative aligned with Godwin's form of communism and anarchism, but also with the hope for the triumph of nurture; the contra-population-growth or natural-limits argument was that of property rights' advocate Malthus.

Godwin's 1820 *An Essay on the Principle of Population* was a response to Malthus's critique, and in many ways it set up later debates about the possibility of human progress. As he saw things:

> If I were to say that the globe would maintain twenty times its present inhabitants, or, in other words, that for every human creature now called into existence, twenty might exist in a state of greater plenty and happiness than with our small number we do at present, I should find no one timid and saturnine enough to contradict me. In fact, he must be a literal and most uninventive speculator, who would attempt to set bounds to the physical powers of the earth to supply the means of human subsistence.

> The first thing therefore that would occur to him who should survey 'all the kingdoms of the earth,' and the state of their population, would be the thinness of their numbers, and the multitude and extent of their waste and desolate places. If his heart abounded with 'the milk of human kindness,' he would not fail to contrast the present state of the globe with its possible state; he would see his species as a little remnant widely scattered over a fruitful and prolific surface, and would weep to think that the kindly and gracious qualities of our mother earth were turned to so little account. If he were more of a sober and reasoning, than of a tender and passionate temper, perhaps he would not weep, but I should think he would set himself seriously to enquire, how the populousness of nations might be increased, and the different regions of the globe replenished with a numerous and happy race.[194]

Although largely forgotten today, the most widely read book on economics in the nineteenth century was Henry George's *Progress and Poverty* (1879),[195] in which the author was adamant that 'everywhere the vice and misery attributed to over-population can be traced to the warfare, tyranny, and oppression which prevent knowledge from being utilized and deny the security essential to production.'[196] Reacting to John Stuart Mill's pessimistic views, he argued

> that in any given state of civilization a greater number of people can collectively be better provided for than a smaller. I assert that the injustice of society, not the niggardliness of nature, is the cause of the want and misery which the current theory attributes to over-population. I assert that the new mouths which an increasing population calls into existence require no more food than the old ones, while the hands they bring with them can in the natural order of things produce more. I assert that, other things being equal, the greater the population, the greater the comfort which an equitable distribution of wealth would give to each individual. I assert that in a state of equality the natural increase of population would constantly tend to make every individual richer instead of poorer.[197]

Among the more recent influential works broadly supportive of this position from a free-market perspective are Harold Barnett and Chandler Morse's 1963 *Scarcity and Growth*[198] and Julian Simon's 1981 and 1996 editions of *The Ultimate Resource*.[199] Both showed, among other things, that the inflation-adjusted prices of most natural resources, such as minerals, metals and agricultural products, have decreased over time. To an economist, falling prices translate to a lower demand or a greater abundance; conversely, resources for which prices fall in time are not becoming increasingly scarce. As John Dryzek put it: 'When limits to growth argument and associated [pessimist] survivalist discourse arrived with such a bang in the early 1970s, Promethean [optimist] economists did, then, have a ready-made argument and plenty of data to throw back at the survivalists.'[200] In short, 'survivalism denies agency to populations, which are treated as problems to be controlled. Promethean (optimistic) discourse, in contrast, celebrates the people who compose populations. If individuals are problem solvers, all potentially contributing to the betterment of humanity's lot, then the more people the better... [201] 'Indeed, Julian Simon saw individuals as 'the ultimate resource... skilled, spirited, and hopeful people who will exert their wills and imagination for their own benefit, and inevitably... benefit not only themselves, but the rest of us as well.'[202]

In line with Marx's rejection of Malthus, traditional Marxists and Marxist regimes also stood against the pessimist population discourse in the period after World War II. In more recent times, however, their economic failures and incapacity to provide for growing numbers sometimes led Communist rulers – in China and Cuba for example – to embrace population-control policies. At the same time, proponents of eco-Marxism and various other radical leftists have used ecological apocalypse rhetoric as a handy method to indict the capitalist system.[203] To give but a few instances, a generation ago the founder of the Institute for Social Ecology, Murray Bookchin, declared that 'the immediate source of the ecological crisis is capitalism' and that 'the color of radicalism today is not red, but green.'[204] An influential recent spin on this perspective was penned by Arizona State University scholar Benjamin Fong, who argued in a *New York Times* op-ed that the 'real culprit of the climate crisis is not any particular form of consumption, production or regulation but rather the very *way* in which we globally produce, which is for profit rather than for sustainability.' As long as this order is maintained, Fong argued, 'the crisis will continue and, given its progressive nature, worsen.' He further observed that 'climate change has made anticapitalist struggle, for the first time in history, a non-class-based issue.'[205] Finally, anti-racist, pro-immigrant and social justice activists have opposed the pessimist prescription on the grounds that it was 'designed to control and discriminate against those ethnic groups whose numbers are increasing most rapidly,'[206] while feminists and ecofeminists have found patriarchal control of female fertility equally disturbing.[207]

Apart from orthodox Marxist regimes, the most vociferous and organized opposition to population control policies have historically come from traditionalist or fundamentalist branches of major world religions,[208] with the Roman Catholic Church having proven especially effective in this regard.[209] (Recently, however, the theology of Pope Francis is said to have veered towards a more pessimistic interpretation of human life as '[t]he Earth, our home [...is] beginning to look like an immense pile of filth.'[210]) Although many, if not most, governmental bureaucracies in mixed economies have historically embraced the pessimistic narrative, some openly and effectively stood up against it, a prime example being the United States Geological Survey, especially under the directorship of Vincent Ellis McKelvey in the 1970s.[211]

In recent decades in the United States, however, most individuals who have effectively challenged pessimist thinking were affiliated with a few think tanks, most prominently the mainstream Resources for the Future (RFF) until the mid-1970s,[212] and pro-market organizations such as the American Enterprise Institute, the Hudson Institute, the Heritage Foundation, the Cato Institute and, later on, the Property and Environment Research Center and the Competitive Enterprise Institute.[213] Similar organizations in other English-speaking countries, such as the Institute of Economic Affairs in the United Kingdom and the Fraser Institute in Canada, along with other free-market think tanks in other parts of the world, also stood up for optimism.[214]

What follows is our summary of the key optimistic arguments about population growth, improved standards of living and environmental remediation.[215]

Key arguments

A larger population that engages in trade and the division of labour will deliver greater material abundance per capita.

> Population growth increases the size of the market and encourages economies of scale and an ever more minute and sophisticated division of labour. One hundred people with 100 different skill sets who specialize in what they do best and who trade with each other will produce and consume far more than 100 self-sufficient individuals.

The British economist Edward Cannan observed a century ago that, as an old proverb said, with 'every mouth God sends a pair of hands.' Why then shouldn't an 'increased number of people be able to grow a proportionately increased amount of produce?' Indeed, why couldn't they produce proportionally ever more as 'they would be able to draw greater advantage from [the] division of labour?'[216]

In 1821 the French economist Jean-Baptiste Say had similarly judged the belief that a reduction in population would 'enable those which are left to enjoy a greater quantity of those commodities of which they are in want' nonsensical because it ignored the fact that a reduction in manpower simultaneously destroyed the means of production. After all, one did not see in thinly populated countries that 'the wants of the inhabitants are more easily satisfied.' On the contrary, it was 'abundance of productions, and not the scarcity of consumers, which procures a plentiful supply of whatever our necessities require.'[217] This is why the most populous countries were generally better supplied.

In 1879, Henry George observed in similar vein that while one could see 'many communities still increasing in population,' they were also 'increasing their wealth still faster.' Indeed, 'among communities of similar people in a similar stage of civilization,' the 'most densely populated community is also the richest' and the evidence was overwhelming that 'wealth is greatest where population is densest; that the production of wealth to a given amount of labour increases as population increases. These things are apparent wherever we turn our eyes.' In the end, the 'richest countries are not those where nature is most prolific; but those where labour is most efficient – not Mexico, but Massachusetts; not Brazil, but England.' Where nature is niggardly, George commented, '[t]wenty men working together will…produce more than twenty times the wealth that one man can produce where nature is most bountiful.' This was because the 'denser the population the more minute becomes the subdivision of labour, the greater the economies of production and distribution, and, hence, the very reverse of the Malthusian doctrine is true; and, within the limits in which we have reason to suppose increase would still go on, in any given state of civilization a greater number of people can produce a larger proportionate amount of wealth, and more fully supply their wants, than can a smaller number.'[218]

One of the best short overviews of the anti-Malthusian stance can be found in an anonymous essay published in 1889 in the *Westminster Review*:

> The Malthusian theory does not accord with facts. As population grows, instead of production being less per head, statistics clearly prove it to be greater. The intelligence which is fostered in large communities; the advantages of the division of labour; the improved transit, which increases in efficiency with an enterprising people in proportion as numbers become large, and is impracticable until population has developed – are more than a match in the competition of production for any advantage a thinly scattered community may in some respects gain on a virgin soil. Malthus and his followers, while bringing prominently forward the needs of an increasing population, keep out of view the increasing means of supply which the additional labour of greater numbers will produce.… and so long as there are a pair of hands to provide for every mouth, with intelligence and energy ample production is assured, unless society erects artificial barriers by means of its laws regarding the distribution of wealth.[219]

A century later the development economist Peter T. Bauer made similar points when arguing that:

> population growth can have favourable external effects. It can facilitate the more effective division of labour and thereby increase real incomes. In fact, in much of Southeast Asia, Africa, and Latin America, sparseness of population inhibits economic advance. It retards the development of transport facilities and communications, and thus inhibits the movement

of people and goods and the spread of new ideas and methods. These obstacles to enterprise and economic advance are particularly difficult to overcome.[220]

More recently, science writer Matt Ridley described the shortcomings of the Malthusian position on population growth and local resource limitations by noting that it is not just the propensity to manage goods by trading goods and services, but the incentive to specialize in order to trade more efficiently, thus utilizing each individual's unique comparative advantage, that best refutes the Malthusian argument. The fewer efficiency-boosting solutions and ways to employ individual skills, the fewer unique goods to trade: the fewer incentives to trade, the more are humans reduced to a niche-limiting self-sufficiency:[221]

> [G]ood old-fashioned Malthusian population limitation does not really apply to human beings, because of their habit of exchange and specialisation. That is to say, instead of dying from famine and pestilence when too numerous for their food supply, people can increase their specialisation, which allows more to subsist on the available resources. On the other hand, if exchange becomes harder, they will reduce their specialisation, which can lead to a population crisis even without an increase in population. The Malthusian crisis comes not as a result of population growth directly, but because of decreasing specialisation. Increasing self-sufficiency is the very signature of a civilisation under stress, the definition of a falling standard of living.

Urban theorist Jane Jacobs not only dismissed any direct causal link between population control and poverty reduction, but also turned the arguments on its head:

> So little does this [relationship between population and resources] seem to be understood, that it is becoming conventional (especially among the very well-off) to assume that poor and unproductive people cause their own poverty by multiplying – that is, by their very numbers. But if it is true that poverty is indeed caused by overpopulation, then it follows that poor people ought to prosper wherever populations decline appreciably. Things do not work out that way in the real world. Entire sections of Sicily and Spain have become almost depopulated by emigration. Yet the people remaining do not prosper; they remain poor... One wonders how much a population is supposed to be reduced before prosperity ensues.[222]

Human creativity can deliver increasing returns

> Human beings are creators of new and better (or progressively less damaging) ways of doing things that increase the efficiency of key economic sectors such as agriculture, resource extraction, industry, transportation and communications.

A long-standing tenet of population growth optimism is that knowledge, or creative application of the human brain, is the key factor in overcoming scarcity and diminishing returns.[223] As Barnett and Morse observed two generations ago: 'Recognition of the possibility of technological progress clearly cuts the ground from under the concept of Malthusian scarcity' and the historical evidence 'mainly show[ed] increasing, not diminishing, returns.'[224] As Jane Jacobs put it:

> A developing economy needs increasing numbers of workers, which of course means a growing population. And a developing economy also increases the natural resources it can draw upon for its population, rather than diminishing its store of resources. When people added grain culture and animal husbandry, they were expanding, not diminishing, the natural resources they were capable of using. Modern men have done the same by adding chemical fertilizers and oil drills and thousands of other goods and services; and future developing economies will surely tap immense new resources in the sea, among others.[225]

What has also long been understood by optimistic writers is that a greater division of labour also favours the development of new ways of doing things. Writing in 1857, the social theorist Herbert Spencer observed: 'By increasing the pressure on the means of subsistence, a larger population again augments these results; seeing that each person is forced more and more to confine himself to that which he can do best, and by which he can gain most. Presently, under these same stimuli, new occupations arise. Competing workers, ever aiming to produce improved articles, occasionally discover better processes or raw materials.'[226] Spencer not only believed this made possible the development of better alternatives to what existed before, but also the development of things not possible before. For instance, the replacement of stone tools by similar bronze tools paved the way to the development of new things that could not have been made out of stone. These advances would increase the manipulative skill, comfort and intelligence of the population, in turn refining 'their habits and tastes,' transforming 'a homogeneous society into a heterogeneous one' and ultimately resulting in social and political progress.

In 1879 Henry George commented that 'even if the increase of population does reduce the power of the natural factor of wealth, by compelling a resort to poorer soils, etc., it yet so vastly increases the power of the human factor as more than to compensate.'[227] A decade later the American entrepreneur, inventor and economic writer Edward Atkinson observed that the 'mind of man when applied to the direction of natural forces is the principal agent in material production, in fact, the controlling element. Those who claim that labor is the source of all production are utterly misled because they do not admit this fundamental principle.'[228] The basic Malthusian hypothesis was thus 'utterly without warrant either in fact or in experience' because 'Malthus appears to have had no imaginative faculty, a very essential quality in dealing with economic questions.' As Atkinson saw it, Malthus 'could not forecast the future nor foretell the wonderful results that would be attained through the new scientific discoveries and the better understanding of the art of production and distribution which had begun even in his own day to work a profound change in the relations of men to each other.'[229] Atkinson further discussed the case of land that 'itself may be exhausted when treated as a mine,' but 'may be maintained when worked as a laboratory' and might one day be potentially enriched through the diversion of 'nitrogen and carbon from the atmosphere and converting these elements into food for man and beast.'[230]

The Scottish agricultural writer James Anderson made a similar argument over eight decades earlier, when he observed that human creativity could deliver increasing returns despite less valuable lands being brought under cultivation:

> Nothing can be more certain, than that the productions of a country can be increased by human exertions; and that this increase of produce can, by judicious management, be gradually augmented in a country which admits of being cultivated almost without any limitation. If these facts be admitted, it will follow, that by due attention to carry forward improvements in agriculture, the population of a country may be gradually increased to an indefinite degree, and the people still find abundant subsistence from the productions of their own fields, even where there seemed to be no superabundant produce at the time the population began to increase.[231]

A few years before he co-authored the *Communist Manifesto*, the young Friedrich Engels argued that the 'productive power at mankind's disposal is immeasurable' and the 'productivity of the soil can be increased ad infinitum by the application of capital, labour and science.'[232] In later decades, several German and Russian writers expanded on this point.[233] Lenin thus argued that the law of diminishing returns 'does not at all apply to cases in which technology is progressing and methods of production are changing' and 'has only an extremely relative and restricted application to conditions in which technology remains unchanged.'[234]

At about the same time Edward Cannan opined that while one might occasionally observe 'diminution of returns,' these were typically only temporary until the development of 'inventions and the introduction of better methods.' Indeed, the belief that 'diminishing returns was the general rule throughout history' was 'so contrary to the results of direct observation that it seems difficult to believe that it could ever have been accepted.' As a matter of fact, 'no reasonable person can have any doubt that the productiveness of agricultural industry has enormously increased' and that 'the population of the civilized world is much better fed, and yet has to spend far less a proportion of the whole of its labour on the acquisition of food.' If returns had actually diminished in agriculture, a 'larger and ever larger proportion of the world's labour would clearly have to be expended in producing food,' something that was obviously not the case in the early years of the twentieth century.[235]

Writing in 1945, the agricultural economist Karl Brandt observed:

> During World War I and immediately after, the belief was common among scholars and statesmen that Malthus' doctrine was still valid and that, owing to the progressive propagation of man, scarcity of food was not only inevitable in the long run but characteristic also for the second quarter of the twentieth century. A few years after the war the situation in world markets contradicted those assumptions. The war had fostered rapid progress in farm technology. It brought the internal combustion engine into general use for agriculture, first in America and later elsewhere. The truck, tractor, and combine [harvester] were some of the machines in which it was applied. Millions of horses were replaced, and millions of feed acres were released for food production. Enormous savings in manpower and in production costs became possible. New varieties of plants made available for crop production many areas that previously could be used only for scanty grazing. Research in animal nutrition and genetics also led to much greater efficiency in converting feed into animal products. The really revolutionary progress in food production technology revealed the economic fallacy of the more than century-old secular 'law of diminishing returns,' as commonly applied to food production. It became apparent that technological progress made increasing economic returns and a lowering of the costs of food production possible within sufficiently wide boundaries.[236]

One can identify at least two key arguments on the benefits of growing population numbers in terms of delivering increasing returns.

The first is that the more human brains, the greater the likelihood of new beneficial inventions. As the British political economist William Petty observed over a century before Malthus, it was 'more likely that one ingenious curious man may rather be found out amongst 4,000,000 than 400 persons.'[237]

Edward Cannan similarly disagreed with the notion that agricultural productivity would have been greater in his time if population numbers had remained small because fewer brains meant that fewer advances would 'have been discovered and introduced.'[238] More recently, the physicist Robert Zubrin asked which one of either Louis Pasteur or Thomas Edison should not have been born in order to improve the lot of mankind.[239]

The second key argument is the cumulative nature of technological development: the fact that present and future advances build on past ones. The economist Fritz Machlup perhaps put it best over half a century ago when he distinguished between the 'retardation school' of technological change, whose proponents believed that 'the more that has been invented the less there is left to be invented,' and the 'acceleration school', according to which 'the more that is invented the easier it becomes to invent still more' because 'every new invention furnishes a new idea for potential combination with vast numbers of existing ideas' and the 'number of possible combinations increases geometrically with the number of elements at hand.'[240]

In a personal reply to and further face-to-face conversation with Malthus, the American diplomat Alexander Everett suggested that an expanded division of labour not only made people more productive, but further laid the foundation for 'the invention of new machines, an improvement of methods in all the departments of industry, and a rapid progress in the various branches of art and science'[241] that resulted in a level of labour productivity that far exceeded the proportional increase in population numbers. A belief in decreasing returns, he argued, ultimately assumed that 'labor becomes less efficient and productive in proportion to the degree of skill with which it is applied; that a man can raise more weight by hand, than by the help of a lever, and see further with the naked eye than with the best telescope.'[242]

In 1844, Friedrich Engels stood Malthus on his head by observing that 'science increases at least as much as population. The latter increases in proportion to the size of the previous generation, science advances in proportion to the knowledge bequeathed to it by the previous generation, and thus under the most ordinary conditions also in a geometrical progression.'[243] Harold J. Barnett and Chandler Morse similarly commented in 1963 that 'a strong case can be made for the view that the cumulation of knowledge and technological progress is automatic and self-reproductive in modern economies, and obeys a law of increasing returns' as '[e]very cost-reducing innovation opens up possibilities of application in so many new directions that the stock of knowledge, far from being depleted by new developments, may even expand geometrically.'[244]

Reformulating this insight, with the bluntness of 21st-century discourse, Matt Ridley coined his signature phrase by observing that: 'Ideas are having sex with other ideas from all over the planet with ever-increasing promiscuity.[245] He went on to add that: 'Henry Ford once candidly admitted that he had invented nothing new. He had "simply assembled into a car the discoveries of other men behind whom were centuries of work". So objects betray in their design their descent from other objects: ideas that have given birth to other ideas.'[246]

Innovation writer and podcaster Steven Johnson, on the other hand, did not place agency for innovation with the seemingly random and promiscuous behaviour of disembodied idea memes. In his *Where Good Ideas Come From: The Natural History of Innovation*,[247] he described several conditions that both environments and their human inhabitants needed to meet, or at least approximate, in order to accelerate the generation of ideas. Johnson cleverly built his concepts with what he borrowed from chemistry, physics, evolutionary biology and computer science, and he readily acknowledged their intellectual pedigree as if to show how natural and productive it was for ideas to travel along 'liquid networks'[248] – once these were available – in order to expand 'the adjacent possible'.[249] Johnson's constructs derived their creativity partly from the limits of their original definitions: 'The adjacent possible is a kind of shadow future, hovering on the edges of the present state of things, a map of all the ways in which the present can reinvent itself. Yet it is not an infinite space, or a totally open playing field... What the adjacent possible tells us is that at any moment the world is capable of extraordinary change, but only certain changes can happen.'[250] These are the changes that work with human goals, needs, incentives, and the current state of the environment, but each change transforms the adjacent possible to open up new states in an ongoing process.

Human standards of living are not constrained by local resources

> Optimistic outlooks on population and resources reject the application of biological metaphors or ecological constraints (such as carrying capacity[251]) on economic systems because of humans' trading, creative and adaptive abilities in the right institutional context.

Henry George famously observed that of 'all living things, man is the only one who can give play to the reproductive forces, more powerful than his own, which supply him with food.'[252] Other animals survive on what they find and can only grow as numerous as their food sources allow, but increases in human numbers are possible because of their ability to produce more food. As George saw things:

> If bears instead of men had been shipped from Europe to the North American continent, there would now be no more bears than in the time of Columbus, and possibly fewer, for bear food would not have been increased nor the conditions of bear life extended, by the bear immigration, but probably the reverse. But within the limits of the United States alone, there are now forty-five millions of men where then there were only a few hundred thousand,[253] and yet there is now within that territory much more food per capita for the forty-five millions than there was then for the few hundred thousand. It is not the increase of food that has caused this increase of men; but the increase of men that has brought

> about the increase of food. There is more food, simply because there are more men.[254]

George added that a key difference between animal and man was that both 'the jay-hawk and the man eat chickens, but the more jay-hawks the fewer chickens, while the more men the more chickens.' Similarly, 'both the seal and the man eat salmon, but when a seal takes a salmon there is a salmon the less, and were seals to increase past a certain point salmon must diminish.' Humans, however, 'by placing the spawn of the salmon under favorable conditions' can increase their number to such an extent as to more than make up for their catches. In the end, George argued, 'while all through the vegetable and animal kingdoms the limit of subsistence is independent of the thing subsisted, with man the limit of subsistence is, within the final limits of earth, air, water, and sunshine, dependent upon man himself.'[255] The ultimate limit to human population was therefore physical space.

Another writer who made this point forcefully nearly a century later is Jane Jacobs:

> Wild animals are strictly limited in their numbers by natural resources, including other animals on which they feed. But this is because any given species of animal, except man, uses directly only a few resources and uses them indefinitely. Once we stopped living like the other animals, on what nature provided us ready-made, we began riding a tiger we dare not dismount, but we also began opening up new resources – unlimited resources except as they may be limited by economic stagnation. Analogies of human population growth to animal population growth, based on the relation of population to current resources, are thus specious. The idea that, under sensible economic planning, population growth must be limited because natural resources are limited is profoundly reactionary. Indeed, that is not planning for economic development at all. It is planning for stagnation.[256]

Historically, one of the main ways to break local limits was to increase agricultural outputs on the same piece of land, either by introducing new crops, developing new crop rotations, improving the productivity of existing crops or by enriching the soil through various means. Commenting on the latter case, the anarchist theorist and geographer Pyotr Kropotkin observed in the late nineteenth century that the high agricultural productivity of Belgian farmland had nothing to do with some inherent superior fertility of the local soil because:

> to use the words of Laveleye, 'only one half, or less, of the territory offers natural conditions which are favourable for agriculture;' the other half consists of a gravelly soil, or sands, 'the natural sterility of which could be overpowered only by heavy manuring.' Man, not nature, has given to the

> Belgian soil its present productivity. With this soil and labour, Belgium succeeds in supplying nearly all the food of a population which is denser than that of England and Wales...[257]

Commenting on the market gardens that surrounded Paris, Kropotkin wrote that in 'market-gardening the soil is always made, whatever it originally may have been.' It was therefore a 'usual stipulation of the renting contracts of the Paris *maraîchers* [market gardeners] that the gardener may carry away his soil, down to a certain depth, when he quits his tenancy' because he had created it.[258]

More generally, optimistic writers typically dismissed the notion of 'natural resources.' The German-born economist Erich Zimmermann thus observed over eight decades ago that, before the emergence of humans, 'the earth was replete with fertile soil, with trees and edible fruits, with rivers and waterfalls, with coal beds, oil pools, and mineral deposits; the forces of gravitation, of electromagnetism, of radio-activity were there; the sun set forth his life-bringing rays, gathered the clouds, raised the winds; but there were no resources.'[259] He argued that resources are in reality:

> ...highly dynamic functional concepts; they are not, they become, they evolve out of the triune interaction of nature, man, and culture, in which nature sets outer limits, but man and culture are largely responsible for the portion of physical totality that is made available for human use... knowledge is truly the mother of all resources.[260]

Writing in 1973, the economist Colin Clark similarly commented that while humanity had used up 'large and increasing quantities of food, fibres, timber, wood pulp and so on,' these were not 'natural resources' but rather 'products obtained by applying our labour, equipment and skills to the land, whose soil and climate constitute the genuine 'natural resources.'[261]

As uber-doomslayers Julian Simon and futurist Herman Kahn put it over a generation ago, because 'of increases in knowledge, the earth's 'carrying capacity' has been increasing throughout the decades and centuries and millennia to such an extent that the term 'carrying capacity' has by now no useful meaning. These trends strongly suggest a progressive improvement and enrichment of the earth's natural resource base, and of mankind's lot on earth.'[262] In the end, as economist Jacqueline Kasun observed in 1988: 'In the same territories in which earlier men struggled and starved, much larger populations today support themselves in comfort. The difference, of course, lies in the *knowledge* that human beings bring to the task of discovering and managing resources.'[263] The regional scientist Peter J. Taylor used an evocative phrase from archaeology: 'the release from proximity,'[264] to describe this unique human ability to transcend the limitations of local resources.

Past successes are grounds for optimism

Past achievements are grounds for cautious optimism.

Over a century ago Edward Cannan took issue with John Stuart Mill's ambivalence as to whether or not future improvements could overcome decreasing returns. The problem with Mill, he argued, is that he limited his discussion to 'fairly recent times' in which 'it does not appear to be possible either to prove or disprove [the argument].'[265] Fortunately, Cannan observed, a longer-term perspective yielded a more promising outlook. While commodity prices go through cycles, in the long run valuable resources typically become less scarce and less expensive. Because of historical precedents, he added, pessimistic future projections based on very recent trends should not be taken seriously.

In his 1964 prognosis of the needs for and the availability of natural and industrial materials, the economist Hans Hermann Landsberg commented that 'the indications are that the American people can obtain the natural resources and resource products that they will need between now and the year 2000' because 'neither a long view of the past, nor current trends, nor our most careful estimates of future possibilities suggest any general running out of resources in this country during the remainder of the century.'[266]

Two decades later Julian Simon dismissed critics who viewed 'all the evidence of history [as] merely "temporary" and must reverse "sometime"' as being 'outside the canon of ordinary science.'[267] Quoting the development economist Peter T. Bauer, he firmly believed that 'it is only the past that gives us any insight into the laws of motion of human society and hence enables us to predict the future.' If the future was going to differ, he added, 'the bias is likely to be in the direction of understating the rate at which technology will develop, and therefore underestimating the rate at which costs will fall.'[268] In a critique of the Carter administration's *Global 2000 Report to the President*, Simon lamented its authors' 'lack of historical perspective' and reliance on the work of analysts such as Paul Ehrlich and Garrett Hardin who typically ignored 'contradictory historical evidence.' In Simon's perspective, 'experience is to be preferred to pure logic as a policy guide' and the most 'important aspect of the relevant historical experience is that humans use their imaginative and creative powers to change their situation when caught in a resource bind, and the final result is usually that we are left better off than before the problem arose.'[269]

Prescription

A few decades ago Robert Heilbroner described a set of common beliefs among his optimist opponents, such as the 'self-evident importance of efficiency, with its tendency to subordinate the optimum technical scale,' the need to 'tame' the environment, and the 'priority of production itself, visible in the care both systems lavish on technical virtuosity and the indifference with which both look upon the aesthetic aspects of life.'[270] While one might quibble with the latter statement, belief in the absolute necessity of technological advances has long been shared by optimistic writers, whatever their political preferences.

On the one hand, traditional Marxist theorists had rejected the notion that poverty was a natural outcome of growing population numbers. Unlike Malthusians, who believed in a universal law of population independent of time or location, Marx and his followers argued that each mode of production has its own law of population that arises and disappears with it. In the context of capitalism, the problem is not too little food or too many people, but socially unjust practices that result from the concentrated ownership of the means of production.[271] As population and birth control advocate Margaret Sanger observed nearly a century ago:

> The earlier Marxians, including Karl Marx himself, expressed the bitterest antagonism to Malthusian and neo-Malthusian theories. A remarkable feature of early Marxian propaganda has been the almost complete unanimity with which the implications of the Malthusian doctrine have been derided, denounced and repudiated. Any defense of the so-called 'law of population' was enough to stamp one, in the eyes of the orthodox Marxians, as a 'tool of the capitalistic class,' seeking to dampen the ardor of those who expressed the belief that men might create a better world for themselves. Malthus, they claimed, was actuated by selfish class motives. He was not merely a hidebound aristocrat, but a pessimist who was trying to kill all hope of human progress. By Marx, Engels, Bebel, Karl Kautsky, and all the celebrated leaders and interpreters of Marx's great 'Bible of the working class,' down to the martyred Rosa Luxemburg and Karl Liebknecht, Birth Control has been looked upon as a subtle, Machiavellian sophistry created for the purpose of placing the blame for human misery elsewhere than at the door of the capitalist class. Upon this point the orthodox Marxian mind has been universally and sternly uncompromising.[272]

Indeed, in the 1970s many Marxists accused the 'population bombers' of diverting 'attention from the real issues and pav[ing] the way for world-wide race war and genocide.'[273]

Although other left-wing thinkers might have favoured more decentralized approaches, orthodox Marxists' proposals typically revolved around the socialization of the means of production and central planning.

By contrast, Julian Simon argued that the real problem was not 'too many people, but a lack of political and economic freedom.'[274] Indeed, he even stated that 'India is poor and underdeveloped for many reasons, and it might be even more so if it had a smaller population.'[275] Peter T. Bauer suggested more broadly that '[p]overty in the Third World is not caused by population growth or pressure' and that economic progress depends 'on people's conduct, not on their numbers.'[276] Free-market economists have also long emphasized the role of the price system as a feedback mechanism. In short, in a market economy characterized by freely determined prices and secured property rights, a rise in the price of a valuable resource could only be temporary, as it would provide incentives for people to look for more of it, to produce and use it more efficiently, and to develop substitutes. Figure 2.1 summarizes these processes.

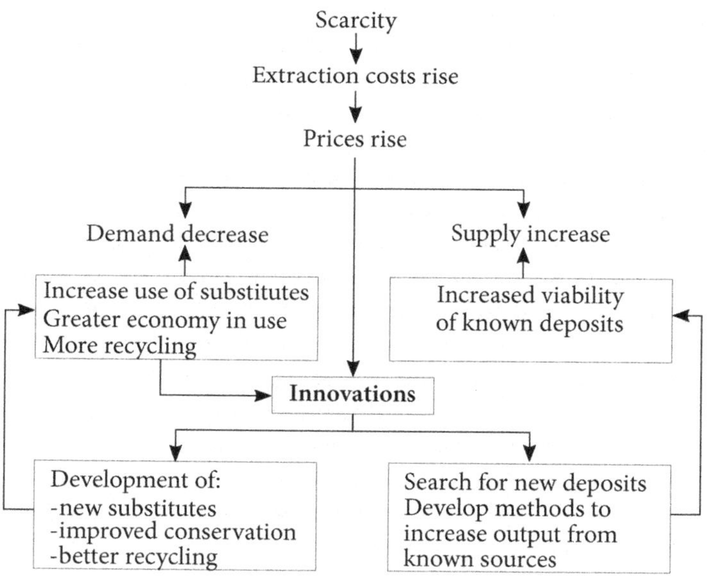

Figure 2.1: Market response to resource scarcity.

Based on Rees (1985, Fig. 2.8).

As the economist Carl Kaysen observed in his 1972 critique of *Limits to Growth*, although these processes might now not always have functioned as smoothly as in textbooks, they had historically proven 'sufficiently powerful to mediate very large shifts in use of resources location, of population and patterns of consumption.' For instance, new land 'can be created by new investment, as when arid lands are irrigated, swamps drained, forests cleared. Similarly, new mineral resources can be created by investment in exploration and discovery. These processes of adding to the supplies of 'fixed' resources have been going on steadily throughout human history.'[277]

Julian Simon perhaps put it best when he wrote:

> More people and increased income cause problems in the short run – shortages and pollutions. Short-run scarcity raises prices and pollution causes outcries. These problems present opportunity and prompt the search for solutions. In a free society, solutions are eventually found...In the long run the new developments leave us better off than if the problems had not arisen.[278]

For Simon, Bauer and others, no special policies are required to provide for humanity's future wants beyond proper institutions and governance, including not interfering with the price system when the value of a commodity shoots up. In the long run, resources – including non-renewable ones – will become less scarce as they are ultimately created by the renewable and ever-expanding human intellect.

Looking at the empirical evidence, Barnett and Morse noted in 1963 that, with the exception of forestry, resource scarcity was not a meaningful issue. Not only had unit costs gone down in all other sectors, but also economizing or saving resources for future generations was deemed nonsensical as 'the economic magnitude of the estate each generation passes on – the income per capita the next generation enjoys – has been approximately double that which it received.' The most important legacy, they argued, was not 'stocks of untapped resources,' but 'knowledge, technology, capital, instruments, and economic institutions' that allowed for the future creation of new resources.[279] In this context, as Jane Jacobs put it a few years later, birth control as an economic development and poverty alleviation tool was not only unnecessary, but counterproductive inasmuch as it distracted from the real causes of poverty:

> Birth control has much to recommend it...Birth control is also perhaps a major human right, although certainly not so vital as the right to have children. But birth control as a prescription for overcoming economic stagnation and poverty is nonsense. Worse, it is quackery. It carries the promise that something constructive is being done about poverty when, in fact, nothing constructive may be happening at all. The economies of people are not like the economies of deer, who wax fat if their numbers are thinned.[280]

We now turn to an historical assessment of the capacity of both perspectives to predict future developments.

3 Contradictory forecasts: an assessment

Numerous writers on population and the environment, many of them highly credentialed and experienced, have for over two centuries made general and sector-specific forecasts and predictions about availability of natural resources and the outlook for human societies. As will be demonstrated in this chapter, pessimists have been repeatedly and decisively proven wrong, typically sooner rather than later.[281]

Eager to demonstrate the value of an historical perspective on the topic, the economist Julian Simon once urged pessimistic analysts to learn 'from the great economist Jevons' scholarly 1865 prediction of cessation of growth for England by 1900 due to lack of fuel' and to remember Jevons' dismissal of petroleum as a potential substitute for coal.[282] Not mentioned by Simon is that Jevons further rejected the notion that technological advances would ever deliver acceptable substitutes. He was especially critical of the Irish scientific writer Dionysius Lardner's statement that 'long before such a period of time shall have rolled away, other and more powerful mechanical agents will supersede the use of coal.'[283] Once the United Kingdom had lost its 'main agent of industry,' Jevons maintained, its inhabitants would 'either sink down into poverty,' adopt 'wholly new habits,' or witness an exodus of their youth to better-endowed countries like the United States.[284]

As is obvious in retrospect, Lardner's optimistic prediction – made in his 1840 treatise on the steam engine – proved prescient. He first described in great detail how revolutionary the new technology was, for it had 'penetrated the crust of the earth, and drawn from beneath it boundless treasures of mineral wealth, which, without its aid, would have been rendered inaccessible; it has drawn up, in measureless quantity, the fuel on which its own life and activity depend.'[285] He added that the 'enormous consumption of coals produced by the application of the steam engine in the arts and manufactures, as well as to railways and navigation, has of late years excited the fears of many as to the possibility of the exhaustion of our coal mines.'[286] However, he deemed 'such apprehensions... altogether groundless' as 'probabl[e], if not certain progress of improvement and discovery ought not to be overlooked' for, in time, 'other and more powerful mechanical agents' would run on different fuels.[287]

Lardner's great optimism was grounded in the 'vigour, activity, and sagacity with which researches in [the physical science] are prosecuted in every civilised country, the increasing consideration in which scientific men are held, and the personal honours and rewards which begin to be conferred upon them.' All of this, he believed, justified 'the expectation that we are on the eve of mechanical discoveries still greater than any which have yet appeared.'[288] Indeed, Lardner went so far as to predict that 'the steam engine itself... will dwindle into insignificance in comparison with the energies of nature which are still to be revealed; and that the day will come when that machine, which is now extending the blessings of civilisation to the most remote skirts of the globe, will cease to have existence except in the page of history.'[289]

As we will now discuss in more detail, the outcome of the Jevons–Lardner conflict of visions was typical of the long-standing debate between pessimists and optimists.

3.1 Pessimists

In 1912 the eugenicist Edward Isaacson cited a study according to which 'the whole earth will be populated up to the limit of the food supply in A.D. 2180.'[290] He further commented that once the possibility of feeding their population through food imports was no longer feasible, over-populated countries that had not given up on their industrial development and population growth would experience a 'distress [that] will be something beyond all human experience.'[291]

Writing a decade later, the Harvard plant geneticist and eugenicist Edward Murray East speculated on the state of the world at the end of the twentieth century if an expansionist policy remained the order of the day. Describing the result as 'not a pretty picture,' he believed that 'the China and India of to-day' provided an accurate reflection of 'the world of to-morrow when the world as a whole reaches the same population status.'[292] As he imagined it:

> Food exportation had ceased some thirty years before, except for the exchange of specialties; all temperate regions had then reached the era of decreasing returns in agriculture. The tropics are being populated as fast as their submission to the hand of man makes it possible. Gradual reduction in population increase has occurred, due to the intensity of the struggle; yet there are 3,000 million people in the world. Migration has

> ceased; the bars have been put up in every country. Those nations where there is still a fair degree of comfort wish to retain it as long as possible. Food is scarce and costly. Man works from sun to sun. When crops are good there is unrest but no rest, there is privation and hardship; when crops are bad there is mass starvation such as China and Russia had experienced long before. Agricultural efficiency has risen 50 per cent during the past half-century through the pressure of stern necessity, yet the food resources of each individual are smaller than ever before. Where war occurs, it is war of extermination, for only by extermination can the conquerors profit; where peace remains it is under the shadow of a struggle as grim as war.[293]

In their influential 1945 essay *Population Roads to Peace or War*, academic sociologist Elmer Pendell and Guy Irving Burch, then director of the American Eugenics Society and a past founder of the Population Reference Bureau, exhibited the same spirit. As they argued in the revised 1947 edition, entitled *Human Breeding and Survival*, the land was already full, 'while our population is large and rapidly growing.' By 1951 one could see 'forming for the American people, a future marked by conditions like those which prevailed in the times of scarcity and want which Europe used to know so well in past centuries and under which it now suffers.'[294]

In 1948, their friend Fairfield Osborn described environmental collapse as being 'eventually [more] deadly'[295] than World War II, for 'man's destructiveness has turned not only upon himself but upon his own good earth – the wellspring of life.'[296] In this context, man's 'avoidance of the day of atonement that is drawing nearer as each year passes' implied that he had to quickly learn 'to work with nature in understanding rather than in conflict.'[297] Failure to change would not only 'point to widespread misery such as human beings have not yet experienced,' it would also, in the end, threaten 'even man's very survival.'[298] Humanity had 'now arrived at the day when the books should be balanced.'[299]

The same year, William Vogt wrote that '[w]e must accept change' and 'adjust our lives to it, if we are to survive,' for a failure to understand some basic relationships 'of man with his environment' would 'almost certainly smash our civilization.'[300] Vogt also predicted famines in the next three decades in countries such Great Britain, Japan and Germany[301] while the 'exhaustion of our own [American] oil wells [was] in sight.'[302]

In 1967, the authors of the US President's Science Advisory Committee's report *The World Food Problem* believed that '[u]nless the rate of population increase can be sharply diminished, all the efforts to augment agricultural production will merely postpone the time of mass starvation, and increase its agony when it inevitably occurs.'[303] Soon afterwards, Paul Ehrlich wrote the famous opening lines of his *The Population Bomb*: 'The battle to feed all humanity is over. In the 1970s and 1980s hundreds of millions of people will starve to death in spite of any crash program embarked upon now. At this late date nothing can prevent a substantial increase in the world death rate...'[304] A few months later, he forecasted that '[m]ost of the people who are going to die in the greatest cataclysm in the history of man have already been born. More than three and a half billion people already populate our moribund globe, and about half of them are hungry. Some 10 to 20 million will starve to death this year [1969].'[305]

As evidenced by his most recent writings and interviews – including a readable take on the alleged errors of optimistic writers[306] – Ehrlich's certainties and philosophical outlook remain unchanged.[307] For instance, he told a *New York Times* reporter that while he 'would not echo everything that he once wrote,' he 'remains convinced that doom lurks around the corner,' that what 'he wrote in the 1960s was comparatively mild' and that his 'language would be even more apocalyptic today.'[308] Indeed, he claimed on a HuffPost Live webcast that in the near future humans would have to contemplate 'eat[ing] the bodies of [their] dead' in order to survive.[309]

In their influential 1972 tract *A Blueprint for Survival*, the editors of *The Ecologist* magazine and over thirty prominent British scientists wrote that the 'ethos of expansion' of industrial society 'is not sustainable' and that, although 'the precise time and circumstances are in doubt,' its 'termination within the lifetime of someone born today is inevitable', either 'in a succession of famines, epidemics, social crises and wars' or radical changes imposed by the 'present increases in human numbers and per capita consumption' that were then 'disrupting ecosystems [through pollutants] and depleting resources.'[310] They added:

> It should go without saying that the world cannot accommodate this continued increase in ecological demand. Indefinite growth of whatever type cannot be sustained by finite resources. This is the nub of the environmental predicament. It is still less possible to maintain indefinite exponential growth – and unfortunately the growth of ecological demand is proceeding exponentially (i.e. it is increasing geometrically, by compound interest).[311]

Although he did not use the dramatic language of either Ehrlich or the editors of *The Ecologist*, the economist Robert Heilbroner reflected the pessimistic spirit of many of his contemporaries[312] when he observed in 1974 that in the previous years people had struggled with 'a visible decline in the quality of the air and water,' a 'series of man-made disasters of ecological imbalance,' and a 'mounting general alarm as to the environmental collapse that unrestricted growth could inflict. Thus, even more disturbing than the possibility of a serious deterioration in the quality of life if growth comes to an end is the awareness of a possibly disastrous decline in the material conditions of existence if growth does not come to an end.'[313]

3.2 Optimists

Optimistic writers traditionally based their stance on future technical advances. For instance, Alexander Everett observed in 1823 that 'because labour productivity depends almost entirely on skill and science, the introduction of new skills would in time deliver an abundance of products in ways that are 'unbounded and incalculable".'[314] More than six decades later, Edward Atkinson suggested that 'as the mental faculties of man are more developed and are more intelligently applied to the conversion of the forces of nature into material products, the general struggle for life will become less and not greater.'[315]

One result of these advances would be the elimination of the most important wants and problems, at least in peaceful times. The author of an anonymous essay published in 1889 in the *Westminster Review* thus argued that:

> [s]tatistical evidence incontrovertibly proves that a large community, other things being equal, is capable of producing more food and more wealth generally, man per man, than is possible in a smaller community. Europe has overgrown the dread of famine, and no doubt in future days will outlive the dread of pestilence. Famines are objects of terror in the early stages of social growth when numbers are numerically weak. Thus the last great famine that visited England was in the fourteenth century. At the present day, with a population in round numbers eleven times greater, a famine is so exceedingly improbable that such a calamity is no longer feared.[316]

In 1904, the outgoing president of the American Association for the Advancement of Science, Carroll D. Wright, mentioned that the Malthusian doctrine and related perspectives had been superseded by scientific and technological advances and theories 'more rational and more in line with the facts.' The law of diminishing returns, he observed, had been overshadowed by countless innovations, such as the introduction of electric light in greenhouses. Although geographical expansion had been the 'immediate means of depriving the doctrine of its force,' it was 'intensive agriculture and the discoveries of science' that mattered. Apart from agricultural production, relevant scientific advances included steamships, railroads, and telegraphy that resulted in famines being 'avoided or minimized,' 'prices [being] equalized,' and the state of the 'markets of the world [being] known every day.' Wright, however, believed that while Malthusian theory might be revived at some future date, it would not be 'in our day, nor will it be in our century.'[317]

In his 1944 book *Enough and to Spare*, the Harvard geologist Kirtley Fletcher Mather reminded his readers that the 'subtle hold upon the populace secured by the totalitarian dictators of Germany, Italy, and Japan [was] due in large part to the apparent validity of the [Malthusian-inspired] argument that virile, capable, and ambitious nations must 'grab while the grabbing is good' because the day is close at hand when 'there will not be enough to go around.'"[318] While he agreed that 'peace, prosperity, and security' were unattainable if Malthus was right, it was fortunately not the case. Although this was obvious with advances such as the use of synthetic nitrogen fertilizer in agriculture and hydropower, Mather contended that the supply of minerals would last a few hundred and perhaps even a few thousand years.[319] True, the 'discovery of new oil fields [was] no longer keeping pace with the exhaustion of the older fields,'[320] but deficiencies in local production could be made up by 'imports from abroad or by synthetic products from other domestic sources,' by the development of valuable resources out of oil shale and lower grade deposits, or else by substituting 'other forms of power for that derived from gasoline.'[321] 'Summing it all up,' Mather wrote:

> for nearly all of the important nonrenewable resources, the known or confidently expected world stores are thousands of times as great as the annual world consumption. For the few which like petroleum are available in relatively small quantities, substitutes are known or potential sources of alternative supply are at hand in quantities adequate to meet our current needs for many thousands of years. There is no prospect of the imminent exhaustion of any of the truly essential raw materials, as far as the world as a whole is concerned. Mother Earth's storehouse is far more richly stocked with goods than is ordinarily inferred.[322]

The bottom line, as stated on the book's dustcover, was that the nation or the man looking to conquer 'breathing room' at the expense of his neighbor instead of cooperating with him was doomed. Malthusian theory that had 'frightened mankind into warfare had no basis in fact and the abundance of the earth's nonrenewable resources guaranteed "enough and to spare" for this generation and generations to come.'[323]

Economist Julian Simon's well-known stance was that 'people in the future will live longer lives than they do now, with higher incomes and better standards of living, and the costs of natural resources will be lower than at present.'[324] His outlook was arguably best summed up in his (in)famous 'long-run forecast in brief:'

> The material conditions of life will continue to get better for most people, in most countries, most of the time, indefinitely. Within a century or two, all nations and most of humanity will be at or above today's Western living

> standards. I also speculate, however, that many people will continue to think and say that the conditions of life are getting worse.[325]

3.3 Balance of evidence

The big picture

Over ten millennia the human population surged from a few millions to well over seven billion individuals.[326] While not much changed during most of this period, in the relatively recent past, human numbers, wealth, health and nutritional intake have improved to such an extent that, according to the Nobel laureate economist Robert Fogel and his collaborators, 'in most if not quite all parts of the world, the size, shape and longevity of the human body have changed more substantially, and much more rapidly, during the past three centuries than over many previous millennia,'[327] meaning that humans are now taller, stronger and healthier than ever before. Gregg Easterbrook summarized this development as follows: 'The increased life expectancy means twice as much time on earth for the typical person. The economist Julian Simon called the fast rise in the life expectancy for typical people "the greatest single achievement in history".'[328]

This achievement had a corollary outcome that, superficially at least, played into the hands of the pessimists even more than it vindicated the optimists:

> It is ever increasing life expectancy, and surely not birthrates, that caused the population explosion of the late twentieth century, as it took the planet thousands of decades, until the year 1970, to reach a human population of three billion, then just three more decades, from 1970 to 2001, to leapfrog to six billion. Birthrates and fertility declined almost everywhere during the very period when the global census was doubling; steadily, fewer children were being born per woman. But death has declined and longevity improved at even faster rates than fertility decline, the net being ever more people alive. 'The population explosion,' the analyst Nicholas Eberstadt has written, 'is really a health explosion.'[329]

To give but a few uncontroversial data points, in the last 200 years the world's population went from approximately 1 billion to over 7.5 billion individuals.[330] The share of the global population living in extreme poverty fell from approximately 84% in 1820 to well below 10% today.[331] Global life expectancy rose from approximately 30 years in 1900 to almost 70 today and no country at the present time has a lower life expectancy than the countries with the highest life expectancy in 1800, as seen in Figure 3.1.[332]

Remarkable progress can also be observed in food production, yields and environmental quality measures, such as air and water pollution or forest cover,

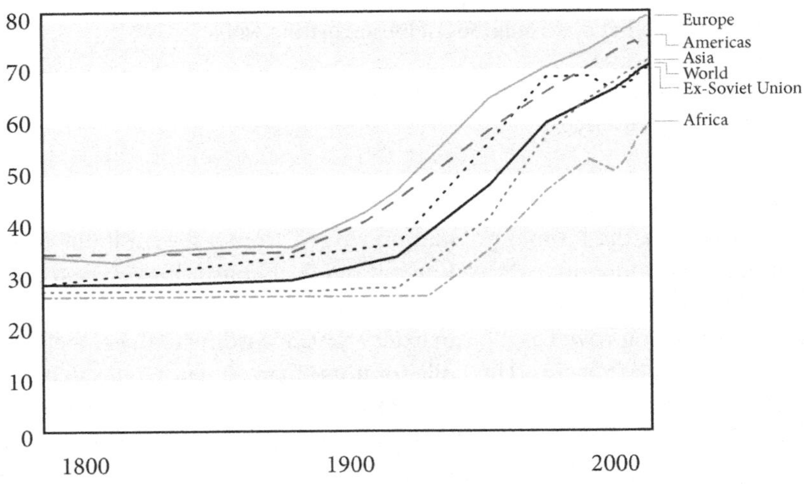

Figure 3.1: Life expectancy globally and by world regions 1770–2015.

Souce: Roser (2017).

with much evidence suggesting that, from a global perspective, 'human systems such as agriculture have proven extraordinarily resilient to environmental and social challenges, responding robustly to population pressures, soil exhaustion, and climate fluctuations over millennia.'[333] In the meantime, non-renewable resources have become less scarce than ever before while, over the long run, their price has become more affordable.[334] In fact, the Australian economic forecaster Stefan Hajkowicz, in his 2015 overview of the seven megatrends the world is facing in the near future, described the 'more from less' trend of more efficient resource utilization and waste reduction in the following terms:

> The world doesn't have a problem of food scarcity. But it does have a problem about food distribution. As a general rule the world has enough food, water, energy and minerals to meet the needs of current and future forecast populations. But there is an important 'if'. We have enough if, and only if, we're smart about how we develop, utilise and share our resources... Nevertheless, the world is heading in a better direction. This contradicts some environmental doomsday predictions that foresee humans running out of resources, leading to a subsequent Armageddon. By and large I think these predictions are incorrect or at most unlikely. That's because innovations in technology, changes to lifestyles – which needn't involve a loss of quality of life – and better governance achieve not only

> more from less but enough from what we have. I think the future is, or at least can be, bright.[335]

Virtually all of Hajkowicz's solutions to achieve 'more from less' involve technological and social innovations that improve efficiency, find new substitutes and 'mine above ground'[336] for underutilized waste. We will review many of these processes in Chapter 4.

A statistical bestiary

Several scientists, analysts and writers have documented and synthesized recent trends using a vast array of credible sources. The following articles summarize many relevant milestones and provide references as well as additional links:

Rosling In a column published in 2013, the late Hans Rosling, then professor of global health at the Karolinska Institutet (Sweden), introduced his readers to 'five ways the world is doing better than you think':

- fast population growth is coming to an end;
- the 'developed' and 'developing' worlds have gone (i.e., 'so many of the formerly 'developing' group of countries have been catching up that the countries now form a continuum');
- people are much healthier;
- girls are getting better education;
- the end of extreme poverty is in sight.[337]

Ausubel In a 2015 essay, Rockefeller University scientist Jesse Ausubel documented how 'over the past several decades, through technological innovation, Americans now grow more food on fewer acres, eat more sources of meat that are less land-intrusive, and used water more efficiently so that water use is lower than in 1970. The result: lands that were once used for farms and logging operations are now returning as forests and grasslands, along with wildlife.'[338]

Hajkowicz In his 2015 book, Commonwealth Scientific and Industrial Research Organisation (CSIRO) economic planner and forecaster Stefan Hajkowicz brought together quantitative research from around the world to present some milestones:

- Between 1990 and 2010 the proportion of people who were living in extreme poverty (on less than $1.25 a day) fell by 25 percentage points to 22%.

- Children's mortality fell by 41% to 51 deaths per 1000 children in 2011.
- 15% of the world's population was hungry in 2012 versus 23.2% in 1990.
- 89% (up from 76% in 1990) of the world's population had access to good-quality drinking water in 2010.[339]

Bailey In a 2018 column, science journalist Ronald Bailey wrote about how the US has long passed 'peak water' withdrawal, that wind and water erosion of soil have fallen by 44% in the US since 1982; that farmers are getting more crops from less land; that the area covered by forests in the US has increased from 721 million acres in 1920 to 766 million acres in 2012; that of the 44 overfished stocks examined, 19 showed significant increases in rate of biomass recovery; none of the 44 showed statistically significant declines in rate of biomass recovery; that the Environmental Protection Agency reports that air pollution has fallen by 67% since 1980, although water pollution trends are not as positive. [340]

Mann In the March 2018 issue of *The Atlantic*, the science journalist Charles Mann observed that in 1970 about one out of every four people was hungry (or 'undernourished'), a proportion that is now approximately one in ten. In the last five decades, the global average life span has risen by more than 11 years, with most of the gains occurring in less developed countries. Hundreds of millions of people in Latin America, Asia and Africa have lifted themselves from destitution into a status approaching middle class, an unprecedented surge of well-being in human history.[341]

Pinker and Epstein In data-filled books, Harvard psychologist Steven Pinker described how the 'world has improved by every measure of human flourishing over the past two centuries, and the progress continues',[342] while philosopher Alex Epstein has stated that the problem of the current sustainability discourse is not so much that pessimists 'predicted a disaster and got half a disaster – it's that they predicted disaster and got dramatic improvement.'[343]

The pessimists' (partial) concessions

Interestingly, past advances were also acknowledged by many among previous generations of analysts, including pessimistic ones (who quickly added that positive trends would soon come to an end). For instance, the economic historian Arnold Toynbee (1852–1883) prepared lectures intended in part as a rebuke to Henry George's optimistic view on population growth. Toynbee observed that Malthus' proposition that 'population tends to outstrip the means of subsistence', if interpreted as meaning that 'population *does* increase faster than the means of subsistence', was clearly 'not true of England at the present day' as the 'average quantity of food consumed per head is yearly greater.' It was also debatable in the case of India, where it would have been true 'in certain districts' only.[344]

In 1889 Edward Atkinson admitted that while 'a century or less is quite insufficient to warrant absolute inductions from experience, yet it may well be considered that there has not been a single decade, since the hypothesis of Malthus was first presented, in which the means of subsistence have not gained very rapidly upon the population of the world.'[345] Nearly 30 years later, the economist Albert Benedict Wolfe commented that for decades before World War I 'the problem of population had [slumbered] in innocuous desuetude. Indeed, the popular impression was that a population problem in an economic or Malthusian sense no longer existed.' While organized labour favoured immigration restriction for fears it would result in low wages and unemployment among the native population, 'any suggestion that immigration would tend to produce overpopulation would have been laughed at.'[346]

In 1954 Harrison Brown acknowledged that the 'disaster which Malthus foresaw for the Western World did not occur. Instead, Western populations [are] far beyond the levels he would have considered possible, and the poverty and deprivation so widespread in Malthus's time [have] enormously decreased.' Brown even added that 'so widely divergent were the predictions from the actual course of events that, if we were to look only at the predictions divorced from the reasoning, we would be inclined to say that he was incompetent.'[347] The following year, biologist and population pessimist Marston Bates confessed that human population had multiplied threefold since the days of Malthus 'without disastrous consequences' and that people 'in many parts of the world are much better off, by any measure, than they were 150 years ago.'[348] Two decades later, another pessimist, economist Robert Heilbroner, felt compelled to write that:

> in the last century or so...great masses of people have moved 'up' the scale – each generation consuming food in quantity and quality superior to that of the classes above them in the preceding generation, each generation clothed in materials whose variety, color, fineness, and abundance surpassed the garb of all but the very wealthiest figures of their youth, each generation able to enjoy a degree of mastery over death that would have appeared miraculous to its progenitors, each generation able to move about the surface of the earth or to command the powers of nature in ways that would have struck the previous generation with awe...[349]

Finally, the environmental activist Bill McKibben acknowledged in a 1998 book entitled *Maybe One* (child) that 'Each new generation of Malthusians have made new predictions that the end was near, and they have been proven conclusively wrong...So Malthus is wrong. Over and over again he is wrong. No prophet has ever been proved wrong more times. In each generation Malthusians have risen up to say he is about to be proved right, and in each generation they have been left looking silly.'[350]

We now consider more specifically how spontaneous market processes delivered such positive results while elite opinion argued it could not be achieved.

4 How market processes simultaneously deliver economic and environmental benefits

4.1 On the spontaneous greening of market economies

One illustrative device used to convey the notion that increased wealth can be compatible with improved environmental indicators is the inverted U-shaped 'environmental Kuznets curve' (EKC), which shows how the emissions and/or concentrations associated with many pollutants first rise with economic development, but then fall as income exceeds a threshold level (Figure 4.1).

The most common explanation for EKCs is that a high standard of living allows people to attach increasing value to environmental amenities, which in turn leads to more stringent environmental standards, the development of technologies to meet them, and regulatory machinery to enforce them. As the economist Colin Clark observed in 1973, at a time when many activists blamed population growth for pollution problems:

> Pollution of the environment...is found in all industrial countries. It is serious in France, and also in Sweden. Swedes are finding the whole of the Baltic Sea contaminated by industrial effluents. Why mention these two countries in particular? Because, for a long time, they have had very little population growth.
>
> It is our handling, or rather mishandling of sewage and industrial wastes, which causes pollution. If population growth stopped, but present industrial practices continued, pollution would continue. The converse is also true. An increasing population, with proper organisation of waste treatment could be quite free from pollution.[351]

Similar observations could be made in the context of urban agglomerations. For instance, air pollution in London was not only much worse in 1900 than in 2000, but it was also arguably worse than in large urban agglomerations of the

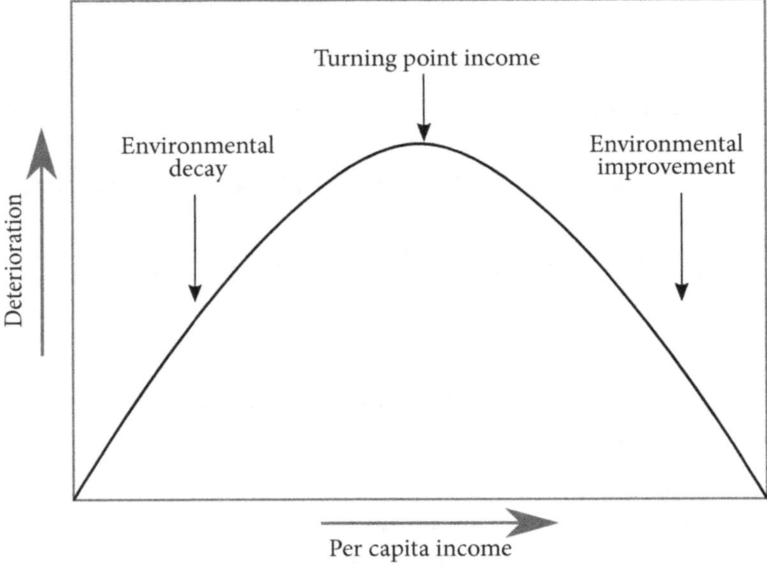

Figure 4.1: Environmental Kuznets curve.

Source: Yandle *et al.* (2002, p.3).

developing world today.[352] As the journalist Charles Mann observed recently, the Ehrlichs opened their *Population Bomb* with a vivid description of the over-populated and polluted conditions they had observed in New Delhi in 1966. The Indian capital at the time had a population of approximately 2.8 million. Paris, by contrast, had a population of about 8 million. 'No matter how carefully one searches through archives,' Mann writes, 'it is not easy to find expressions of alarm about how the Champs-Élysées was 'alive with people.' Instead, Paris in 1966 was an emblem of elegance and sophistication.'[353] Needless to say, in 1900 the then much smaller Parisian population had to contend with a much more significant form of pollution, namely horse manure.[354]

Using a large array of data, electrical engineer and policy analyst Indur Goklany suggested an 'environmental transition' hypothesis.[355] Unlike EKC theorists, Goklany postulated that economic growth *and* technological change acting in conjunction initially cause environmental degradation, but that it is later reversed as quality of life improves. In the first stage, individuals are able to meet their basic needs: food, clean water, sanitation, basic medical and public health services, education, and so on. Once this is achieved, they address environmental concerns resulting from both previous poverty – for example, deforestation or indoor air pollution – and later industrialization, for example outdoor air and water pollution.

Other possible explanations for EKC-type outcomes include an economy-wide structural change to service- and information-based activities that are less polluting than physical production. This hypothesis, however, is doubtful in light of the growth of manufacturing value and output in advanced economies such as the United States.[356] The same can be said about the alleged displacement of dirty industries from advanced to less-developed economies for environmental – as opposed to economic (cost) – considerations. The reality of this practice is questionable, if only because the cost of improving the environmental performance of manufacturing operations is typically but a small fraction of the costs of moving operations to jurisdictions with lower environmental standards but less reliable power supplies, skilled labour shortages, poor information, transportation and communications infrastructures, and bad governance.[357]

Be that as it may, advances in public health policies and pollution control technologies have certainly played a role in addressing environmental problems.

Less widely known and understood, however, is the relative (or weak) and absolute (or strong) decoupling between a growing population, its consumption of resources and its environmental impact. In short, *relative decoupling* refers to environmental impacts growing at a slower rate than population or consumption while an *absolute decoupling* describes declining overall impacts independent of population and consumption trends.[358]

These processes were summarized by Linus Blomqvist, the Director of Conservation at the Breakthrough Institute: 'Humans spare nature by more efficiently using land to produce food, wood, and other goods, and by substituting technology for ecosystem goods, such as going from bushmeat to farmed meat, wild fisheries to aquaculture, fuelwood to modern fuels, and from organic to synthetic fertilizer.'[359]

Another important process that has gone largely unnoticed is the longstanding and constant development of valuable by-products out of what used to be polluting production waste.

The drivers of these processes are straightforward. As the engineer and historian of technology Henry Petroski explained, the 'form of made things is always subject to change in response to their real or perceived shortcomings, their failures to function properly. This principle governs all invention, innovation, and ingenuity; it is what drives all inventors, innovators, and engineers.' Furthermore, 'since nothing is perfect, and, indeed, since even our ideas of perfection are not static, everything is subject to change over time. There can be no such thing as a 'perfected' artifact; the future perfect can only be a tense, not a thing.'[360] In practice, as the Canadian engineer and communist activist H. Dyson Carter observed nearly eight decades ago, this means that commercially successful inventions must display at least one of the following characteristics: save time, lower costs, last longer, do more, work better and sell more easily.[361] While not all of these characteristics have environmentally beneficial implications, most do. In other words, a widespread feature of successful market innovations is that they mandate the creation of smaller or less important problems than those that existed previously. This occurs mainly through the following processes:

- increased efficiency via dematerialization/intensification
- resource creation through substitution or transmaterialization
- resource recovery through by-product development.

Increased efficiency via dematerialization/intensification

Numerous studies on the increased efficiency of material use have demonstrated how, in a competitive context, creative individuals have every incentive to develop production processes that generate more or better output using less input.[362] This is especially obvious in agriculture, where, over the centuries, farmers have gone from one harvest every 10 years to two or three harvests per year, using up to 30 times less land to produce the same amount of food.[363] While in the past bringing more land under cultivation was often a prerequisite to increased food production, in the last century most of the progress can be attributed to increasing the yields of land under cultivation through technological advances such as mechanization, crop rotation, better drainage and irrigation, and improved seeds, livestock, fertilizers and pesticides.[364]

To give but two cases, one can look at the long-term cereal yields in the United Kingdom over the last eight centuries, as shown in Figure 4.2, and corn yields, total production and acreage in the United States over the last century and a half, as shown in Figures 4.3 and 4.4. As environmental analyst Jesse Ausubel points out, 'crucially, rising yields have not required more tons of fertilizer or other inputs. The inputs to agriculture have plateaued and then fallen – not just cropland but nitrogen, phosphates, potash, and even water', as seen in Figure 4.5.[365]

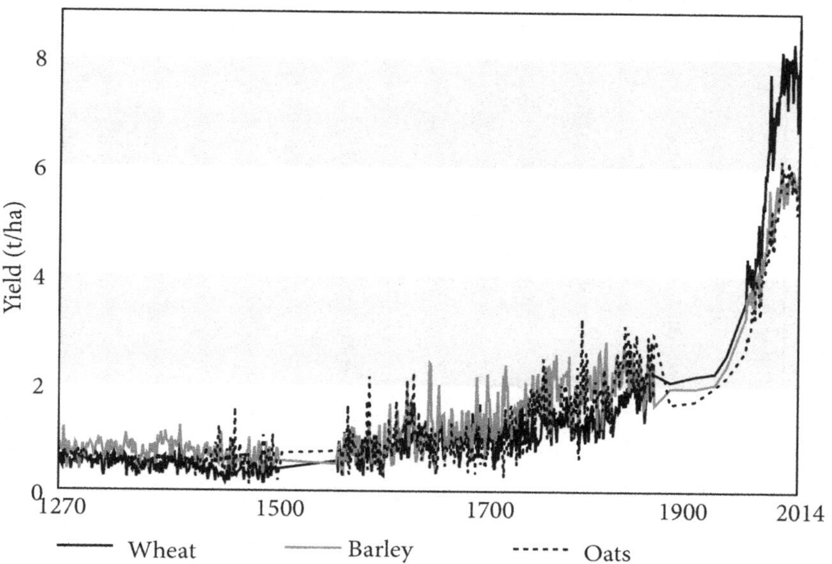

Figure 4.2: Long-term cereal yields in the United Kingdom.

Source: Roser and Ritchie (2018b).

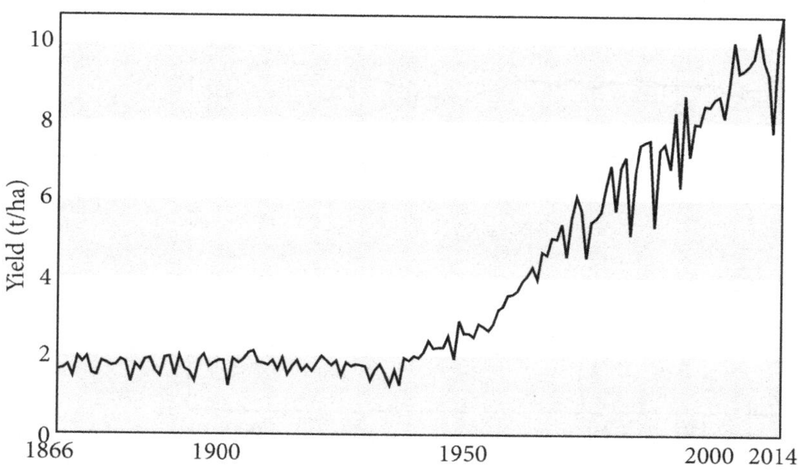

Figure 4.3: Average corn yields in the United States, 1866–2014.

Source: Roser and Ritchie (2018b).

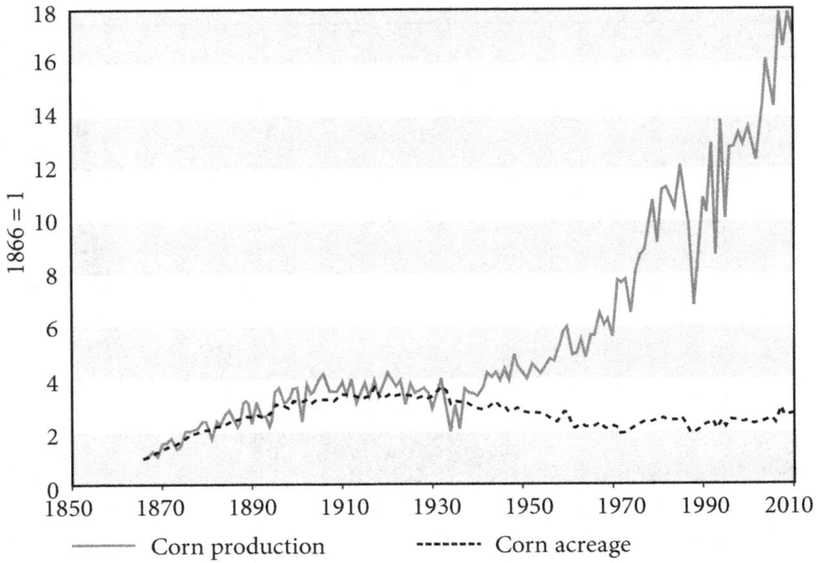

Figure 4.4: Decoupling of US corn production from area farmed.

Source: Ausubel (2015).

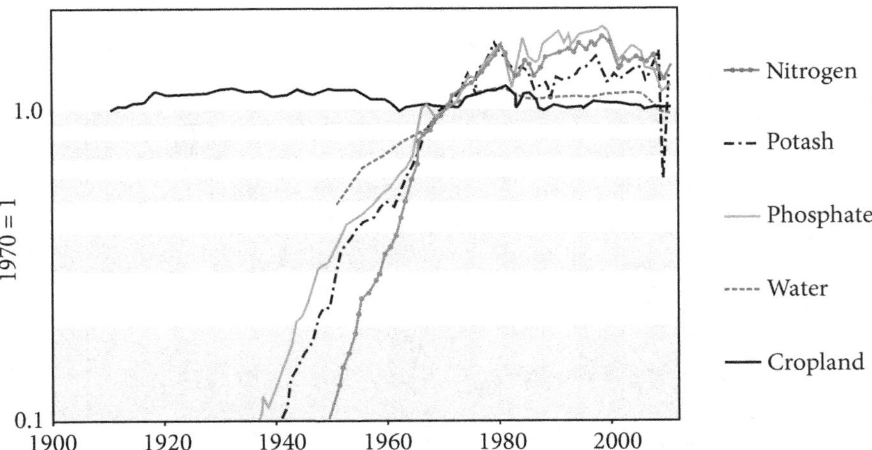

Figure 4.5: Absolute US consumption of five agricultural inputs.

Note: while the x-axis is a linear scale, the y-axis is logarithmic, so the spacing is proportional to the logarithm of the number. Source: Ausubel (2015).

While increased efficiency is most easily illustrated in the agricultural sector, numerous other data points also demonstrate dramatic efficiency improvements:

- *Energy use*: The amount of energy used to produce a good or service in the US economy has, on average, fallen every year since about 1800.
- *Energy generation*: Over the last three hundred years, the efficiency of generators has gone up from 1% of their apparent limit to about 50%.
- *Per unit output*: Over the last two centuries, the ratio of weight to power in industrial boilers has decreased almost 100 times.
- *Carbon use in fuels*: In 1860, globally, about 1.1 tons of carbon went into the primary energy produced by the energy equivalent of one ton of oil then in the fuel mix; this amount had decreased to about 0.7 tons by 1990.[366]

The concept of *dematerialization* is now often used to characterize the decline over time of the weight of materials used in industrial end products. *Intensification* conveys the reality of higher yields or returns on investment in the production of biomass such as plants and livestock. Both processes explain why the impact of wealthier consumers on the environment is not necessarily greater than that of much poorer people. For instance, while 'the average Northern European consumes more food and a larger variety of foods than the average West African,' both regions 'actually require a similar amount of cropland, per capita, for food production, because they use very different agricultural technologies.'[367]

Resource creation through substitution or transmaterialization

In a market economy, a sustained price increase for any resource not only encourages individuals to use it more efficiently, but also to look for more of it and to develop substitutes. As a result, despite the physical finiteness of the earth:

- most resources for which there is a sustained demand over time have become more plentiful and affordable;
- human ingenuity tends to substitute smaller volumes of higher quality or technologically more sophisticated materials for larger volumes of lower quality materials, a process sometimes referred to as *transmaterialization*.

In the former case, economic incentives reward the development of innovative resource extraction processes that open up newly profitable deposits, such as offshore drilling, oil sands, or shale. In the latter case, similar economic incentives stimulate the development of new inputs with some combination of advantages over earlier alternatives, such as being more powerful and/or abundant; stronger and/or lighter; and/or easier to produce, handle, transport and/or store. As Barnett and Morse explained over five decades ago, the 'increasing scarcity of particular resources fosters discovery or development of alternative resources, not only equal in economic quality but often superior to those replaced.'[368] For instance, when:

> coal, petroleum, hydroelectric power, and the atomic nucleus replace wood, peat, and dung as sources of energy, when aluminum yields its secrets to technology and is made to exist, as never before, in the form of metal; when the iron in taconite, once held there inseparably, becomes competitive with that in traditional ores – when all this happens, can we say that we have been forced to shift from resources of higher to those of lower economic quality?[369]

One aspect of transmaterialization rarely, if ever, discussed is that it often involves the development of new products out of what was previously considered industrial waste, a topic we will now address.

Resource recovery through by-product development

According to environmental engineer James D. Ward and his collaborators, the only way to achieve sustainable growth would be 'via permanent absolute decoupling,' an outcome that 'remains elusive', although it can sometimes be observed through resource substitution.[370] Yet, as argued in Chapter 3, the available empirical evidence suggests that environmental remediation and a cleaner environment are more often than not associated with greater wealth production and consumption.

One other component of the answer to this apparent conundrum was provided nearly three decades ago by economist and demographer Mikhael Bernstam in his analysis of the diverging environmental performance of open competitive markets such as the United States, as compared to centrally planned economies such as the Soviet Union. As was then obvious, over time the former had become wealthier and cleaner, while the latter stagnated, or even regressed, and became increasingly polluted. Bernstam considered this outcome the 'most important reversal in economic and environmental history since the Industrial Revolution.'[371] He attributed it to the cost minimization paradigm of market economies as opposed to the input maximization of centrally planned ones.[372] His key insight, however, concerned waste: uselessly processed resources and economically useless production, such as scrap, spills, slag, discards, refuse and other processing losses, destroyed primary resources and losses of intermediary and final output in transportation and storage. It was this, rather than increased production or consumption, that was the ultimate determinant of the impact of economic growth on the environment. As Bernstam put it, 'as [market] economies grow, discharges to the environment increase rapidly, then decelerate, and eventually decline.'[373]

Bernstam, however, didn't discuss the creation of valuable by-products out of polluting production residuals, a phenomenon that has long been widespread and significant.[374] For example, a scientific retrospective published in 1887 highlighted 'the utilization of waste materials and by-products' as a 'leading feature of the Victorian epoch.'[375]

A year earlier, an encyclopedia entry described how, 'in the earlier days' of many manufacturing branches, 'certain portions of the materials used have been cast aside as "waste"', but over time 'first in one branch and then in another, this "waste" material has been experimented upon with a view to finding some profitable use for it; and in most instances the experiments have had more or less satisfactory results.'[376] Writing in 1904, the American industrial chemist Leebert Lloyd Lamborn observed:

> If there is one aspect more than any other that characterizes modern commercial and industrial development...it is the utilization of substances which in a primitive stage of development of any industry were looked upon as worthless. They were secondary products incurred in the manufacture of the main commodity, for which the industrial acumen of the age found no use; or if a use were known, the prejudices and conservatism of society allowed them to languish in the shadow of a similar commodity already strongly intrenched.[377]

As the journalist Frederick Talbot commented nearly a century ago: 'To relate all the fortunes which have been amassed from the commercialization of what was once rejected and valueless would require a volume. Yet it is a story of fascinating romance and one difficult to parallel in the whole realm of human activity.'[378] A former president of the Federation of British Industries similarly commented at the time: 'In the days of my childhood, 'waste not, want not' was a lesson inculcated upon all young people. Whether there was at once a suitable response in the nursery I am now too old to remember, but the same wise saying has had the constant consideration of every progressive manufacturer for at least a century.'[379]

We can illustrate this principle with some examples. In 1931 Sir Harry McGowan, chairman of Imperial Chemical Industries Ltd, could declare:

> No one can read of the early days of chemical manufacture without being struck by the extravagance and wastefulness of its methods. It is difficult to visualize to-day the possibility of great tracks of lovely country being laid waste by fumes. These same fumes have now been caught and snared to become valuable money-making products.[380]

A similar pattern of outcome was observed with cottonseed, which typically accounted for between two-thirds and three-fourths of the weight of the cotton as it was picked in nineteenth-century America. It was originally considered an unmitigated nuisance, which attracted vermin, polluted streams, rotted in the soil, poisoned most livestock and was a significant fire hazard. Indeed, the increasingly large volume of this natural waste product caused so many problems that it led to the adoption of the first environmental regulations in the United States. For a time, there were even a few calls to abandon the cultivation of cotton altogether because of the severity of cottonseed disposal problems. At first, the main marketable uses of cottonseed were as adult ruminant feed or fertilizer for depleted cotton and corn fields located close enough to production sites to cover transportation costs. By 1889, however, the prolific technical writer Robert Grimshaw commented that cottonseed, having long been 'considered a refuse for which there was no use; long burned or thrown away,' had been turned into a 'main and by-products... now very important elements in our national industries. The garbage of 1800 became the fertilizer of 1870, the cattle food of 1880, and is now made to yield table food and useful articles of industrial pursuits.' The oil – 'more widely known throughout the world and used for a greater variety of purposes than any other oil' – was by then most valuable, but the 'residuum after its expression' was a valuable fertilizer and the 'best cattle food,' the ashes of the hulls delivered 'potash of high commercial value,' and the refuse from the refining of the crude oil provided a 'most excellent stock for laundry and toilet soaps.'[381] In time, these by-products were not only eliminated as sources of pollution but became crucial to the financial survival of countless cotton growers.[382]

One can get a glimpse of the wide range of useful substances created from various industrial residuals at the time through figure drawn in 1919 by the prominent US animal ecologist Victor E. Shelford (see Figure 4.6).

Although lawsuits and regulations sometimes provided additional motivation,[383] the key factor behind these developments was the profit motive, which, far from rewarding wasteful behaviour through the release of pollutants, actually gave corporate managers a strong incentive to turn waste into wealth, in the process improving the profitability and viability of their operations while delivering incidental environmental benefits.[384] In the words of Karl Marx: 'With the advance of capitalist production the utilization of the excrements of production and consumption is extended' and the 'so-called waste plays an important role in almost every industry' because finding new uses for previously unmarketable residuals ultimately increased 'the rate of profit.' In Marx's opinion, industrial waste recovery had become 'the second great branch of economy in the conditions of production' after economies of scale.[385]

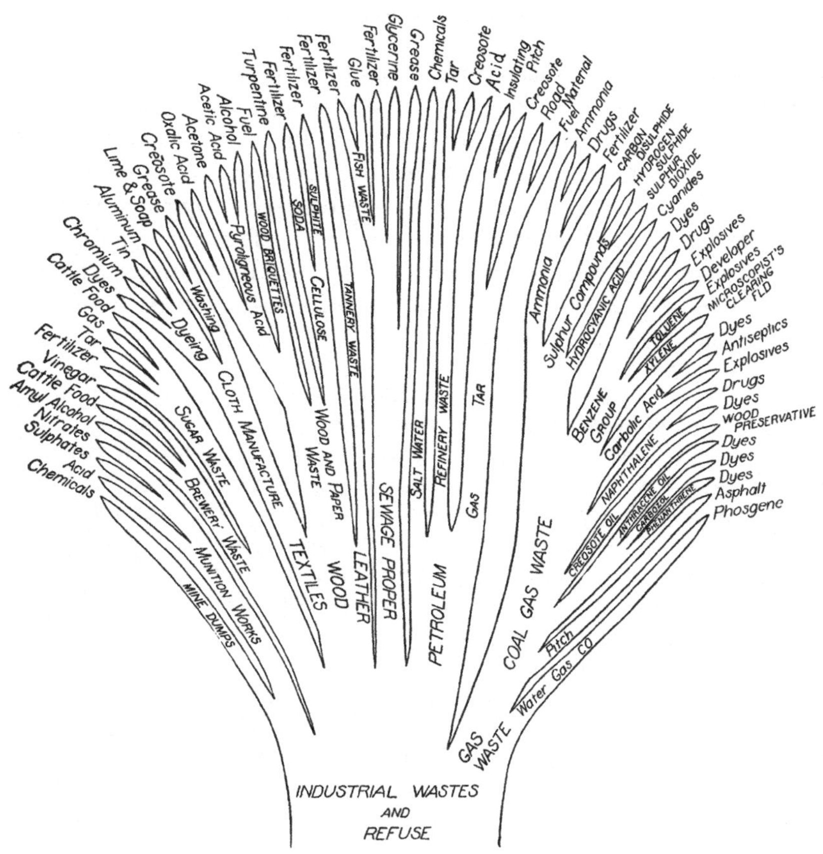

Figure 4.6: Wastes and the useful substances into which they may be manufactured or which may be obtained from them.

Source: Shelford (1919, p. 100).

The various developments described in this chapter will now be examined in more detail through a number of historical advances in the production and processing of carbon fuels.

4.2 Carbon fuels and the greening of planet earth

Energy scholar and analyst Vaclav Smil[386] lucidly synthesized the history of humanity's adventure with energy by tracing our energy transitions. He noted: 'Fundamentally, no terrestrial civilization can be anything else but a solar society dependent on the Sun's radiation, which energizes a habitable biosphere and produces all our food, animal feed and wood...The origins of fossil fuels are also in the transformation of solar radiation...'[387] He then pointed out what was uniquely efficient about our society's use of fossil fuels: two crucial innovations we were able to accomplish beyond merely burning these high energy density materials for heat and light.

> The transition to fossil fuels has...entailed two classes of fundamental qualitative improvements, and only their accumulation and combination have produced the energetic foundations of the modern world. The first category of these advances was the invention, development, and eventually mass-scale diffusion of new ways to convert fossil fuels: by introducing new prime movers – starting with steam engines and progressing to internal combustion engines, steam turbines, and gas turbines – and by coming up with new processes to transform raw fuels...The second class of inventions used fossil fuels to produce electricity, an entirely new kind of commercial energy.[388]

Smil followed up these facts with an essential and often overlooked insight: Innovating and exploring new energy sources is heavily dependent on the existing energy infrastructure. Energy transitions cannot be decoupled from their parent energy sources too quickly:

> [E]very transition to a new form of energy supply has to be powered by the intensive deployment of existing energies and prime movers: the transition from wood to coal had to be energized by human muscles, coal combustion powered the development of oil, and...today's solar photo-voltaic cells and wind turbines are embodiments of fossil energies required to smelt the requisite metals, synthesize the needed plastics, and process other materials requiring high energy inputs.[389]

Sustainable development theorists and environmental activists often assume that some power sources and commodities are inherently sustainable because of their renewable character. Conversely, these individuals typically consider minerals and hydrocarbons as inherently less desirable because they are non-renewable. Paradoxically, human history provides many examples of renewable resources being exploited unsustainably (e.g. loss of topsoil to erosion, water pollution, water table depletion, deforestation and defaunation) while continuing to show that our supply of non-renewable resources for which there is a significant demand keeps increasing over time. This is especially obvious with carbon fuels.[390]

While the dominance of coal, petroleum and natural gas in our modern energy mix is both overwhelming and long-standing, discussions of the beneficial social and environmental outcomes that are a result of their large-scale use is now virtually non-existent in popular and academic discourses. We address these issues in the next section, along with some further illustrations of the processes described in the previous section (dematerialization, transmaterialization and by-product development), which also contributed to beneficial environmental outcomes. As such, they provide striking illustrations of economist Julian Simon's belief that:

> [t]he main fuel to speed the world's progress is our stock of knowledge, and the brake is our lack of imagination. The ultimate resource is people – skilled, spirited, and hopeful people – who will exert their wills and imaginations for their own benefit as well as in a spirit of faith and social concern. Inevitably they will benefit not only themselves but the poor and the rest of us as well.[391]

Historical overview

The rise of carbon fuels

Until the 1890s, renewable power sources, including human and animal power, water, wind, solar and biomass sources such as fuelwood, charcoal, animal dung and crop residues, dominated the world's energy supply. While some quantities of coal, petroleum and bitumen had been used, their overall contribution worldwide was marginal. Among other problems, before the development of better combustion technologies, the burning of coal filled household and production sites with noxious smoke and gases, and people who could afford to do so relied instead on fuelwood and wood-derived charcoal. While some quantities of (sometimes distilled) crude oil and bitumen had been used as architectural adhesives, ship caulking, medicinal laxatives, road surfacing materials, lamp oil and domestic fuel, unreliable supplies and lack of markets for most fractions of crude oil prevented their large-scale development and exploitation.[392]

Beginning with the development of coal stoves, steam engines and coking technologies,[393] carbon fuels made possible new economic activities and the scaling up of earlier ones to unprecedented levels because of their capacity to deliver much more plentiful and reliable heat, power and feedstock in more advantageous geographical locations than renewable alternatives. In turn, new and better energy sources, new processes and new resources developed to meet a particular need paved the way to other applications.[394]

Let us examine a few illustrations of the social and environmental benefits of carbon fuels. The most obvious was the substitution of coal for biomass, as it was the shortage of fuelwood and charcoal in the vicinity of cities and towns that initially motivated the switch to coal. In short order, as Jevons observed in 1865, 'forests of an extent two and a half times exceeding the whole area of the United Kingdom would be required to furnish even a theoretical equivalent to [the country's] annual coal produce.'[395] More generally, as Edward A. Wrigley observed:

> The [organic economy] escaped from the problem of the fixed supply of land and of its organic products by using mineral raw materials. Thus the typical industries of the [Industrial Revolution] produced iron, pottery, bricks, glass and inorganic chemicals, or secondary products made from such materials, above all an immense profusion of machines, tools and consumer products fashioned out of iron and steel. The expansion of such industries could continue to any scale without causing significant pressure on the land, whereas the major industries of an organic economy, textiles, leather and construction, for example, could only grow if more wool, hides or wood were produced which in turn implied the commitment of larger and larger acreages to such ends, and entailed fiercer and fiercer competition for a factor of production whose supply could not be increased. Meeting all basic human needs, for food, clothing, housing and fuel, inevitably meant mounting pressure on the same scarce resource.[396]

Other considerations explain the rapid abandonment of older power sources. Writing in 1838, American economist Francis Wayland observed that water power – all of which would now be classified as small scale – could be capable of 'exerting great mechanical force', all the while being 'cheap [and] tolerably constant.' Unfortunately, it could only be used 'in situations where it has been created by nature,' which were often 'at a considerable distance from the seaports whence the manufacturer derives his supplies, and whence he exports his products,' thus often adding significant transportation costs to the price of manufactured goods. Furthermore, water could not always 'be commanded in sufficient quantity' and '[v]ery few mill-seats [were] secure from the liability to suffer from the want of water', such as in 'seasons of drought' when 'a large number of the laborers must be unemployed, and a large portion of the expenses of the establishment must be incurred, without yielding any remuneration to the proprietor.' Water power was also liable to 'dangers from inundation.'[397] Of course, severe freezing conditions would also have been problematic, as would be dams that silted up. Later analysts would estimate that the shops, factories and mills of the time could not depend upon their waterwheels more than 160 days a year because of these reasons.[398]

The British economist Richard Jones commented a few years after Wayland that while water power was 'cheap,' it was also 'uncertain' which is why 'more certain and continuous' – and in most cases much more powerful – coal-powered steam engines proved more desirable.[399] Wayland further observed that while steam engines were more costly (mostly because of the price of the engine, fuel and maintenance), the advantages of coal-powered steam engines over water wheels were overwhelming. Steam power, he remarked:

- could be used 'to create any required degree of mechanical force'
- was 'perfectly under human control'
- could 'be created in any place where fuel can be obtained'
- could 'be used at will, either as a stationary, or a locomotive power'
- could 'be made to act with perfect regularity.'[400]

In later decades, technical advances of all kinds led to a significant expansion of large-scale water power, but in more distant and/or less problematic locations and conditions. For instance, the development of better turbines made it possible to harness much more powerful rivers. As one observer noted, the idea of developing Niagara Falls had occurred to many people long before the end of the nineteenth century, 'but with the [water] wheels then available it was like trying to bind a giant with a thread.'[401] The use of concrete for the building of dams and the development of electricity, as opposed to the ropes, wires and transmission belts used in older mills, were also instrumental in harnessing rivers and lakes once too remote, yet extremely reliable and powerful. While governments subsidized some of these projects, large-scale hydroelectric output produced in the best locations proved an economically viable proposition from the turn of the twentieth century onward.

Nothing of the sort happened with wind, once used to power mills and pump water. In 1865, Jevons elaborated on the advantages of coal-generated steam over this then old-fashioned way of doing things:

> The first great requisite of motive power is, that *it shall be wholly at our command, to be exerted when and where and in what degree we desire.* The wind, for instance, as a direct motive power, is wholly inapplicable to a system of machine labour, for during a calm season the whole business of the country would be thrown out of gear. Before the era of steam-engines; [sic] windmills were tried for draining mines; [sic] 'but though they were powerful machines, they were very irregular, so that in a long tract of calm

> weather the mines were drowned, and all the workmen thrown idle. From this cause, the contingent expenses of these machines were very great; besides, they were only applicable in open and elevated situations.'[402]

Jevons further added, 'No possible concentration of windmills' could ever 'supply the force required in large factories or iron works.'[403] With coal, on the other hand, 'almost any feat is possible or easy' and going without it would mean his contemporaries would have been 'thrown back in the laborious poverty of earlier times.'

In later years, petroleum products – gasoline, diesel, kerosene and bunker fuel – proved a superior alternative to coal in the transportation sector while, when available and affordable, natural gas turned out to be preferable to coal and fuel oil in electricity production and home heating. These substitutions occurred because crude oil and natural gas have a number of technical (and therefore economic) advantages over coal, including, in petroleum's case:

- higher energy density (the amount of energy stored in a unit of volume);
- cleaner combustion with less-polluting gases and particulate matter;
- greater ease of extraction, because it requires no underground work by humans;
- greater ease of handling, transport and storage in a variety of applications and therefore much lower labour costs;
- more affordable feedstock for the production of a wide range of synthetic items.[404]

In each case, these transitions occurred without government support, because new developments were truly superior to older ways of doing things.

The two key advantages of carbon fuels – constancy (or non-intermittent controlled operation) and the sparing of land from energy production – have made it possible to establish a greener and more reliable electricity-powered industrial infrastructure, complete with high-temperature and high-throughput metal smelting and processing. As Vaclav Smil[405] further pointed out, it is this infrastructure that enabled the manufacture of wind turbines[406] and solar cells,[407] two land-based and intermittent energy sources that cannot manoeuvre past the non-intermittence and land-sparing advantages of carbon fuels. Indeed, gigantic wind turbines would be unthinkable without petroleum products: powered heavy equipment to dig their foundations, natural-gas-fired kilns to bake their concrete and coal-forged steel to erect their towers.[408]

As we will now discuss, the fundamental realities that mandated the development and increasing reliance on carbon fuels are still very much with us and will not go away despite wishful thinking and governmental support of inferior alternatives.[409]

Carbon fuels in the current energy mix

Carbon fuels have long accounted for over 80% of the commercial energy used worldwide, as shown in Figures 4.7–4.9.

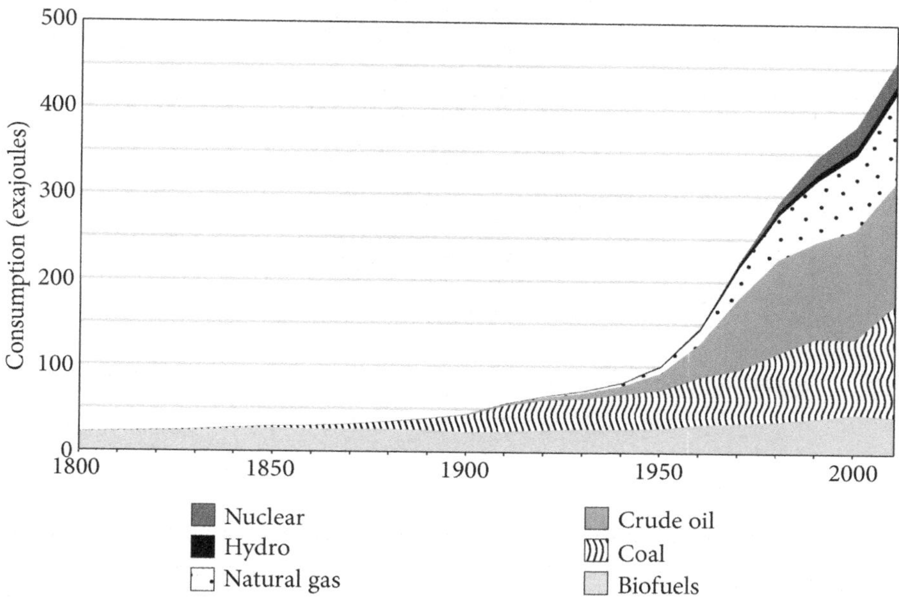

Figure 4.7: World energy consumption by source, 1800–2008.

Energy consumption unit: 1 exajoule = 1018 joules http://www.convertunits.com/info/exajoule. Roser (2015).

Despite repeated numerous government-sponsored initiatives, the share of global primary energy consumption represented by non-hydroelectric renewable energy sources – wind, geothermal, solar, biomass and waste – still accounts for less than 8% of global electricity generation, a significant portion of which now takes the form of logging and wood-processing waste and wood pellets, which do not display some of the key shortcomings of wind and solar technologies (most notably intermittency). For instance, in 2012 about 47% of the electricity generated from renewable technologies in the European Union came from wood, with figures ranging from 80% in Finland and 52% in Sweden to approximately 36% in Germany.[410] In some countries such as the United Kingdom, wood pellets need to be imported from North American and Russian forests in order to meet renewable quotas, while Brazil is on its way to becoming

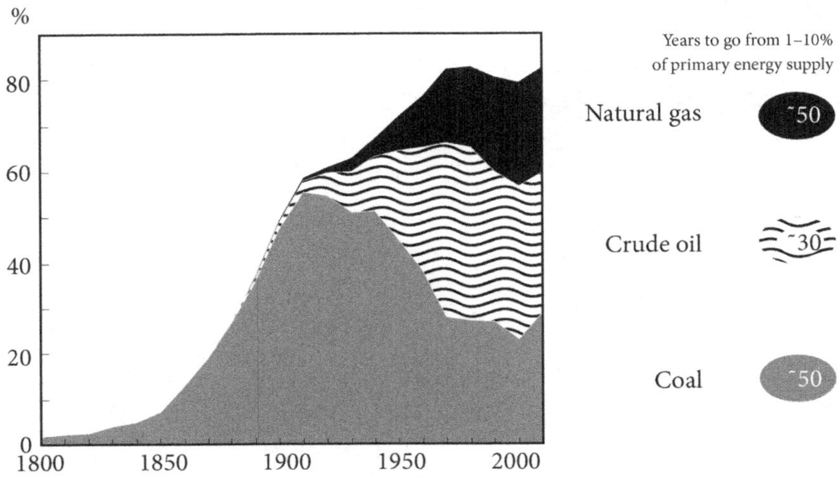

Figure 4.8: Share of primary energy supply (coal, oil, natural gas).

Source: Adapted from Dobbs *et al.* (2011, p. 26).

an important player in this sector.[411] Interestingly, in spite of their renewable character, wood pellets are now thought to produce more greenhouse gas emissions than the burning of coal once the entire lifecycle of the resource has been factored in.[412]

In the end, the long-standing constraints that once mandated the development of carbon fuels and the abandonment of renewable power sources in favour of non-intermittent, controllable and land-sparing fossil fuels are still too formidable to be ignored. No matter how much politicians spend on 'green shift' policies, the entirely predictable and unavoidable problems inherent to wind, solar and geothermal power generation – intermittency, low power density, (much) higher capital and operating costs, limited capacity, limited number of suitable locations, large (above- ground) surface area, lack of affordable storage options, required back-up power generation and additional delivery infrastructure – remain insurmountable. True, some news reports claimed that in 2014 Germany produced half of its electricity (not to be confused with total energy output, which includes petroleum products in the transportation sector) using solar power. Citing analysis by the Fraunhofer ISE research institute, however, Vaclav Smil observed that this peak production figure 'lasted for only one hour' and that this 'record share (50.6%) was due not only to hot, sunny weather, but also to the fact that that particular day was a public holiday with

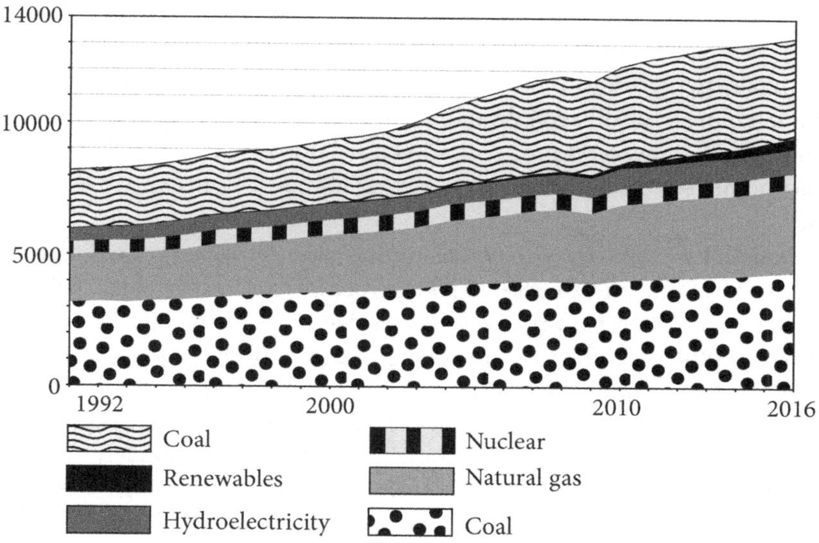

Figure 4.9: World primary energy consumption by fuels (million tonnes equivalent), 1991–2016.

Source: BP (2017, p. 10).

lower than normal demand – and, most fundamentally – to the fact that solar and wind have legal priority over fossil fuels and, when available, must be used to the maximum possible extent.'[413]

The shortcomings of wind and solar power sources also defeated Google's Renewable Energy Cheaper than Coal (RE<C) initiative launched in 2007, an effort to drive down the cost of renewable and clean energy with a particular emphasis on geothermal and solar power technology.[414]

Among other crucial issues lost on many commentators, wind and solar power can only generate electricity and thus cannot provide valuable substitutes to transportation fuels, to say nothing of feedstock for the creation of synthetic and other products, such as asphalt for roads. While biomass can be turned into ethanol, biodiesel or plastics, none of these products is either technologically preferable or scalable enough to meet more than a tiny fraction of the overall market demand currently supplied through petroleum and natural-gas-derived feedstock.[415] Indeed, apart from being damaging to most engines and having inherent limitations, such as the low extraction power density of liquid fuel from biomass, producing enough ethanol and biodiesel to power a modern economy would require up to 10,000 times more cultivation area than is currently occupied by oil-extracting and producing infrastructures.[416] Furthermore, unlike energy transitions achieved spontaneously through many trials, errors and failures, subsidized jobs in the wind, solar and biomass sectors have come at a tremendous economic cost and has resulted in massive job losses in other economic sectors while creating a less reliable and more expensive power supply.[417]

Sustainability proposals based on technological approaches once discarded by decentralized and incremental market processes are preordained failures. What activists and theorists misunderstand is that market outcomes are not determined by ruthless displays of corporate power, but by a selection process in which alternative technologies are pitted against each other, with the best (or least bad) in terms of a wide range of trade-offs eventually being adopted and continually improved upon. As energy analyst Vaclav Smil concluded, 'Today's great hope for a quick and sweeping transition to renewable energy is fuelled mostly by wishful thinking and a misunderstanding of recent history.'[418]

Resource creation, efficiency and by-product development

Resource creation

Historically, carbon fuel producers have always exploited the best deposits available at the time. Once these were no longer productive in light of both the available technologies and market prices, they moved elsewhere. Yet, one cannot infer from this that petroleum producers were forever left scraping the bottom of the barrel, nor that petroleum became inexorably more expensive to find, extract, refine and bring to market, resulting in higher production costs, declining availability and increased environmental damage.

The first people to collect crude oil gathered it in locations where it naturally seeped to the surface of ponds and streams. From then on, if there was typically nothing 'easy' about pumping large amounts of petroleum out of the ground, human ingenuity always found ways to keep costs reasonable over time, even in the absence of exceptional discoveries such as the Persian Gulf deposits. As energy analysts Peter Huber and Mark P. Mills observed a decade ago: 'Oil extracted today from beneath 2 miles of water and 4 miles of vertical rock, with 6 additional miles of horizontal drilling beyond that, costs less than the 60-foot oil Colonel Drake was extracting a century ago and about the same as one-mile oil cost in 1980.'[419] To be more specific, the American petroleum pioneer Edwin Drake only had access to percussion (cable-tool) drilling technology, which severely limited the depth he could reach and the type of rocks he could bore through when he went looking for crude oil in northwestern Pennsylvania in the late 1850s. In later decades, the development of rotary drilling, offshore technologies and other advances of all kinds made it possible to tap into ever more remote and deeper oilfields. The 'easily accessible oil' of yesterday only seems so in light of later technological advances.

Needless to say, in the last two decades the world has witnessed the so-called 'fracking revolution' which was, as are all innovations, the result of the combination of existing technologies and much development work, most notably the prior knowledge that shale rock contains gas (as evidenced by 'shows' or bursts of gas when drilling through shales to reach deeper oil deposits), the hydraulic fracturing of rock (first introduced in the 1940s), horizontal drilling technologies (introduced in the 1970s) and advances in seismic exploration technologies that had benefitted from innovations in everything from computer to sensor technologies.

Thanks to shale oil and gas development, hydrocarbon reserves are now at an all-time high.[420]

Over time, as the energy economist Morris Albert Adelman famously observed: 'A stream of investment creates additions to proved reserves from a very large inground inventory. The reserves are constantly being renewed as they are extracted. How much was in the ground at the start and how much will be left at the end are unknown and irrelevant.'[421] This insight is also conveyed by what is known as a 'McKelvey box', which illustrates the distinction between the (typically unknown) total physical availability of a resource and the economically recoverable portion of it at any given point in time in light of market prices and available technology – in other words, a reserve – as shown in Figure 4.10.[422]

This interplay between physical deposits, technological innovation and fluctuating market prices explains why, in spite of their non-renewable nature, the economically recoverable amounts of crude oil and natural gas have increased substantially over the last two decades, as illustrated by Figure 4.11. It is also why the same cannot be said about coal, which has become less economically valuable due to the increased availability of natural gas.

Efficiency gains over time

As the then chief chemist of the US Bureau of Mines wrote nearly a century ago, 'the object of all fuel research is either to eliminate waste and increase efficiency in the mining, preparation and utilization of fuels, or to convert the raw fuel by treatment or processing into a more convenient or effective form for use with, in many cases, the recovery of valuable by-products for other purposes.'[423] One striking illustration of the results of these efforts is the fact that, over a three-

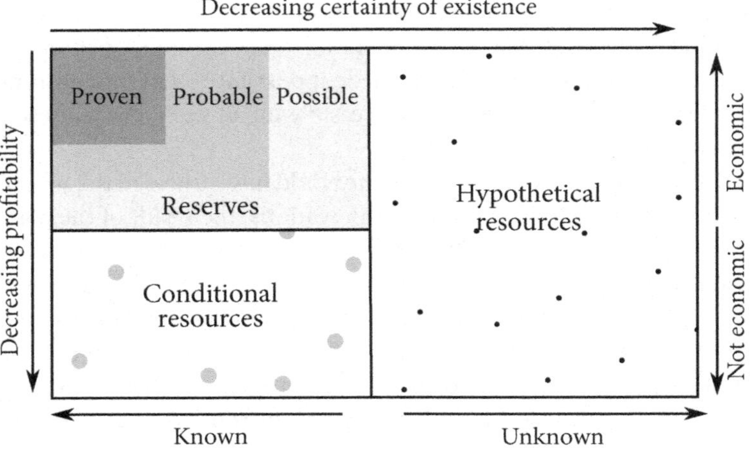

Figure 4.10: McKelvey box.

Source: Hanania *et al.* (2015).

hundred-year period, the efficiency of generators went from 1% (early steam engines) to about 50% of their apparent limit (gas turbines).[424] Figure 4.12 presents the logarithmic relationship between the work/efficiency of different coal-fired engines over time.

The search for increased efficiency in the use of resources was also the main rationale in the creation of the Standard Oil Company of Ohio in 1870 and the creation of the Standard Oil Trust in 1872, bringing nearly all the refining firms located in Cleveland under one consolidated umbrella.[425] As industry analysts observed in 1916:

> The purposes of this alliance were to cheapen transportation, both local and to the seaboard; to manufacture a better grade of illuminating oil at less expense by uniting the knowledge, experience and skills of all parties, as well as their various secret processes and patents; to unite with the business of refining the business necessarily collateral thereto (manufacture of barrels, tin cans, boxes, paint glue and sulphuric acid); to obtain and utilize the best scientific skill in investigating and experimenting upon the obtaining of new and useful products from petroleum, and to cheapen illuminating oils by obtaining profits from the by-products; to employ agents and send them through the world to open up markets; and by all the means enumerated to increase the supply of petroleum products and lessen their price to the consumer.[426]

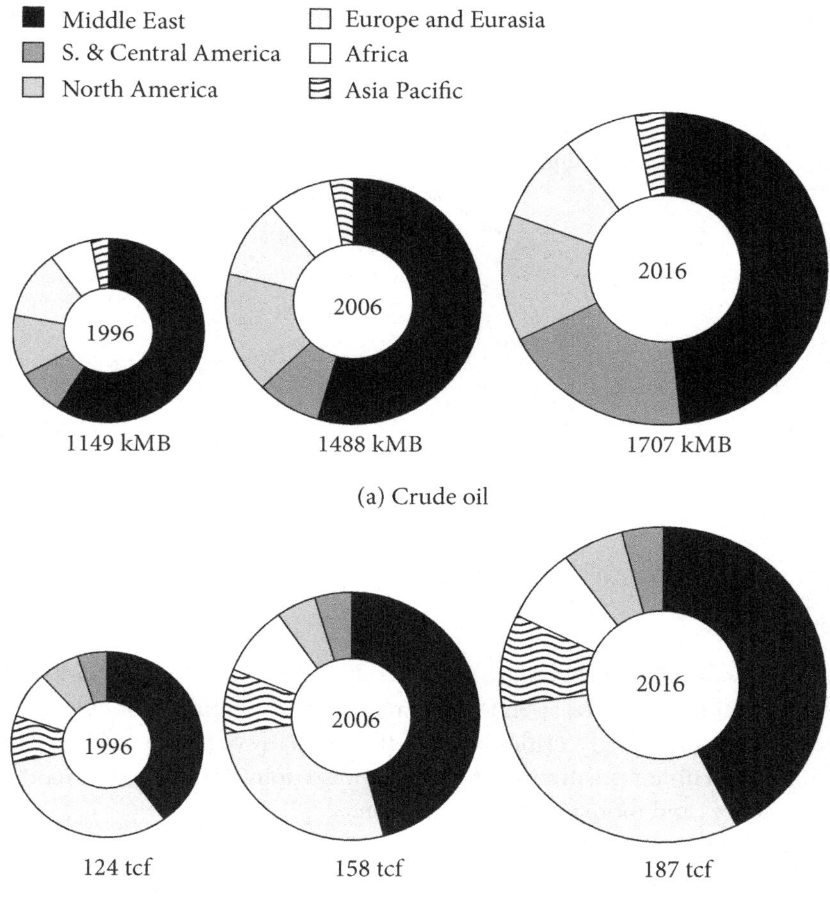

Figure 4.11: Fossil fuels, distribution of proved reserves 1996, 2006, 2016.

kMB, thousand million barrels; tcf, trillion cubic feet. Source: BP (2017, pp. 13,27).

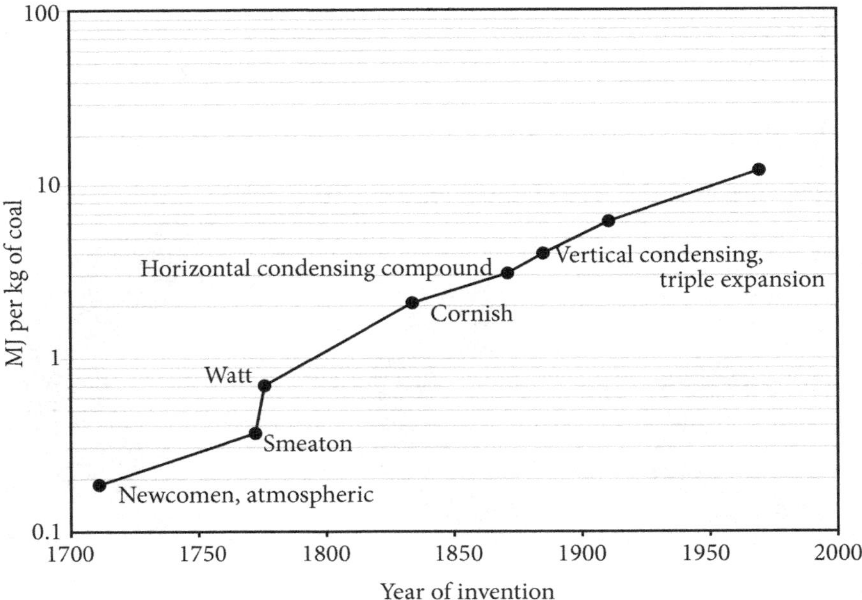

Figure 4.12: Steam engine efficiency over time.

The y-axis is logarithmic. Source: Brander.

Upon its foundation, Standard Oil controlled 4% of the refining market, but a decade later its share had risen to 90%, a position it maintained for about two decades. Not surprisingly, critics accused the company of having achieved this result through unfair practices,[427] while defenders pointed to superior management practices and more innovative behaviour.[428]

In an 1899 governmental hearing, John D. Rockefeller explained the rapid growth of his business as being the result of an ever more efficient use of resources:

> I ascribe the success of the Standard to its consistent policy to make the volume of its business large through the merits and cheapness of its products. It has spared no expense in finding, securing, and utilizing the best and cheapest methods of manufacture. It has sought for the best superintendents and workmen and paid the best wages. It has not hesitated to sacrifice old machinery and old plants for new and better ones. It has placed its manufactories at the points where they could supply markets at the least expense. It has not only sought markets for its principal products, but for all possible by-products, sparing no expense in introducing them

> to the public. It has not hesitated to invest millions of dollars in methods of cheapening the gathering and distribution of oils by pipe lines, special cars, tank steamers, and tank wagons. It has erected tank stations at every important railroad station to cheapen the storage and delivery of its products. It has spared no expense in forcing its products into the markets of the world among people civilized and uncivilized. It has had faith in American oil, and has brought together millions of money for the purpose of making it what it is, and holding its markets against the competition of Russia and all the many countries which are producers of oil and competitors against American oil.[429]

Rockefeller further argued that 'the object and the success of the Standard Oil Company has been due to the fact that their effort is continually to reduce the cost of manufacturing and distributing of oil; and we sell it as cheaply as we can, based on that cost, to the consumer, and thereby increase the volume of our business by cheapening the cost to the consumer.'[430]

On this count the evidence backs Rockefeller's account: Standard Oil's output of kerosene quadrupled between 1870 and 1880, while between 1870 and 1885 the price of refined kerosene dropped from 26 cents to 8 cents per gallon, primarily because Standard Oil refiners had managed to reduce the costs per gallon from almost 3 cents in 1870 to 0.45 cents in 1885.[431]

By-product development over time

The modern synthetic world was born with coal gasification by-products, later superseded by more affordable chemical intermediates derived from petroleum and natural gas.[432] The diversity of synthetic products, shown in Figure 4.13, which now surrounds us from our birth to our death, is as remarkable as it is taken for granted.

Synthetic products are typically frowned upon by sustainable development theorists and environmental activists because of the carbon-based raw materials from which they are derived, their persistent nature and their non-renewable character. Yet, as Edward A. Wrigley observed nearly fifty years ago, they allowed 'the by-passing of the bottleneck caused by the problems of expanding organic raw material supply' when 'at various dates between the sixteenth century and the present day inorganic materials [were] substituted for organic [ones] across a very broad spread of industrial products.' In each instance, Wrigley wrote, 'another sector became independent from the soil.' [433]In other words, synthetic products replaced resources harvested from the surface of our planet with better substitutes manufactured from underground resources, in the process relieving the environmental impact of human activities. Refined petroleum products thus reduced harvesting pressure on wild resources such as whales

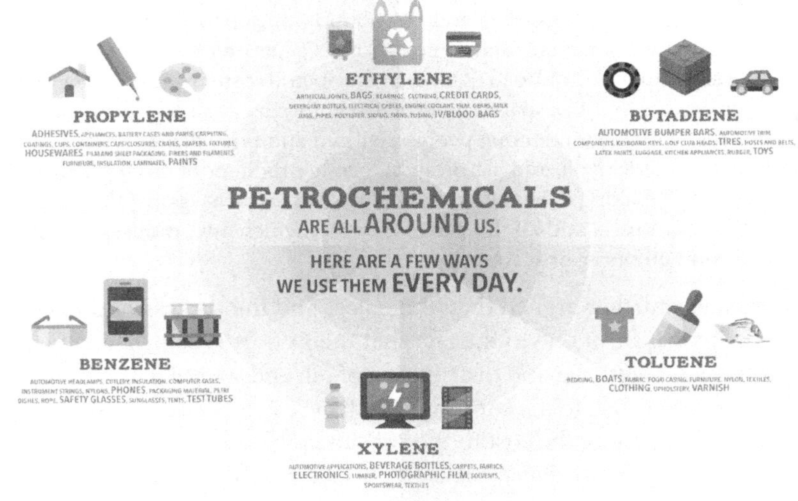

Figure 4.13: Products made from petrochemicals.

American Fuel and Petrochemical Manufacturers. Why petrochemicals matter to you. https://outreach.afpm.org/Petrochemicals/why-petrochemicals-matter-to-you-2.html. For a (much) more detailed list of products, see American Fuel and Petrochemical Manufacturers. Chart of Products Made from Petrochemicals http://www.afpm.org/policy-positions-petrochemicals/.

(whale oil, perfume base),[434] trees (lumber, firewood), birds (feathers), agricultural products (fats and fibres derived from animals and plants, leather from livestock) and other wildlife (ivory, furs, skin).[435]

What follows is a brief history of some of these developments and their beneficial environmental impact, thus illustrating one way by which a market economy can simultaneously deliver increased wealth and environmental remediation.

Coal gas residuals

'King coal' fueled the Victorian engine.[436] While almost all of the United Kingdom's production was either consumed in industrial, transportation and domestic uses, or exported to other countries, a small percentage was heated with the addition of various amounts of steam and air in order to generate different varieties of lighting and fuel gas. Apart from the hydrogen-based gas (and excluding waste products generated from gas purifiers), coal gasification generated three residual substances. The first was a carbon-rich coke, for which there was from the beginning a large demand to power engines and wherever a cheap smokeless fuel was needed, such as in railroad transportation. The second was dirty water, rich in ammonia. The last, and by far most problematic, was a thick black viscous substance known as coal (or gas) tar.[437]

The first practical uses of coal gas were in English cotton mills, beginning in 1805 and 1806, as well as street lighting in 1813, where its 'brilliant lustre' provided a superior alternative to 'miserable oil lamps.'[438] Its adoption in homes, however, was met with considerable resistance. Replacing tallow candles and oil lamps by natural gas streaming through pipes was indeed quite a challenge because of the difficulties involved in removing a number of substances that were invariably mixed with it and, when burnt in a closed room, caused headache and sometimes respiratory problems. According to chemist Lyon Playfair, the gas not only had an intolerably stale odor, but was noxious when burned, discoloured curtains, tarnished metals, ate through the covers of books, and covered everything with its fuming smoke.[439]

As Talbot would later observe, early 'cynics, critics, and caricaturists' lost no opportunity to suggest that the fumes released in rooms in which gas was burned caused a grave danger to the health and, in some cases, the lives of the occupants.[440]

Just as problematic were the dirty gas water and foul-smelling residual tar. When discharged into rivers, coal tar floated in 'ghastly blue patches' known as 'Blue Billy' and killed all aquatic life. When buried, it destroyed the surrounding vegetation. If burned, it generated a heavy black smoke that poisoned the atmosphere over large distances. Not surprisingly, early coal tar disposal practices generated numerous complaints as well as costly litigation for gas companies; reckless disposal practices were soon prohibited. Indeed, despite an initially limited and very polluting use as a fuel in gas plants, gas producers were more than willing to give coal tar away for free to anyone who would cart it away and it remained a nuisance for more than a generation after the first introduction of gas-lighting.

Despite initial failures, hundreds of remunerative by-products derived from these substances would eventually become the original building blocks of our modern synthetic world. As Talbot observed while pondering the advent of electrification, the gas generated from the destructive distillation of coal had by then become, for all intents and purposes, a by-product without which 'the world could roll along very comfortably' as all the real value then came from former production residuals.[441] Such developments, however, had required tremendous entrepreneurial and developmental initiative.

Apart from early and often problematic uses as a protective coating for the hull of wooden ships and ropes, fuel and for roofing, the first highly significant demand for coal tar followed the introduction of the wood pressure impregnation (or Bethell) process in 1838. This 'pickling' or 'creosoting' of timber – a process through which dried timber was placed in a container, subjected to partial vacuum and impregnated with heavy oils from coal tar – soon thrived on a large scale as a result of the increasing demand for wooden sleepers from the railroad industry, for wooden poles from the telegraph industry and from builders of various coastal structures that incorporated a significant amount of timber. This industry not only saved the situation as far as tar disposal was concerned, but also significantly reduced both the cost of maintaining wooden structures and, by tripling or quadrupling its useful life, the consumption of wood.[442] Wood preservation techniques also made it possible to use inferior species of wood that had previously been unsuitable for use as railroad crossties because they decayed too rapidly. As historical geographer Sherry Olson observed, 'such techniques not only increased the useful life of crossties but expanded substantially the wood supplies upon which it became possible to draw.' This is how 'mixed hardwoods, sappy pines, and Douglas fir' previously of no interest as bridge timber, ties and for other uses, became, once treated, 'roughly equal to the best white oak' in their desirability.[443]

Of course, creosoting also created problems, but it seems fair to say that these were much less important than those solved in the first place.

Other uses for tar creosote were eventually developed. The most prominent was arguably the preparation of cattle washes, sheep dips, and general disinfectants. It was also used as a fuel in diesel engines and for lighting, in the production of lamp-black, for softening or 'revivifying' hard pitch (the hard black residue left once the liquid fractions had been removed from the coal tar), and for scrubbing coal and coke-oven gas for the recovery of benzene and toluene. The heavier liquid fractions of coal tar found further outlets in the preservation of iron, bricks and stone, in the preparation of roofing felt and, when produced in isolated plants where they could not be recovered economically for further processing, burnt more cleanly and efficiently than before.

Originally, however, no markets existed for the remaining lighter fractions of tar oil, which, while much less significant in terms of volume, proved too volatile for civil engineering applications. Early users of the Bethell process converted these into 'coal-tar naphta' ('naphtha' is the modern spelling) for burning and dissolving rubber and gutta percha,[444] and for a few additional uses. These applications, however, resulted in only a limited demand for a product that was rapidly increasing in supply. As a result, the lighter fractions were originally 'in much about the same industrial position as the tar itself before its application as a timber preservative.'[445]

Valuable uses for this waste material would eventually come on the heels of chemical advances that allowed their use in the preparation of benzene and nitrobenzene on an industrial scale. The latter found an early use as a substitute for the essential oil of bitter almonds, a coloring and perfuming agent. Beginning with William Henry Perkin's *mauve* in 1856, the synthetic dyes industry soon provided significant markets for these previously useless residues. Actually, this industry's reliance and willingness to pay for a growing number of coal tar derivatives ensured that 'the other products of tar-distilling could be sold at low rates and new markets could be opened out for them.'[446] In time, advances in synthetic dye making served as a technological springboard for the creation of other tar-derived products, ranging from explosives, medicines and perfumes, to flavoring materials, sweeteners, disinfectants and antitoxins, as well as tracing and photographic agents. In much the same way, the replacement of various dyeing substances previously extracted from plants (principally madder and indigo), lichens, trees, insects, mollusks, minerals and guano by synthetic dyes simultaneously reduced extractive pressures while allowing increased food production.[447] Examining the details of the developmental work, environmental benefits and – typically unknown at the time – more problematic aspects of these activities is beyond the scope of this book.

The residual hard 'pitch' eventually led to the development of products ranging from substitute asphalt, black varnish, and hard pavements to disinfectants, roofing-felt and electrical insulation. One of its most successful markets was created in 1832 by French entrepreneurs Auguste Ferrand and Émile Marsais,[448] who mixed it with coal-dust formerly wasted in mining operations, in the process producing a commercially successful 'patent fuel' of which between two and three million tons were manufactured annually in the UK and continental Europe by the end of the nineteenth century.[449] According to one commentator, legislative mandates to curtail smoke emissions from locomotives originally facilitated the sale of this product, as the supply of gas coke was at one point in time insufficient and more expensive. As a result, railway companies obtained their coke more cheaply than was formerly the case, coal owners made 'something out of a (commercial) nothing' and the land surrounding some coal pits became increasingly 'freed from an incumbrance.'[450]

The ammonia-rich residual water, formerly wasted, similarly became the basic input of valuable goods such as carbonate of ammonia (produced with the addition of quicklime); sal-ammoniac (produced with the addition of a strong acid, such as hydrochloric acid – itself a residual of alkali production); and sulphate of ammonia (through the addition of sulphuric acid). These were all valuable inputs in industries ranging from pharmaceuticals and dyeing to printing and fertilisers. While the purging of ammonia was done for 'sanitary reasons' as well as 'to meet wise legislative demands,' it was typically in the corporate interest to act in this manner as all ammoniacal products were 'easily sold' and brought a 'fair price.'[451]

Finally, the refuse of combustion, such as clinker, soot and ashes, proved valuable in the preparation of mortar, roads and manure.

Since creative destruction is the foundation of market economies, illuminating gas was eventually displaced by electricity, fuel gas by natural gas (which, consisting essentially of methane, had a much higher heating value) and hundreds of tar-based derivatives by components from natural gas and petroleum.

Petroleum by-products

The first significant commodity created out of petroleum in the late 1850s was kerosene, then and for nearly four decades used as a substitute for whale oil in lighting in locations where coal gas, and later electricity, wasn't available.[452] No matter how they distilled petroleum, however, early refiners were left with a residue – about half of the original material – which was then of no commercial value. As the geographers Robert C. Estall and Robert O. Buchanan observed, despite the very high quality of western Pennsylvania crude, these leftover portions 'were waste products, and the main problem was how to dispose of them,' something that typically occurred through dumping or burning.[453] Although in time improvements in refining raised the marketable yield to about 75%, the large quantity of production residuals mandated that refineries remained located close to oilfields or in locations with relatively cheap access to crude supplies, for example Pittsburgh and Cleveland.[454]

Beginning in the mid-1860s, a few by-products were created out of the liquid residue, most notably lubricating oil, grease, paraffin, petrolatum (or petroleum jelly, better known by the trademark Vaseline), candles, insect repellents and solvents. These new commodities, however, were largely extracted from what was referred to as the 'middle of the barrel.' By contrast, gasoline (found in the lighter portion that accumulated at the 'top of the barrel') and most heavy residuals (found in the 'bottom of the barrel') remained problematic, save the use of some heavy crude and residuum as fuels in refining operations and buildings in oil-producing regions when alternatives, such as coal, were more expensive. As refining specialist William Leffler put it, consumers originally used:

> ...petroleum products for what we now consider basic needs – lighting, heating, cooking, and lubricating. When Colonel Edwin Drake... initiated the oil era, his investors were thrilled. They saw the opportunity to compete with whale oil in the illumination market by providing a similar product, kerosene. Gasoline and naphtha were mostly considered waste

> products, often allowed to 'weather,' a euphemism for evaporating into the atmosphere, before the kerosene was recovered. Sometimes refiners just burned the light material in pits or dumped it into nearby streams to get rid of it.[455]

As scientists and innovation scholars Newton Copp and Andrew Zanella wrote somewhat more bluntly: 'The typical solution for this problem was to dump the gasoline into adjacent rivers and hope it would evaporate before the river caught on fire!'[456] The problem was that while gasoline could be used as a solvent for paint and varnish and in air–gas machines,[457] it proved too flammable and too volatile to be used for household lighting and heating. Similarly, while some of the heavier components had limited uses for road surfacing and roofing, no adequate furnace technology had been developed to burn heavy oil for space heating.

As mentioned earlier, John D. Rockefeller and his employees played a key role in developing and/or marketing by-products. In the mid-1870s, Standard Oil began selling paraffin wax for chewing gum and residual oil tar and asphalt for road building. A few years later the company marketed manufacturing lubricants for railroads and machine shops, candles, paints, dyes and industrial acid. In 1880 Rockefeller acquired the Chesebrough Manufacturing Company of New Jersey in order to strengthen its sales of petroleum jelly.[458] By the time of his 1899 testimony, Rockefeller's business sold approximately two hundred by-products, including 'naphtas for local anesthetics, solvents for industry, fuel for stoves and the internal combustion engines, wax for pharmaceuticals and candles, oils and lubricants to free machines from friction, heavy oils for the gas industry.'[459]

In his 1908 book *Wealth from Waste*, the pastor George Powell Perry attributed much of the success of Standard Oil to the 'wise use of that which was once regarded worthless' rather than 'financial shenanigans and deceptive practices.' He supported his contention through a brief account of the development of paraffin out of a 'sticky, slimy stuff... left over from the refining business':

> At first [the residual] was thrown into the river. But soon the authorities complained because of the pollution it produced. Then it was put into a deep trench and they tried to burn it. It made such a furious flame that the heat became unendurable and the strongest wall could not resist it. In great perplexity the company finally sought the help of some expert chemists to see if some way could not be found to get rid of the nuisance. It was at that time that a process was discovered whereby this disagreeable refuse could be converted into paraffine. Then it was found that this troublesome refuse could be made a good source of revenue.[460]

Apart from lubricating oils, early uses of refined paraffin included as an input in wax (with its main market in candle-making) and chewing gum manufacture, and as a sealing agent for jellies and preserves in an age without artificial refrigeration.[461] Paraffin was also used in pharmaceutical, medical, surgical, dental and electrical equipment. To give but a few illustrations of how these new products relieved pressures on biodiversity, in 1861 paraffin was introduced into the pharmaceutical industry as substitute for wax, spermaceti (the highest grade of whale oil), almond oil, and lard in cerates and salves.[462] By 1870 it had supplanted spermaceti as the main laundry sizing in both domestic and commercial uses while gaining market shares in textile manufacturing, being used as a wood preservative and displacing natural rubber in waterproofing tents, boots and coats.[463]

In his early twentieth century history and economic analysis of Standard Oil, the lawyer Gilbert Holland Montague wrote that the main complaint voiced by Rockefeller's competitors was that the new 'improved methods of utilizing by-products' had made them 'as remunerative as the refined oil itself' which gave the company a significant competitive advantage. As was widely understood at the time, the main challenge of by-product development was that it required 'the greatest specialization of methods, encouragement of invention, investment of capital, and extension of plant,' something beyond the capacity of smaller refining operations. In the end, Montague agreed with Rockefeller that the large profits Standard Oil derived from by-products was 'owing entirely to its superior mechanical efficiency and organization.' [464]

The advent of electric lighting – in the late nineteenth century – turned kerosene into a by-product of gasoline refining. Between 1899 and 1914, the share of kerosene dropped from 58 to 25% of refined products, whereas gasoline rose from 15 to 48%, overtaking it in various parts of the world between 1908 and 1911.[465] Writing in 1920, the journalist Frederick A. Talbot observed, somewhat carelessly but colorfully, that the development of the internal combustion engine ensured:

> [The] volatile spirit which hitherto had been spurned and burned wastefully by the refineries was immediately discovered to be invested with a value which had heretofore escaped attention. It formed the ideal fuel for the new motor. Forthwith wanton destruction of the volatile spirit was abandoned. Every drop was carefully collected, and, as time went on and the demand for the light liquid fuel increased, the refiners put forth great effort to wring every possible dram of [gasoline] from the crude petroleum.[466]

Talbot also commented that 'forty years ago the boring of [an oil] well was followed with mixed feelings' as a successful strike would unavoidably 'crash through the roof of an underground reservoir of petroleum gas' that might then blow up and cost the lives of the crew. 'Ignorant of the value of this product, though painfully aware of its danger,' he writes, 'the early seekers for oil led this gas through a pipe to a point some distance away' where it was then ignited and 'allowed to burn merrily in the open air.' It was only when 'the flame flickered and expired' that the 'boring for the precious liquid' would proceed ahead.[467] In time, however, the flaring of natural gas was recognized for what it was, the waste of a valuable resource. As Talbot observed, 'with passing years and progress came enlightenment. The gas is no longer wasted; it is trapped. In some instances, it is led through piping for hundreds of miles to feed hungry furnaces engaged in the making of steel and other products.'

In time, diesel became the dominant fuel for ships, locomotives and road vehicles, while the development of jet and turbo-jet aircrafts eventually provided a new large-scale market for kerosene.[468] To mention but one later instance of by-product development, the boom in plastics production can be traced back to the development of the cracking of crude oil to produce high-quality gasoline, a process which generated residual gases that were first burnt as waste, but which eventually became a cheap feedstock for the production of polymers.[469]

After writing that over 5000 different products had been developed from crude oil, the geographer Joseph Russell Smith and his collaborators observed in 1961:

> The meat-packing industry has long boasted that it uses all parts of a pig except the squeal. The petroleum industry sometimes adds the odor of oil to odorless gas to help detect leaks in pipelines. The petroleum industry claims that it uses everything in crude oil, including the smell.[470]

4.3 On the unique benefits of carbon fuels

To summarize some of the issues raised earlier and to add a few more, the main economic and environmental benefits made possible by humanity's reliance on carbon fuels are set out in the rest of this chapter.[471]

Economic and social benefits

Transportation

Beginning with coal-powered railroad and steamships, carbon fuels made possible, for the first time, large-scale, reliable and affordable long-distance transportation. This paved the way for:

- *improved overall nutrition* by concentrating food production in the most-suitable locations, thus making food more plentiful, diverse and affordable;
- *the eradication of famines* by moving the surplus of regions with good harvests to those that have experienced mediocre ones;
- *large-scale urbanization* and the wealth creation that can only occur when large numbers of people move from the countryside into cities.[472]

Improved nutrition

Improved nutrition was also facilitated by the replacement of draught animals by petroleum products-powered tractors, trucks, combines, generators, as well as by widespread electrification. Fodder once eaten by work horses and mules could be fed to meat and dairy animals. The replacement of charcoal by coke also meant that areas devoted to producing biomass for charcoal could become pastureland. Electricity also made artificial refrigeration possible, greatly increasing the amount of fresh food available for mass consumption.[473]

Public health benefits

Sanitation

Starting with their propensity to kill people through kicking and trampling, and ending with the problem of vermin and flies in urban horse stables, city work horses, their excrement and carcasses were a source of deadly diseases such as typhoid fever, yellow fever, cholera and diphtheria. In the late nineteenth century, New York City horses produced well over four million pounds of manure each day, sometimes piled up to a height of between 40 feet and 60 feet in vacant lots. The replacement of horses by cars and trucks powered by petroleum products thus dramatically improved public health.[474]

Air quality

Kerosene and heavy oil displaced poor-quality (lower energy density) biomass fuels such as firewood and dung, which filled houses with soot, particulates, carbon monoxide and toxic chemicals. These inferior household fuels still kill millions of people who cannot afford higher energy density carbon fuels, or do not have access to advanced electricity infrastructure, where carbon fuels drive prime movers such as steam turbines.[475] The spontaneous market process of shifting away from low energy density and highly polluting household fuels to clean high energy density fuels is best conveyed through the concept of an energy ladder, as depicted in Figure 4.14.

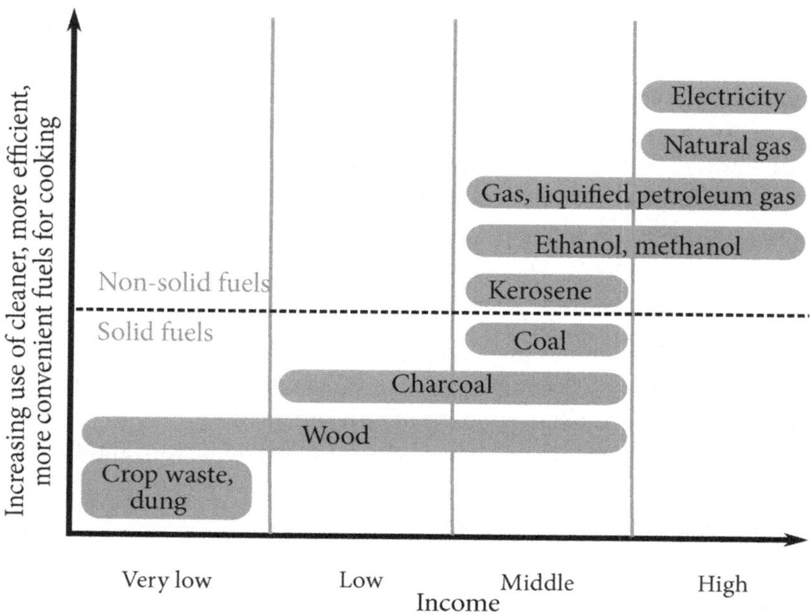

Figure 4.14: The energy ladder – the link between household energy and development.

Source: Paunio (2018).

Water quality

Increased fossil fuel use made possible significant advances in terms of sanitizing drinking water and removing and treating sewage, from building infrastructure to powering treatment plants.[476]

Environmental benefits

Humanity's increased reliance on resources extracted from below the earth's surface helped preserve and promote life forms on the surface in various ways, most notably:

Rewilding and preservation of marginal lands

Larger amounts of food can now be produced on the same piece of land because of inputs ranging from synthetic pesticides and plastic sheeting to electricity and veterinary medicine. Tractors and other machines, which do not get sick, do not require care when not being used, and do not consume more than a fifth of the food they help to grow, have replaced much less powerful and reliable horses and mules. These advances have made marginal agricultural lands, sometimes cultivated through environmentally damaging methods, such as slash-and-burn, available for spontaneous reforestation and tree plantations (in a few selected locations) while sparing many non-cultivated marginal wetlands, grasslands and forestlands from the plough.

Synthetic products have reduced harvesting pressures on biomass

Coal and hydrocarbon-based synthetic products displaced many agricultural products that were once cultivated, harvested or hunted for industrial uses, for example whales hunted to produce lighting oil, plants grown to produce fibres, dyes and rubber, and animals raised primarily for their wool and fur.[477]

Carbon dioxide fertilization effect

Increased availability of atmospheric carbon dioxide, greater rainfall since the middle of the nineteenth century, and, to the extent it can be traced back, a lengthening of the growing season, have contributed positively to the efficiency of photosynthesis, hence to greater plant growth and to increased agricultural productivity.[478] According to a recent study, between a quarter and a half of our planet's vegetated lands has shown significant greening over the last 35 years, largely due to rising levels of atmospheric carbon dioxide.[479] As a result of these processes, all advanced economies and many areas in developing economies, including China, India, Bangladesh and Vietnam, have benefitted from large-scale reforestation and increased biodiversity.[480] This is especially visible in the case of the United States, as shown in Figure 4.15, but is also well documented in other developed countries, as presented in Figure 4.16.

In the end, the ever-increasing use of carbon fuels in various forms turned out to be a crucial component of decoupling and ecosystem preservation or re-wilding. But although humanity's increasing use of carbon fuels has had countless economic, social and environmental benefits, it created a few problems along the way, from urban smog to increased greenhouse gas emissions. While most of these have long since been addressed successfully, the latter remains a cause for concern, a topic we will now discuss in more detail.

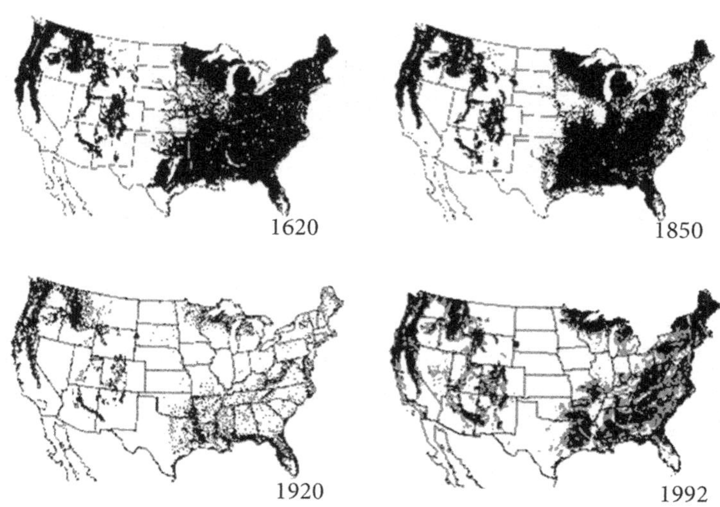

Figure 4.15: Forest land in the United States, 1620, 1850, 1920, and 1992.

All maps from the United States Forest Service. A discussion of the first three (1620, 1850 and 1920) by the then Chief of the US Forest Service is found in Greeley (1925). A higher resolution version of the 1992 map is available at, among other places, USDA – Forest Service https://data.fs.usda.gov/geodata/rastergateway/forest_type/.

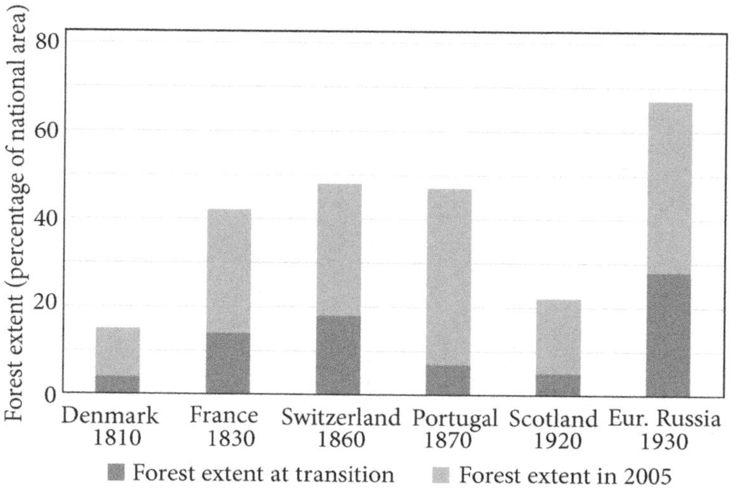

Figure 4.16: Forest transition in some advanced economies.

Source: the authors, based on Kauppi *et al.* (2006).

5 Carbon dioxide emissions as the environmental crisis of last resort

At odds with the longitudinal empirical evidence, many environmental scientists, as well as sustainable development and degrowth theorists, believe that 'the historical record of industrialisation in every country is that economic growth is associated with a wide range of forms of environmental damage – from resource depletion to climate change.'[481] Resources for the Future staffer Henry Jarrett perhaps best summed up their perspective over five decades ago when he wrote that the 'underlying causes' of problems such as 'lowered environmental quality, smoggy atmosphere, polluted streams, noise [and] land skinned by strip mining' were 'to be seen in the same statistics that most of the time are hailed as indicators of economic growth.'[482] Shortly thereafter, economist Kenneth Boulding argued that an abundance of material resources created through technological advances might be problematic, as humanity might run out of 'pollutable reservoirs before our mines and ores are exhausted. There are signs of this happening in the atmosphere, in the rivers, and in the oceans.'[483]

Professional and popular interest in rising carbon dioxide emissions and global warming can be traced back to the 1950s, including efforts by the oil industry to quantify the percentage of these emissions that could be traced back to the combustion of petroleum products. In his 1965 presidential address to the American Economic Association, preeminent American population economist Joseph Spengler suggested that economist 'J.K. Galbraith had better labeled ours an effluent society than an affluent one.'[484] One problem raised by Spengler was carbon dioxide emissions, a concern echoed a few years later by environmental economist Allen Kneese, who worried about the lack of a suitable sink for this greenhouse gas,[485] and by Paul Ehrlich, who in 1969 identified the issue as a 'serious limiting factor' to growth.[486] In short order the Ehrlichs and John Holdren raised fears that carbon dioxide 'produced by combustion of fossil fuels in quantities too large to contain may already be influencing climate' and, as such, constituted one of the 'gravest threats to human well-being... [i.e.] the loss of natural services now provided by biogeochemical processes.'[487]

Closer to us, in 1998 climate change activist Bill McKibben admitted that resource scarcity was not a problem, but that what humanity was 'running out of is what the scientists call 'sinks' – places to put the by-products of our large appetites. Not garbage dumps (we could go on using Pampers till the end of time and still have empty space left to toss them away) but the atmospheric equivalent of garbage dumps.'[488]

Needless to say, from a degrowth perspective 'technology is not viewed as a magical savior since many technologies often accelerate environmental decline.'[489] As leaders in the movement wrote in 2015:

> After careful analysis, those in the degrowth camp have come to the conclusion that the only way for humanity to live within its biophysical limits and mitigate the effects of climate change is to reduce economic activity, to downscale consumerist lifestyles, to move beyond conventional energy sources, to give up on the fantasy of 'decoupling' economic and population growth from environmental impacts, and to rethink the technologies that have gotten us into our current predicament.[490]

Now, as in the past few decades, the basic fears associated with greater use of mineral resources revolve not only around the depletion of finite deposits, but also in the limited capacity of the natural environment to assimilate negative externalities such as polluting emissions. The first section of this chapter will critically examine some influential frameworks that have been built around these themes, and which implicitly equate an expanding population, wealth creation and negative environmental outcomes.

5.1 Overconsumption and environmental degradation: key arguments

The global use of materials has increased substantially in recent decades. According to a recent report on materials flows and resource productivity published by the International Resource Panel of the United Nations Environment Programme (henceforth UNEP IRP), '[o]verall, the global economy expanded more than threefold over the four decades since 1970, population almost doubled and global material extraction tripled,' with annual global extraction of materials growing from 22 billion tonnes (1970) to 70 billion tonnes (2010), much of which can be attributed to the rapid industrialization of China.[491] Another recent study of 57 common goods and services[492] further suggests a widespread 'Jevons' paradox' or 'rebound effect' in each case, because 'no matter how much more efficient and compact a product is made, consumers will only demand more of that product and in the long run increase the total amount of materials used in making that product.'[493]

In later work, the researchers identified six cases in which an absolute decline in materials usage had occurred. With the exception of wool, which has been displaced by synthetic alternatives, these were materials such as asbestos and thallium whose usage had declined due to government intervention rather than market-led innovation.

The authors of the UNEP IRP and degrowth theorists did not believe that a laissez-faire approach to development could deliver a sustainable outcome. Other case studies also questioned the possibility of a global decoupling of economic growth and the environment, even though the authors acknowledged that partial and temporary decoupling is possible through substitutions, such as the reduction in horse manure brought about by the truck and the automobile, or the reduction in greenhouse gas emissions that resulted from the substitution of coal by natural gas in electricity generation.[494] Not surprisingly, increased consumption of raw materials also keeps old fears alive. The authors of the UNEP IRP report thus commented that:

> [d]uring the twentieth century, the economic development that improved material standards of living for hundreds of millions of people was assisted by declining real prices for most materials, including food, fuel and metals. This situation may not be sustained through the twenty-first century as the rapid economic growth occurring simultaneously in many parts of the world will place much higher demands on supply infrastructure and the environment's ability to continue supplying materials.[495]

These analysts further add:

> Extraction of non-renewable materials, most notably of fossil fuels and metal ores, inevitably reduces the global stocks of these materials available for use in the future. At some point, ongoing and increasing exploitation must lead to serious depletion of global deposits of these materials.[496]

In light of declining birthrates, however, numerous academics, bureaucrats and activists now worry more about increased consumption rather than population growth, and question the true impact of lifting millions of people out of poverty so that they can drive cars and consume more meat.[497] These apprehensive individuals issue calls 'for transformative changes in lifestyles and consumption behaviour'[498] among citizens of rich countries. Such concerns, however, are hardly new. For example, in his book *The Population Bomb*, Paul Ehrlich argued that because white Americans do so much ecological damage they should be the prime target of fertility suppression.[499]

In 1970 the Ehrlichs expanded on the problem:

> Because of their impact on the environment, population growth among the affluent in the US and their counterparts in Europe, the Soviet Union, and Japan is the most serious in the world, even though it is not the most rapid. These people are the main consumers of our planet's non-renewable resources and polluters of its environment; their activities threaten to destroy the Earth's life-support systems. In terms of degradation of the environment, the birth of each American child is 50 times the disaster it is for the world as the birth of a child in India. In terms of the consumption of non-renewable resources, an American baby is some 300 times as dangerous to our future well-being as an Indonesian baby…Similarly, poor people in the U.S have far less power to loot and pollute than does the average American. Therefore, they have much less impact upon the environment, despite their slightly higher birthrates.[500]

A few years later, Holdren and the Erhlichs advocated political efforts to launch a 'massive campaign' to 'de-develop the United States' and to divest energy and resources 'from frivolous and wasteful uses in overdeveloped countries to filling the genuine needs of underdeveloped countries.'[501] In 1976, the Nobel economic laureate Jan Tinbergen coordinated the production of a report to the Club of Rome in which westerners were told that their lives had become wasteful, senseless and did not contribute to real happiness; that 'a ceiling [should be placed] on meat consumption;' that they should rely increasingly on public transit; that an official benchmark should be put on consumption; and that anything beyond that was 'not only waste but a conscious action against the welfare of large numbers of poor and disprivileged, their own children, and the prospects for a peaceful world.'[502]

An interesting issue, however, is why increased production and consumption of raw materials was deemed problematic when many environmental indicators simultaneously showed clear signs of improvement over time. One short answer was given over four decades ago by the Ehrlichs and John Holdren when they summarized the gravest 'defects in the cornucopian argument':

- the presumption that advanced technology will make energy very cheap;
- the presumption that abundant, cheap energy – if available – would prove to be a sufficient condition for abundance of all kinds;
- the serious underestimation of the degree of environmental degradation that would be generated by the proposed cornucopian technologies;
- the even more serious underestimation of the impact on human well-being that major environmental disruption portends.[503]

One can also identify at least three basic arguments as to alleged negative environmental impact of 'overconsumption.' The first is that humanity is only able to maintain current standards of living through the depletion of non-renewable and irreplaceable natural capital: high-quality soil, non-replenishable groundwater deposits, irreplaceable biodiversity and so on. Gretchen Daily and Paul Ehrlich thus argued in 1992 that 'the human enterprise has not only exceeded its current carrying capacity, but is actually reducing future carrying capacity.'[504] In a piece titled 'Too many people, too much consumption' published a decade ago, the Ehrlichs once again rejected the belief that 'technological fixes...will allow the population and the economy to grow forever' because humanity had depleted the natural capital of earth, 'in particular its deep, rich agricultural soils, its groundwater stored during ice ages, and its biodiversity.' Human life on earth, they argued, would become 'increasingly untenable because of two looming crises: global heating, and the degradation of the natural systems on which we all depend.'[505]

The second argument is a fundamental belief, as stated by Al Gore a generation ago, that an 'overcrowded world is inevitably a polluted one,'[506] and that citizens of advanced economies are the worst polluters because they consume far more than their fair share of global resources. For instance, the Ehrlichs and their collaborators argued on various occasions that, because of decreasing returns, growing consumption unavoidably results in greater environmental damage:

> [To] support additional people it is necessary to move to ever poorer lands, drill wells deeper, or tap increasingly remote sources to obtain water – and then spend more energy to transport that water ever greater distances to farm fields, homes, and factories. Our distant ancestors could pick up nearly pure copper on Earth's surface when they started to use metals; now people must use vast amounts of energy to mine and smelt gigantic amounts of copper ore of ever poorer quality, some in concentrations of less than one percent. The same can be said for other important metals. And petroleum can no longer be found easily on or near the surface, but must be gleaned from wells drilled a mile or more deep, often in inaccessible localities, such as under continental shelves beneath the sea. All of the paving, drilling, fertilizer manufacturing, pumping, smelting, and transporting needed to provide for the consumption of burgeoning numbers of people produces greenhouse gases and thus tightens the connection between population and climate disruption.[507]

In another article, Paul Ehrlich and John Harte argued that:

> [m]ore people using more fossil fuels means more climate change; more people eating more food means more land conversion (with associated loss of biodiversity), more overdraft of groundwater for irrigation, and more pressure on threatened marine resources; and more people consum-

> ing more material goods potentially means more toxic waste products and more mining.

These problems, they suggested, 'act upon each other in a manner that reinforces the deterioration' such as when, for instance:

> soil loss and desertification force farmers to exploit more marginal lands, resulting in yet more erosion, greater need for irrigation water, fertilizers, and herbicides, and more clear-cutting of valuable habitat, all contributing to further loss of biodiversity. More energy-intensive methods of compensating for any of the above damage result in greater disturbance of the climate and pollute the air and water.[508]

The authors of the recent UNEP IRP report expressed similar fears by suggesting that problems associated with the increased use of materials:

> include the destruction of biodiversity and the eutrophication of waterways. Increasing outputs of forestry products can increase deforestation, with attendant damage to surface and groundwater systems, erosion and changed flooding regimes. Problems associated with mining and quarrying include loss of land to competing land uses, pollution of land and waterways from acid mine leaching, heavy metals liberated from mine tailings, and some chemicals used in mining and refining processes. Secondary and tertiary production processes, and disposal after final consumption, add to waste and emissions downstream.[509]

The last argument is a belief in the existence of widespread market failures that do not factor in the damage done to ecosystems by profit-seeking business. The authors of the Royal Society's *People and the Planet* report thus warn that '[i]t would be imprudent to trust the invisible hand of the market to guide humanity away from environmental thresholds' as, among other alleged problems, there is 'insufficient market pressure to develop substitutes' because '[d]epletion of some resources and exhaustion of some ecosystem services are not smooth and linear' and 'the market might not have time to develop technological alternatives,' some of which might at any rate 'not be socially or politically acceptable.'[510] Of course, global warming (or more recently climate change) is now said to be the main negative externality.

A number of frameworks and models have been built upon these concerns and not surprisingly point to the unsustainability of current practices. One early attempt, described by its author as an 'oversimplification', was William Vogt's 1948 equation $C = B : E$, in which C stood for the carrying capacity of any area of land, B for biotic potential and E for environmental resistance.[511] According to Vogt, humanity could expect E to increase, B to decrease, and C to go in an unending downward spiral as a result of ever growing human pressures.

As one critic put it at the time: 'If the validity of the equation is accepted…along with the definitions of terminology, then, by syllogism, the conclusions are inevitable.'[512] This, however, did not make it valid and relevant to real-world conditions. We now turn to a discussion of more recent and similarly fundamentally flawed frameworks.

5.2 Overconsumption: frameworks, evidence and criticism

The notion that current levels of population and affluence are already exceeding natural limits has been expressed and elaborated upon in a number of influential frameworks, which, because of their built-in assumptions, equate smaller population numbers and greater material poverty with lesser environmental impact. While it is beyond the scope of this work to examine the details of these frameworks and of the arguments raised by their critics, it is necessary to say a few words about some of their core assumptions and shortcomings.

IPAT

$I = PAT$ (or $I = P \times A \times T$) is a formula that equates humanity's environmental impact (resource depletion and environmental pollution) to the product of three factors: population (size), affluence (typically GDP per capita), and technology (typically the amount of pollution per unit of GDP).[513]

The formula was originally proposed in 1971 by Paul Ehrlich and John Holdren as $I = P \times F$, where I = total impact, P = population size and F = impact per capita. It was described in a piece titled 'Impact of population growth,'[514] which was intended to re-emphasize the environmental impact of population growth as opposed to the alleged polluting and resources-depleting character of modern technologies. Not surprisingly, Ehrlich and Holdren assumed that 'each human individual has a negative impact on his environment' whether he lives in an agrarian or technological society[515] and that negative environmental impact would result from any combination of population growth, increased affluence and technological change. Ehrlich has maintained this stance ever since. As he put it a decade ago, the IPAT equation 'is not rocket science. Two billion people, all else being equal, put more greenhouse gases into the atmosphere than one billion people. Two billion rich people disrupt the climate more than two billion poor people. Three hundred million Americans consume more petroleum than 1.3 billion Chinese. And driving an SUV is using a far more environmentally malign transportation technology than riding mass transit.'[516] The IPAT framework is also the foundation on which recent studies suggest that 'growth in GDP ultimately cannot plausibly be decoupled from growth in material and energy use, demonstrating categorically that GDP growth cannot be sustained indefinitely.'[517]

One of the problems with the use of the IPAT formula in social science research is the relative difficulty of interpreting its key terms, such as affluence and technology: 'In other words, no one actually knows how to assign values to two of the four terms in IPAT, a fatal problem for anyone who hopes to measure their effects.'[518] As a consequence, most researchers either assume IPAT to be true and use it without testing its assumptions, or avoid the equation altogether.[519] One of the most passionate critiques of IPAT was formulated in 1993 by H. Patricia Hynes, professor of environmental health, anti-war activist and a social justice, eco-feminism and indigenous perspectives scholar. Hynes indicted IPAT for its simplistic treatment of people and their activities without factoring in human agency, motivation, or inequalities in power, affluence and access to technology. As she put it: 'The most telling shortcoming of IPAT is its singular view of humans as parasites and predators on the natural environment. I, or the impact of humans on the environment, is fundamentally a negative measure of degradation and destruction of natural resources, calculated in units of pollution.'[520] Hynes thus saw IPAT as a 'truncated, culture-bound view of humans in their environment.'[521]

Donella Meadows, an early IPAT supporter and one of the lead authors of the 1972 *The Limits to Growth*, wrote a response to Hynes' work that is a rare example of recalibration based on new information in the pessimist discourse [capitals in the original]:

> I didn't realize how politically correct this formula had become, until a few months ago when I watched a panel of five women challenge it and enrage an auditorium full of environmentalists, including me. IPAT is a bloodless, misleading, cop-out explanation for the world's ills, they said. It points the finger of blame at all the wrong places…As I listened to this argument, I got mad. IPAT was the lens through which I saw the environmental situation. It's neat and simple. I didn't want to see any other way. IPAT is just what you would expect from physical scientists said one of the critics, Patricia Hynes of the Institute on Women and Technology in North Amherst, Massachusetts…There are no AGENTS in the IPAT equation, said Patricia Hynes, no identifiable ACTORS… Population growth and consumption and technology don't just happen. Particular people make them happen, people who shape and respond to rewards and punishments, people who may be acting out of desperation or love or greed or ambition or fear. Unfortunately, I said to myself, I agree with this.[522]

Among more recent critiques of IPAT, the Australian ecosocialist Ian Angus and eco-justice activist Simon Butler similarly complained [italics in the original]: '[p]opulationists isolate one number – population size or growth – and claim it is the underlying cause for all the rest. Population increased; economic activity expanded and environmental degradation increased; so population must have caused the expansion and the degradation. That only shows *correlation*, not *causation*.'[523] Angus and Butler shrugged off the IPAT reliance on single numbers, and the lack of nuance of the simplistic expression, noting that [italics in the original]: 'IPAT isn't a formula at all – it is what accountants call an *identity*, an expression that is always true *by definition*. Ehrlich and Holdren didn't *prove* that impact equals population times affluence times technology – they simply *defined* it that way. Not surprisingly, their definition was based on their opinion that population growth is the ultimate cause, the universal multiplier, of other problems.'[524]

As further evidence of the fact that population numbers neither cause, nor correlate with, carbon emissions, Angus and Butler discussed the outcomes of an International Institute for Environment and Development study by David Satterthwaite, showing that 'the correlation between emissions growth and population growth, a connection that seems obvious when we consider only global figures, turns out to be an illusion when we look at the numbers country by country. Almost all the population growth is occurring in countries with low emissions; almost all of the emissions are produced in countries with little or no population growth.'[525] Satterthwaite, in fact, went as far as noting that '[t]he much-used formula of $I = P \times A \times T$...should be $I = C \times A \times T$ when applied to global warming impacts, with C being the number of consumers, not the number of people. In addition, it is neither fair nor accurate to suggest that population growth or urbanization (growth in the proportion of a national population living in urban areas) necessarily cause increases in GHGs.'[526] To further decouple population from carbon emissions, Satterthwaite noted that 'perhaps up to one-sixth of the world's population has incomes and consumption levels that are so low that they are best not included in allocations of responsibility for GHG emissions.'[527]

Even results derived from a faithful use of the IPAT framework often strayed considerably from Ehrlich and Holdren's original emphasis, some going as far as suggesting that technologies created a greater negative environmental impact than population growth while others actually demonstrated techno-optimistic results. In the end though, researchers who have stayed true to Ehrlich's vision have typically ignored the fact that increasing affluence can come as a result of better technologies and that widely disparate outcomes can be attributed to the nature of social institutions and culture in which human actions take place.[528] In other words, these researchers ignored the considerable evidence against the usefulness of IPAT and simply carried on relying on it.

Ecological footprint

The ecological footprint (henceforth, EF) is an extension of the concept of carrying capacity that takes the form of the biologically productive area required to satisfy people's needs.[529] Like previous concepts such as 'ghost acres' (or acreage) and 'shadow areas', the EF takes into account the amount of external land used to supply a national or regional economy with natural resources and agricultural products. Unlike these earlier formulations, however, the EF has a second component: the theoretical area of forested land, beyond existing oceans and forest land, required to sequester or disperse the resulting pollution and waste, primarily carbon dioxide emissions.[530] It thus has a 'strong sustainability' perspective, in which the resulting atmospheric concentration of carbon dioxide should be the same as would have occurred in the absence of human activities.

The brainchild of the University of British Columbia ecologist William E. Rees and his graduate student Mathis Wackernagel,[531] the EF is now mostly associated with the Global Footprint Network,[532] the WWF Living Planet reports,[533] and the Earth Overshoot Day website.[534] It is the method behind several spectacular claims, such as when the spokespersons for Earth Overshoot Day claimed on August 2, 2017 that humans 'have used more from nature than our planet can renew in the whole year' through 'overfishing, overharvesting forests, and emitting more carbon dioxide into the atmosphere than forests can sequester.'[535] EF-based analysis have also been used to claim that 'if everyone on the planet consumed as much as the average US citizen, four earths would be needed to sustain them.'[536] The WWF summarized the main takeaway of the EF as follows:

> For more than 40 years, humanity's demand on nature has exceeded what our planet can replenish. We would need the regenerative capacity of 1.6 earths to provide the natural resources and ecological services we currently use. This is possible only in the short term. Only for a brief period can we cut trees faster than they mature, harvest more fish than the oceans can replenish, or emit more carbon into the atmosphere than the forests and oceans can absorb. The consequences of 'overshoot' are already clear: habitat and species loss, and accumulation of carbon in the atmosphere.[537]

As Rees acknowledged, the ecological footprint framework was developed 'specifically to assess the assertions made by some economists that, because of technological advances, the human economy is 'dematerializing' or 'decoupling' from the natural world.' If true, Rees conceded, 'this implies that modern society is becoming less dependent on nature and can be used to justify further economic growth. If false, the additional stress likely to be imposed on the natural world will be disastrous.'

Rees and Wackernagel's approach, however, has never been about measuring actual environmental quality – air and water pollution, farmland erosion, deforestation, state of local biodiversity and so on – but is rather about equating sustainability with local ecological self-sufficiency. More relevant to our purpose, the EF is built on the conviction that 'the most technologically advanced nations are the most energy- and material-intensive and have the largest per-capita ecological footprints. Hence, the consumer lifestyles of their average citizens (and of the wealthy residents of the developing world) *are the least ecologically sustainable on earth, and cannot be safely extended to humans everywhere*' (our emphasis).[538]

Because of this belief and the 'strong sustainability' assumption for carbon dioxide emissions, the EF has de facto always been an 'energy footprint', in which greater energy use is inherently unsustainable. As the WWF itself acknowledged, 'carbon from burning fossil fuels has been the dominant component of humanity's Ecological Footprint for more than half a century and its share continues to grow.'[539] In other words, spectacular overshoot numbers are entirely driven by the theoretical forested area required to absorb all of humanity's carbon dioxide emissions, not from any real need for additional agricultural or forested land or fishing grounds. As critics observed in 2013, 'if one excludes carbon, global biocapacity exceeds the footprint of consumption by about 45% in 2008... and by an average of 69% over the period from 1961 to 2008. These figures appear to indicate a sustainable pattern of consumption, with productivity rising to meet growing demand.'[540]

Another consideration missing from the EF is that it views energy-powered, highly efficient modern agricultural technologies as inherently unsustainable. As one critic put it:

> The footprints of all the industrialized countries are artificially inflated by [the Global Footprint Network], purely because they are efficient and get high yields. And the higher the yield, the higher the penalty. A country producing wheat at four times the global average wheat yield has its wheat footprint multiplied by four. And conversely, if a country has a yield that is lower than the global average, their footprint gets artificially shrunk. Shrunk! Some countries use more hectares than the rest of the world for a unit of production, and for that the number of hectares of their footprint is reduced?[541]

In short, the countries with the lightest (carbon) footprints are those with the poorest, less urbanized and less healthy populations who struggle with the most significant deforestation, indoor air pollution and public health problems, as shown in Figure 5.1.[542] The fact that the EF contains no economic, social or truly meaningful environmental indicators might explain the silence of its proponents on these issues. In the end though, one must question the value of a measure of sustainability – which is supposed to factor in human welfare – when its most desirable outcome is an ever less numerous and poorer world population that has reverted to environmentally damaging subsistence agriculture.

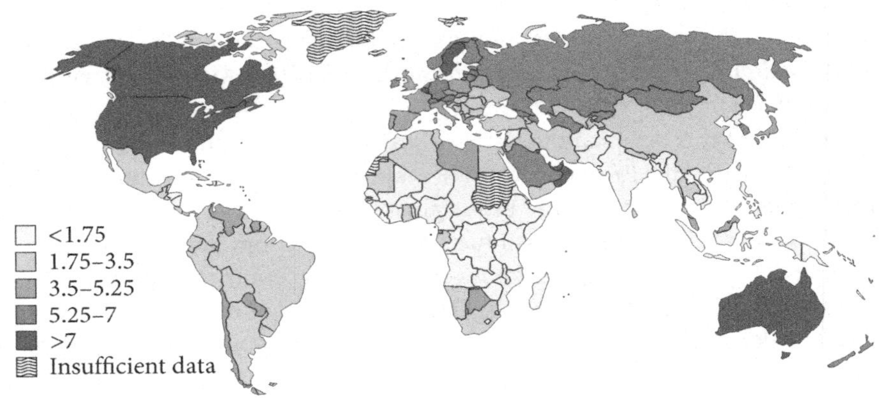

Figure 5.1: Mapping the ecological footprint of consumption.

Ecological footprint per person in 2012 (except Norway, Burundi, 2011). Figures in global hectares. Source: WWF (2016).

Planetary boundaries

The planetary boundaries framework[543] (henceforth PBF) was introduced in 2009 by Swedish researcher Johan Rockström and various collaborators, some of whom are among the most well-known pessimistic earth-system and environmental scientists.[544] It was updated in 2015.[545]

The PBF outlines nine interdependent planetary boundaries, 'within which ...humanity can operate safely,' meaning without reducing the ability of global systems to provide essential natural services and goods. Moving beyond the safe-operation regime, it is argued, risks disturbing the relative stability of the climate and natural systems that characterized the Holocene: the 12,000-years since the end of the last Ice Age. Conversely, operating within the limits set by the PBF allows these global systems to maintain themselves for several thousand years. In the 2015 PBF update, the boundaries were as follows:

- climate change
- change in biosphere integrity (biodiversity loss and species extinction)
- stratospheric ozone depletion
- ocean acidification
- biogeochemical flows (phosphorus and nitrogen cycles)
- land-system change (for example deforestation)
- freshwater use
- atmospheric aerosol loading (microscopic particles in the atmosphere that affect climate and living organisms)
- introduction of novel entities, such as organic pollutants, radioactive materials, nanomaterials, and micro-plastics.

Because of 'a rapidly growing reliance on fossil fuels and industrialized forms of agriculture,' however, human activities are said to 'have reached a level that could damage the systems that keep Earth in the desirable Holocene state.'[546] According to Rockström and his collaborators:

> The exponential growth of human activities is raising concern that further pressure on the Earth System could destabilize critical biophysical systems and trigger abrupt or irreversible environmental changes that would be deleterious or even catastrophic for human well-being. This is a profound dilemma because the predominant paradigm of social and economic development remains largely oblivious to the risk of human-induced environmental disasters at continental to planetary scales.[547]

The PBF is said to lay the groundwork for moving beyond 'essentially sectoral analyses of limits to growth aimed at minimizing negative externalities' towards the 'estimation of the safe space for human development' that would avoid 'major human-induced environmental change on a global scale.'[548] According to the 2015 update, 'four of nine planetary boundaries have now been crossed as a result of human activity.'[549] Figure 5.2 summarizes the extent of humanity's transgressions.

The PBF contributors' policy stance is in line with those of the creators of past approaches that they built upon, most notably limits-to-growth, safe minimum standards, the precautionary principle and tolerable windows.[550] In a recent contribution based on this framework, a group led by the the ecological economist Daniel W. O'Neill suggests that 'If all people are to lead a good life within planetary boundaries, then our results suggest that provisioning systems must be fundamentally restructured to enable basic needs to be met at a much lower level of resource use.' They further acknowledge that these findings 'represent a substantial challenge to current development trajectories' and that the 'challenge will be even greater in future if efforts are not also made to stabilize

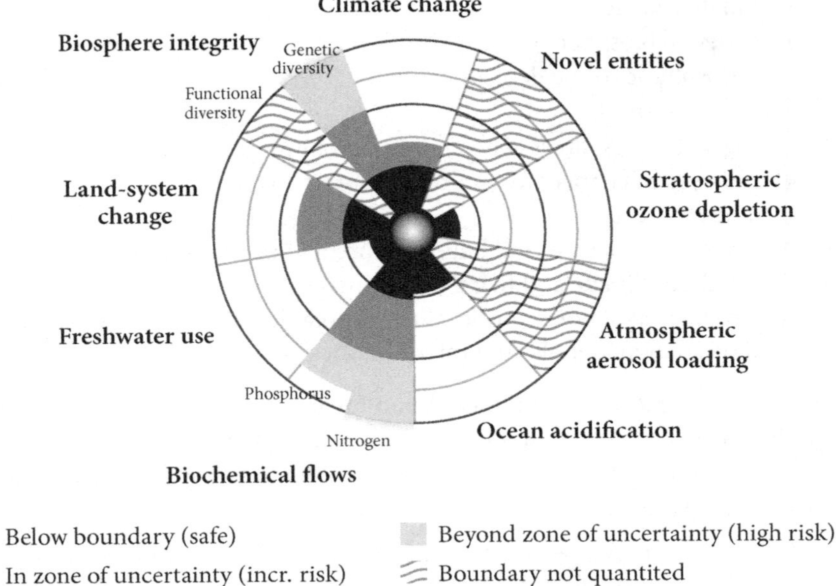

Figure 5.2: Estimates of how the different control variables for seven planetary boundaries have changed from 1950 to present.

The darkest area represents the safe operating space. Source: redrawn from Steffen *et al.* (2015).

global population.'[551] In another paper, Rockström and two collaborators suggest ways to 'limit continued growth of the material economy on a finite planet,' question the need to respect national sovereignty and openly call for global governance:

> Ultimately, there will need to be an institution (or institutions) operating, with authority, above the level of individual countries to ensure that the planetary boundaries are respected. In effect, such an institution, acting on behalf of humanity as a whole, would be the ultimate arbiter of the myriad trade-offs that need to be managed as nations and groups of people jockey for economic and social advantage. It would, in essence, become the global referee on the planetary playing field.[552]

As could be expected, the PBF has drawn its share of criticism.[553] Arguably the most fundamental complaint is the assumption that the natural conditions of the Holocene are an optimal baseline for human flourishing. As analysts associated with the Breakthrough Institute point out: 'Since so much variance from the Holocene has been good for humans, future environmental change cannot be assumed, as planetary boundaries does, to be negative for our welfare.'[554] The geographer Erle C. Ellis similarly observed: 'It was not planetary boundaries, but human system boundaries that constrained human development in the Holocene.'[555] In other words, the remarkable advances in standards of living observed over the last two centuries were entirely contingent upon, among other things, converting more land to agricultural and other uses, damming rivers, increasing carbon dioxide emissions through the burning of carbon fuels and capturing large amounts of nitrogen from the atmosphere while increasing its concentration in the biosphere through the use of synthetic fertilizers.

Other problems include the subjective and arbitrary nature of global boundaries (including whether some of those used in the PBF even actually exist) and whether or not crossing global thresholds will result in global (as opposed to local or regional) tipping points.[556] For instance, it is difficult to conceive how significant problems related to biodiversity, water, land and fertilizer use in one part of the world will somehow affect distant ecosystems. As critics ask:

> Were the planetary boundaries authors suggesting that Africans should wait to use more fertilizer until the Chinese had reduced their use? Not exactly. But in calling for cutting global fertilizer levels by 75 percent, the authors were clearly framing fertilizer as a problem of too much (e.g. in places like China), while leaving the problem of too little fertilizer (e.g. Rwanda) out of the framework.[557]

And while the overuse of fertilizers in some parts of the world may indeed cause problems such as dead marine zones, insufficient use will result in lower yields and the additional conversion of marginal land to agricultural use. As critics explain, with the exception of climate change, ocean acidification and stratospheric ozone, 'characterizing global biotic change with single aggregates is inapt.'[558]

Another problem is that the PBF 'only measures environmental change as negative – as steps in a progression toward supposed biophysical boundaries – and never as positive, either for humans (say, more food) or environments (say, higher yields resulting in less deforestation).'[559] Not surprisingly, as the science journalist Ronald Bailey observed in his discussion of the O'Neill study, countries whose resource use remains well within safe biophysical boundaries are typically economically and socially destitute, be they Haiti, Malawi, Nepal, Myanmar or Nicaragua.[560] As with the environmental footprint framework, the PBF creators arbitrarily adopt a strong sustainability approach in terms of their strict Holocene baseline and view the trade-offs that made human flourishing possible as inherently less sustainable than human misery. Given this limitation, they cannot be said to truly address sustainable *human* development considerations.

Synthesis

Our reading of the evidence on resource availability and the environmental impact of increased consumption can be summarized as follows:

- Non-renewable resources are more abundant than ever before.
- Most environmental indicators in advanced economies and in many developing ones show marked signs of improvement.
- Predictions of future collapse by past pessimistic writers, whether based on resource scarcity or the environmental impact of increased production and consumption, have not come to pass.
- The best predictor of long-term population trends, the total fertility rate, has been declining since the early 1960s.[561] Even though we disagree with the pessimists that human population growth is a problem, the available evidence does not support their alarmist forecasts of critical overcrowding far into the future.
- The problems and threats described by pessimistic writers are typically based on models, scenarios and conjectures rather than time series of environmental data showing actual damage from the use of modern technologies and/or increased consumption.

In short, if the key to truly sustainable development is a reduction of human impact on sensitive ecosystems, then the available evidence suggests that economic development based on ever more globalized trade, greater use of carbon fuels and continuous innovation seems preferable to greater material deprivation and increased reliance on local renewable resources. By contrast, however, the assumptions built into frameworks and models of environmental doom seem more reflective of their authors' lack of understanding or dislike of economic development, market processes (and especially a misunderstanding of the true incentives created by the profit motive), carbon fuels and technological advances rather than actual negative environmental trends.

Be that as it may, in the end the case made by degrowth and sustainable development theorists ultimately relies on computer models in which increased carbon dioxide emissions produced through the combustion of carbon fuels create catastrophic climate warming or climate change.[562] While we claim no expertise in terms of climate modeling, we will now suggest that a broader historical perspective on both alleged anthropogenic climate change and how, over the last three decades, it has become the environmental catastrophe of last resort, should perhaps alleviate some of our worst climate fears.

5.3 Anthropogenic climate change and population growth before the age of global warming

As the biogeographer Philip Stott observed a decade ago, from the 'Babylon of Gilgamesh to the post-Eden of Noah, every age has viewed climate change cataclysmically, as retribution for human greed and sinfulness.'[563] Not surprisingly, environmental and climate scares of all kinds captured the popular imagination over the course of the twentieth century.[564] What follows is a brief historical overview of some of these past concerns and a more elaborate discussion of two of them – soil erosion and global cooling – that paved the way to current calls to curb population growth and economic development in the name of climate change.[565] We then take a critical look at how carbon dioxide emissions and global warming were so readily accepted as high-level threats by the environmental and policy establishments and how quickly what might be termed the 'climate protection institutional apparatus' was created. We conclude with an examination of the rhetoric of the new population-control and climate activists and suggest that it is, in the end, nothing but the latest twist on a long-standing and repeatedly debunked storyline.

Historical perspective

Because of natural factors, such as changes in the axial tilt of the Earth's orbit around the sun, the amount of incoming solar radiation, geological activity (for example, large-scale volcanic eruptions, plate tectonics), changes in atmospheric chemistry as a result of changes in the balance between natural sources and sinks of greenhouse gases, and numerous feedback effects (physical, chemical, and thermal), the earth's climate has always and will remain in a state of flux, no matter how many tons of greenhouse gases are emitted by humans.[566] Needless to say, variations in the local weather have also always been a constant throughout history, no matter the amount of greenhouse gases emitted through human activities.[567] As Aristotle observed over two millennia ago while discussing one area of the Mediterranean basin: 'Sometimes there is much drought or rain, and it prevails over a great and continuous stretch of country. At other times it is local; the surrounding country often getting seasonable or even excessive rains while there is drought in a certain part; or, contrariwise, all the surrounding country gets little or even no rain while a certain part gets rain in abundance.'[568]

As could be expected, many individuals throughout history blamed extreme weather events[569] and climate change on a wide range of anthropogenic causes, be they insufficient offerings to the gods, witchcraft, deforestation, the lightning rod, wireless telegraphy, cannon shots in World War I, atomic tests, supersonic flights, and air pollution (for example, sulphate aerosols).[570] For instance, in 1881 American experts warned that telegraph lines might knock the Earth off its axis, cause earthquakes, melt the poles and cause a 'glacial flood' that would wipe out the human race. A contemporary news report on this hypothesis ended by suggesting that 'Whether this theory prove [sic] correct or not, there cannot be a doubt that something has of late gone wrong with atmospherical arrangements, and perhaps the telegraph wires are not wholly blameless in the matter.'[571] More recently the paleoclimatologist William F. Ruddiman suggested an 'early anthropocene' scenario in which significant human-induced changes in greenhouse gases' atmospheric concentrations began several millennia ago with the widespread diffusion of agriculture in Eurasia rather than the more recent coal-burning activities of the industrial age.[572]

Some human activities were nonetheless thought of as beneficial, such as the idea that 'rain follows the plow'[573] in semi-arid environments, a hypothesis endorsed by respectable scientists in America and Australia during the nineteenth century.

The erosion scare

While past anthropogenic climate scares are now viewed as ludicrous, some human activities did have a noticeable impact, such as extensive and sustained deforestation and flora removal that resulted in dryer (reduced atmospheric humidity) and windier (through the removal of natural wind breaks) local climates.[574] Land mismanagement could also result over time in soil depletion and compaction, siltation, waterlogging, salinization and, in extreme cases, desertification.[575] Such fears caused much alarm among some early twentieth century population control activists, along with rebuttals by more optimistic writers who emphasized the creative capacity of humans to restore nature,[576] but the issue is obviously much older.

As the agricultural economist Dennis Avery put it, soil erosion 'has been threatening since man scratched the first seedbed with a stick.'[577] Fears of deforestation and soil erosion as a result of a growing population are said by some scholars to go back at least four millennia to *The Epic of Gilgamesh*.[578] In the archaic Greek epic poem *The Cypria*, 'countless people' oppressed the 'breadth of the deep-chested earth,' a problem Zeus addressed by fomenting the Trojan war.[579] Plato later lamented that Athens' back country, whose hills had once been 'covered with soil,' the plains 'full of rich earth,' and the mountains displaying an 'abundance of wood,' had been turned after years of abuse into a landscape that could 'only afford sustenance to bees' because all the 'richer and softer parts of the soil [had] fallen away, and the mere skeleton of the land [was] being left.'[580]

By the 1930s, severe droughts created gigantic dust storms on the American plains, one of which blew all the way to Washington DC and prompted the creation of the United States Department of Agriculture's Soil Conservation Service.[581] A 1939 book entitled *The Rape of the Earth: A World Survey of Soil Erosion*[582] reviewed the relevant literature published in the previous two decades. Its British writers, Graham Vernon Jacks and Robert Orr Whyte, argued that 'as the result solely of human mismanagement, the soils upon which men have attempted to found new civilizations are disappearing, washed away by water and blown away by wind' and that the 'destruction of the earth's thin living cover is proceeding at a rate and on a scale unparalleled in history, and when that thin cover – the soil – is gone, the fertile regions where it formerly lay will be uninhabitable deserts.'[583]

In what was arguably the culmination of this genre, William Vogt in his *Road to Survival* argued that, with rare exceptions, man had 'taken the bounty of the earth and made little or no return.' Where he had not lost water and soil, he had 'overgrazed and overcropped, and by the removal of animals and plants, [had] carried away important soil minerals, broken down the all-important soil structure, and generally exhausted the environment.'[584] As he saw it, civilizations were at risk for:

> Fire, the ax, the plow, and firearm have been the four fundamental tools of our modern culture, and in some of the most fertile and productive regions of the earth they have raised the environmental resistance to such a height that the carrying capacity has been brought nearly as low as that of the Gobi or the tundra of Siberia. Hundreds of millions of acres of once rich land are now as poor as – or worse than – the city gardener's sterile plot. Despoiled forests, erosion, wildlife extermination, overgrazing, and the dropping of water tables are unforeseen and unwanted by-blows of a vigorous and adolescent culture on the loose.[585]

One of the most influential erosion doomsayers outside the United States was the Indian sociologist, demographer, population control activist and Union Minister of Health and Family Planning in the cabinet of Prime Minister Indira Gandhi, Sripati Chandrasekhar. A few years after Vogt, he observed:

> The American and Canadian agricultural surpluses are far from typical of the rest of the world. Even these surpluses are obtained at the cost of the longevity and perhaps the very life of the land itself. This wearing away and washing out of the precious soil is not restricted to one country or region. It has spread like an epidemic. With the exception of a few small areas in North Western Europe, forests are not being used on

> a sustained-yield basis; they are being inexorably wiped out. Grasslands almost everywhere are being overgrazed. Water tables are falling; rivers are overflowing and changing their courses. Nature is losing her balance. Man's ignorant and destructive hand has set the ball of disaster rolling. Besides this mismanagement, man's greed for monetary returns prevents him from making the best use of land; perhaps nowhere in the world is land used to produce the crop that is best suited for the soil on a permanent basis. Cash crops that would yield quick returns are raised instead.[586]

Vogt, Chandrasekhar and other catastrophists were criticized by some of their contemporaries, who argued that their diagnosis was utterly at odds with the available evidence. In a scathing review, the agricultural economist Karl Brandt described Vogt's book as:

> '[a] forceful piece of propaganda for the no longer entirely new idea that soil-conservation practices by farmers are needed on many parts of the earth, and for Margaret Sanger's idea that mankind must be saved by birth control. Soil erosion and over-population are treated as the imminent universal threat to the survival of man.

Ignoring all advances in agricultural technologies and practices along with the 'overwhelming evidence to the contrary,' Vogt had produced a 'truly amazing book, not for the knowledge or wisdom it offers the reader, but for its psychological appeal, the emotional reactions it generates, the laudatory reviews it gets from literary critics, and its phenomenal sales.' People knowledgeable about 'farming, land utilization, or the economics of resources' who have 'any critical faculty or plain common sense will be moved to anger by it and may want to throw it into a wastebasket.' The villains in Vogt's story, according to Brandt, were 'the old stand-bys of all left-wing radicals: the white man; the rugged individualist; the free-enterprise system; the capitalistic system; the lumberman who uses an axe; the railroads which contribute the Dust Bowl and the destruction of the forests to modern living.' Vogt had also added some new ones, such as 'the farmers who use moldboard plows; the people who produce children and rear them; and the doctors, chemists, and biologists who reduce mortality and thus help families in over-populating the world. It is the story of the beautiful fertile wilderness, with its ecological balance, gradually and senseless [sic] destroyed by the white farmer and /industrial man-the great illusion.' Brandt urged as many rebuttals to the book as could be mustered to address its abundant scientific errors and 'the nonsense it contains, simply because the basically unsound main thesis of impending catastrophe as the result of universal abuse of land resources and of rapid over-population has profoundly impressed even men of otherwise good judgment.'[587]

The University of Delaware geographer Earl Parker Hanson was equally vociferous in his 1949 book *New Worlds Emerging*. Describing his contribution as a critique of Osborn, Vogt and other 'Jeremiahs of geography, sociology and economics,'[588] the geographer argued that 'it is never a land that is over-populated, in terms of inhabitants per square mile; it is always an economy, in terms of inhabitants per square meal.'[589] Adopting as his motto the 1527 observation of merchant and explorer Robert Thorne that 'there is no land unhabitable, nor sea unnavigable,' Hanson emphasized that much land was still available for development in the Amazon basin and in lower Arctic areas like Alaska. Denouncing the 'hysteria' into which the modern world was 'being stampeded...by the dreadful word *erosion*'[590] and the resurgence of the 'old, mechanistic Malthusian doctrine,'[591] he had no patience for the notions that natural resources should be conserved, 'not sanely by way of making the most of them, but hysterically, as an isolated party of explorers might hoard and ration its dwindling food supplies;'[592] that people should be considered as 'liabilities' rather than 'assets and potential resources;'[593] or that a region would be considered 'over-populated' in terms of a population/space ratio alone without factoring in the potential benefits of economic development that would in time produce 'more in order to have more to go around.'[594] Indeed, throughout history, humanity had met population increases 'not in any one way, but by a complex, interrelated application of three distinct lines of effort, namely migration, change of social and economic organization, and technical invention.'[595]

Hanson was especially critical of Vogt's 'astonishing...tendency to resent all past progress' and lament that 'Adam and Eve [had to leave] the Garden of Eden,'[596] without understanding that 'conservation on [a] large scale...can only be supported by energetic economic development.'[597] As he explained it:

> To proclaim a numerical limit on the world's arable lands, while decrying the technical advances with which that limit can be stretched by many millions of acres, is to turn one's back on reality. Even birth control on a large scale can be accomplished only by raising standards of living through industrialization. Not only do people need money for buying contraceptives, but they need many children for cheap labor so long as they live in poverty and degradation. They will be more likely to think about having fewer children when they are in a position to worry about sending them to college.[598]

In a later article, Hanson would describe the 'currently popular Vogt school of demographers and conservationists' as postulating the twin bogeymen of overpopulation and soil erosion as the price we must inevitably pay for 'conscious efforts to improve human existence.'[599]

Another critical take on Vogt was penned by Merrill K. Bennett, then executive director of Stanford University's Food Research Institute. In a short essay against the 'current [overpopulation] scare' published in *Scientific Monthly*, Bennett targeted the 'conservationists, notably the soil conservationists,' including the 'outstanding, perhaps extreme, examples' of Vogt and Osborn, who seemingly 'uncover[ed]...practically everywhere, evidence of permanent soil erosion by water and wind, and of depletion of soil fertility.'[600] Looking back five decades, a time when 'world population growth was enormous,' Bennett instead saw marked 'evidence of improvement in per capita food supplies.'[601] Toward the end of his essay, he wrote that '[p]essimism about maintenance or improvement of per capita food supply, even where population is densest, is not intellectually necessary, not compelled on the basis of historical fact or logic.' To follow the path traced by Vogt, Osborn, and other pessimists would 'hamper invention, stifle capital accumulation, hinder investment domestically and internationally, and hence to retard the general economic development, one aspect of which is improvement of national diets.' If the paths toward progress and sensible policies – and not only in terms of human reproduction and land use – were followed instead, 'time may prove today's pessimists to have been wrong, as with the pessimists of yesterday.'[602]

Bennett also had a few interesting comments on the political dynamics that made erosion catastrophism such a popular genre. The passage is worth quoting in full:

> There seems to be a degree of historical coincidence in the rise of the soil-conservation school to its present degree of public prominence. Great dust storms afflicted our Great Plains in the middle 1930s. A bit earlier, in 1933, this nation had embarked upon the adventure of curing economic depression in part by supporting farm prices and incomes, and the method first chosen was to make Federal payments directly to farmers in exchange for acreage reduction. When the Supreme Court in January 1936 put a stop to this 'gentle rain of checks,' as a shrewd observer called it, a lawful way to continue became the object of political expediency. And so the payments earlier made to purchase acreage reduction became 'agricultural conservation payment;' politics opened the door of the public treasury to conservationists; the great droughts carried conviction to the public of a crying need for conservation; and increasingly since then political leaders, soil conservationists, and the public seem to have been at one in viewing soil erosion as a dreadful threat domestically. As conservationists proliferated, the perception of threat to food supply through soil erosion spread so as to compass whole continents. The books by Vogt and Osborn provide outstanding, perhaps extreme, examples of literature originating with the ardent-conservation school. That group, of course, cries for 'action now,' and for funds as well. Allusion is made to

> civilizations which, it is claimed, disappeared because their soil was swept away. It is sought to check or control erosion, thus saving civilization. The soil-conservation school adds, to the old concept that the food-producing land of the world is strictly limited in extent the new concept that the land is actually being destroyed, and at a rapid rate.[603]

In hindsight we now know that Brandt, Hanson, Bennett and other optimistic writers were right, as innovative approaches and strategies – many of which preceded the publication of Vogt's eco-catastrophist bestseller – allowed both an increase in agricultural production and environmental remediation.[604]

The global cooling scare

Over four decades ago, fine particles released by industrial activity – airborne soot, and oxides such as sulphates and nitrates – were often invoked to explain a cooling trend observed between the 1940s and the 1970s that was said to depart from the benign climate of the previous century and mark a return to conditions similar to those of the Little Ice Age that lasted from the early fourteenth to the mid-nineteenth century. As with the prior erosion scare, experts often predicted dire effects on global food production, the onset of famines and other catastrophist scenarios.[605]

In 1968, the meteorologist and atmospheric scientist Reid Bryson, arguably the most important proponent of global cooling through his 'human volcano' theory, observed that the 'continued rapid cooling of the earth since World War II is also in accord with the increased global air pollution associated with industrialization, mechanization, urbanization, and an exploding population, added to a renewal of volcanic activity.'[606] A few years later, the energy consultant Wilson Ayers Clark Jr commented that:

> [s]everal schools of thought in climate science interpret existing data in different ways. One argues that, instead of growing warmer, the Earth may enter an Ice Age as a result of man-made fuels combustion. The combustion of fossil fuels releases large quantities of particulate matter into the atmosphere, which may reflect sunlight away from the Earth, thus cooling the planet.[607]

A number of statements by heads and employees of meteorological agencies, academic articles written by prominent scholars and a 1974 CIA report on the state of the art in climatology adopted a similar stance and tone.[608]

Not surprisingly, the coverage in major newspapers, magazines, books and television was often even more alarmist, with extreme weather events typically singled out as signs of a coming ice age.[609] For instance, in his influential 1976 book *The Cooling*, science journalist Lowell Ponte observed that in the northern hemisphere the climate had been getting significantly colder in the past three decades, the consequences of which would probably be 'mass global famine in our lifetimes, perhaps even within a decade. Since 1970, half a million human beings in northern Africa and Asia have starved because of floods and droughts caused by the cooling climate.'[610] Ponte blamed the cooling trend for frost and snow devastating coffee plantations in Brazil, the Sahara Desert advancing south, unusually dry years in France and England, crop failures in the Soviet Union, severe floods in the Mississippi Basin, the Great Lakes, Pennsylvania and New Jersey, and severe droughts in the American southwest. He then argued that global cooling 'presents humankind with the most important social, political, and adaptive challenge we have had to deal with for ten thousand years.'[611] In his 1980 book *The Geography of Famine*, geographer William Dando observed that most climatologists and a declassified CIA report agreed that because of air pollution, the earth was 'entering a period of climatic change' that had already resulted in 'North African droughts, the lack of penetration of monsoonal rains in India and seasonal delay in the onset of spring rains in the Soviet Virgin Lands wheat area.' Global cooling, Dando warned his readers, was 'the greatest single challenge humans will face in coming years' because it would soon trigger 'mass migration and all-encompassing international famines.'[612] Like many others, Dando's preferred policy solutions revolved around population control and reduced economic activities.

Our reading of the global cooling literature suggests, however, that in the absence of an authoritative institution like the United Nations' Intergovernmental Panel on Climate Change (IPCC), allusions to natural causes were arguably more common than in the later age of global warming and that less pressure was brought upon the political establishment to address the issue. Be that as it may, the acceptance of the theoretical underpinning of global cooling among prominent scientists in the 1970s cannot be understated. To give but a few accounts, in 1977 the Ehrlichs and John Holdren wrote that '[m]any observers have speculated that the cooling could be the beginning of a long and persistent trend in that direction – that is, an inevitable departure from an abnormally warm period in climatic history.'[613] As the Ehrlichs would further comment two decades later: 'Predictions of future climate trends by Stephen Schneider and other leading climatologists, based on the prevailing knowledge of the atmosphere in the early 1970s, gave more weight to the potential problem of global cooling than it now appears to merit.'[614] For his part, Julian Simon observed that people worried about a cooling trend:

> ...included *Science*, the most influential scientific journal in the world...; the National Academy of Sciences worrying about the onset of a 10,000 year ice age; *Newsweek* warning that food production could be adversely

affected within a decade; the *New York Times* quoting an official of the National Center for Atmospheric Research; and *Science Digest*, the science periodical with the largest circulation.[615]

Interestingly, the policy solutions suggested to address global cooling were eerily similar to those later suggested for global warming. Perhaps none is more striking than the following excerpt from an editorial published in 1970 in the Owosso (Michigan) *Argus-Press*, reproduced in Figure 5.3.

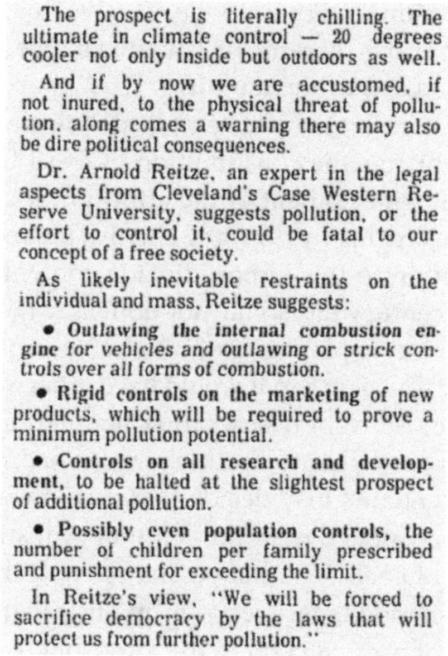

The prospect is literally chilling. The ultimate in climate control — 20 degrees cooler not only inside but outdoors as well.

And if by now we are accustomed, if not inured, to the physical threat of pollution, along comes a warning there may also be dire political consequences.

Dr. Arnold Reitze, an expert in the legal aspects from Cleveland's Case Western Reserve University, suggests pollution, or the effort to control it, could be fatal to our concept of a free society.

As likely inevitable restraints on the individual and mass, Reitze suggests:

- **Outlawing the internal combustion engine** for vehicles and outlawing or strick controls over all forms of combustion.
- **Rigid controls on the marketing** of new products, which will be required to prove a minimum pollution potential.
- **Controls on all research and development**, to be halted at the slightest prospect of additional pollution.
- **Possibly even population controls**, the number of children per family prescribed and punishment for exceeding the limit.

In Reitze's view, "We will be forced to sacrifice democracy by the laws that will protect us from further pollution."

Figure 5.3: Global cooling policy proposal of 1970.

Source: *Argus-Press* (1970).

5.4 From cooling to warming and back to population growth

From cooling to warming

By the late 1970s, it became generally accepted that the modest decline in temperature observed in the last three decades was over, that temperatures seemed to be rising again and that the alleged main causes of global cooling could be scrubbed at source in smokestacks.[616] However, anthropogenic greenhouse gas emissions – emissions produced as a result of human activities such as the burning of fossil fuels, rice cultivation, deforestation, the use of fertilizer in agriculture and production of chlorofluorocarbons – were quickly put at the top of the environmental policy agenda and a wide-ranging institutional apparatus was set up to curb carbon dioxide emissions, said to cause unmanageable global warming. Perhaps most remarkable is the speed at which these developments occurred, especially given that, in the period after World War II, carbon dioxide emissions were not deemed very significant by most climate researchers and, when mentioned more than cursorily in discussion of pollution, were typically a minor policy consideration.[617] For instance, in a 1968 paper climatologist Reid Bryson commented that the reasons for climate change communicated to lay audiences seemed 'as varied as the authors.' True, apart from factors such as changes in sunspots, air pollution and complicated feedbacks between sea and air, some authors did blame 'the consumption of fossil fuels producing an increase in the carbon dioxide content of the atmosphere,'[618] but the tone rarely seemed to be alarmist. Writing in 1973, the chemist and economist Colin Clark deemed that the 'addition to the carbon dioxide content of the world's atmosphere since the 19th century has so far not done any harm, and has probably been beneficial, in increasing plant growth. Probably another effect has been to keep the world slightly warmer than it would have otherwise been.' While Clark acknowledged that the causes of past weather fluctuations were not known, it was clear 'that they are not due to the burning of fuel. However, some centuries hence, our descendants may decide that it is unwise to add further carbon dioxide to the atmosphere, even though they will still probably have very large unused reserves of coal.'[619] A stance that seems to have been common in the early 1970s was re-iterated more recently by Australian geologist Ian Plimer: '[O]nly one molecule of every 85,000 in the atmosphere is CO_2 of human origin, and yet we are asked to believe that this one molecule drives hugely complex climate change systems. We are also asked to believe that the 32 molecules of CO_2 of natural origin in every 85,000 molecules play no part in driving climate change.'[620]

According to climate scientist Richard Lindzen, in the early 1970s:

> [T]he scientific community regularly designated warm periods as 'climate optima'. That carbon dioxide was essential to plants and effectively a fertiliser was also widely understood. Thus, it was not surprising that the early environmental movement chose to promote fear of global cooling, which, not surprisingly, was attributed to industrial emissions (most notably sulphates).[621]

By the late 1970s, however, it became widely recognized that the alleged cause of global cooling could be scrubbed, and that:

> the irreducible product of industrial emissions was carbon dioxide, that carbon dioxide emissions were likely to warm rather than cool, and that

> there was an hypothetical process whereby this warming could be amplified (by what came to be known as the water vapour feedback).[622]

Not surprisingly in light of this context, some commentators have suggested that the rapid adoption of carbon dioxide emissions as a dominant environmental policy concern was certainly helped more by how perfectly it aligned with the belief system and rationale for the existence of certain special interest groups (government-sponsored researchers, renewable energy industry lobbyists, environmental activists and high-level bureaucrats) than by an actual understanding of the real danger fossil fuel combustion might cause in terms of global average surface temperature.[623] As the historian of science Spencer Weart observed, by the 1980s the environmental movement which, up to that point 'had found only occasional interest in global warming,'[624] made the issue one of their top priorities. In his words, 'groups that had other reasons for preserving tropical forests, promoting energy conservation, slowing population growth, or reducing air pollution could make common cause, as they offered their various ways to reduce emissions of carbon dioxide.'[625] Weart added that other voices in this chorus included 'people who looked for arguments to weaken the prestige of large corporations, and people who wanted to scold the public for its wastefulness. For better or worse, global warming became identified more than ever as a "green" issue.'[626]

The redistributive policies of climate treaties were also in accord with the broader social goals of many left-wing activists who had come to embrace environmentalism.[627] A recent case in point is anti-globalization activist Naomi Klein, who concluded that carbon fuels-caused global warming 'changes everything' in terms of 'how we live' and 'how our economies function.'[628] What she meant was it provides a perfect rationale to abolish or severely constrain free markets, change the nature of our energy infrastructure and remake our political system in a way that accords with her prior personal preferences: those she had before she developed an interest in climate change policy.

Be that as it may, the IPCC was created in 1988 with the specific mandate 'to assess scientific, technical, and socioeconomic information that is relevant in understanding *human-induced climate change*, its potential impacts, and options for mitigation and adaptation'[629] (our italics). As such, the IPCC process explicitly directed or limited discussions of climate change to human activities at the expense of natural phenomena, thus creating a more unified narrative on the subject than would have otherwise been the case. Indeed, a number of critics have pointed out that the IPCC has sometimes pushed a climate narrative onto related topics, such as whether global warming will increase the incidence and geographical reach of vector-borne diseases, when there is no evidence to this effect; malaria was once common in northern Europe before it was eradicated through public health campaigns.[630]

To summarize, the core concern is the carbon dioxide emitted as a result of the burning of coal, oil, and natural gas. Some of it is taken up by plants through photosynthesis, chemically combined with rocks or dissolved in the ocean. A not insignificant volume, however, is added to the atmosphere, where its concentration increases and where, when coupled with the feedback effect of water vapour, it is said to be warming our climate beyond humanity's and ecosystems' capacity to adapt, the result of which include calamities such as an extension of the range of infectious diseases and invasive species, rising sea levels, desertification, reduced agricultural yields, extreme weather events, ocean acidification, species extinction, a deterioration of people's health and massive waves of climate refugees.[631] In order to prevent such outcomes, humans across the planet were urged to reduce or forego the use of carbon fuels.[632] As the authors of the Royal Society's *People and the Planet* report commented in 2012, 'industrial development has been founded on cheap and abundant energy from burning fossil fuels. Limits are now being reached, not by shortage of fuels but by the consequent emission of CO_2 and other greenhouse gases causing dangerous climate change.'[633] (Indeed, while the fear of Peak Oil might have come with the hope that a shortage of carbon fuels would mitigate these problems, by the time this report was published, newly abundant fossil fuels made possible by advances in hydraulic fracturing had been denounced as an addiction with lethal societal consequences.[634]) The authors also added that it was 'generally understood that there is an urgent need to switch to alternative energy sources or to capture and store CO_2.'[635]

Critics of this narrative have long argued that current renewable technologies were never a plausible alternative to carbon fuels, that carbon capture and storage technologies have never been economically scalable to a level that would alleviate the fears of climate activists,[636] and that the likely outcome of a policy war against coal, oil and natural gas would be economic and social hardship.[637] Another recurring complaint is that the sole source of belief in 'runaway global warming' – in other words, beyond the range of natural climate variability – is computer-generated scenarios with a poor predictive track record.[638] As climate scientist Judith Curry commented, the 'climate models making dire predictions of warming in the 21st century are the same models that predicted too much warming in the early 21st century, and can't explain the warming from 1910–1945 or the mid-century grand hiatus.'[639] Furthermore, absent fear of global warming, increases in carbon dioxide concentrations would not be problematic as the gas does not impair visibility, is odourless and non-toxic to humans, even at many times current atmospheric levels. And, needless to say, carbon dioxide is, through photosynthesis, the basic building block of the planetary food chain.

The scientific details and economic controversies surrounding the climate change debate have been discussed in much more detail elsewhere,[640] but of greater interest in the context of this book is the striking similarities between the pessimist rhetoric on overpopulation and that on climate change. The first is the simple causality mechanism underlying these narratives:

- population growth → rapidly depleting natural resources and environmental degradation
- aerosols → rapidly cooling climate
- anthropogenic carbon dioxide emissions → rapidly warming climate

The second is that political, academic and foundational support is overwhelmingly skewed towards proponents of catastrophist scenarios. Third, doomsday scenarios are based on theoretical frameworks and computer-generated scenarios rather than longitudinal time series demonstrating actual harm or degradation. Fourth, influential international organizations were set up to help establish a consensus over an allegedly pressing issue (a precedent to the IPCC was the International Union for the Scientific Investigation of Population Problems (IUSIPP), founded in 1928 and still with us today, albeit under a different name[641]). Last but certainly not least, while the environmental problems may change, the solutions remain the same: curbing economic development and population growth. We now turn to a more detailed examination of this last point.

Was global warming always (mostly) about population and economic growth?

While admitting he was not a climate specialist, the economist Julian Simon suspected over two decades ago that global warming was a dubious scare mostly rooted in older concerns about population growth. He observed then that the 'latest environmental justification for slowing or halting population growth is supposed global warming.' Simon cited a World Bank paper on the new 'global negative externality' represented by greenhouse gas emissions, which he summarized as follows: '[The] old rationales for World Bank population control programs – economic growth, resource conservation, and the like – having been discredited, a new 'rationale' has been developed on the basis of speculative assumptions about global warming's economic effects derived from controversial climatological science.'[642] Simon then summarized the position of most environmentalists as follows: 'But isn't it obvious... that additional people and additional economic growth will cause us to use more energy and hence emit more greenhouse gases? Therefore, even if we can't be sure of the greenhouse effect, wouldn't it be prudent to cut back on growth?'[643] The economist Jacqueline Kasun similarly believed at the time that 'by the 1990s the doomsayers had shifted their attack' as they could no longer invoke resource depletion. As she wrote, 'the alarmists didn't miss a step. The problem, they now said, was that people were using too much energy and were causing Global Warming.'[644] Building on similar evidence, the historical climatologist Tim Ball later commented: '[O]verpopulation is still central to the use of climate change as a political vehicle.'[645]

Whether or not one accepts this interpretation, the fact remains that highly placed international[646] and national bureaucrats, activists and public officials with strong limits-to-growth leanings saw the opportunity to connect their beliefs and the catastrophist narrative on climate change in the 1990s and the 2000s, sometimes even stating explicitly that population growth and increased consumption were bigger problems than anthropogenic global warming. The prominent United Nations bureaucrat Maurice Strong[647] (1929–2015), who was described by business journalist Peter Foster as '[m]ore than any other individual... responsible for promoting the [UN] climate agenda,' is a case in point.[648] Among his numerous accomplishments, Strong led the 1972 Conference on the Human Environment in Stockholm (itself part of a 1967 Swedish diplomatic power play to 'use the UN system to shift the diplomatic focus away from a nuclear paradigm towards more concern for international development and environmental protection'[649]); proved pivotal in creating UNEP and then became its first executive director;[650] and organized and led the 1992 'Earth Summit,' the UN Conference on Environment and Development in Rio de Janeiro, Brazil.[651] It was at the latter event that the United Nations Framework Convention on Climate Change (UNFCCC), a treaty approved at the conference, adopted the focus on anthropogenic factors contributing to climate change as its mandate, excluding other potential climate change causes.[652]

Strong's radical views on economic development and population control have long been known. For instance, he first achieved some degree of notoriety in Canada as young deputy minister – a high-ranking civil servant – when he went on the record as stating that 'with a growing global population, we will have to recognise that having children is not just a personal issue but a societal issue and at a certain point we may be faced with a need to have a permit to have a child.'[653] He also referred to the need for 'national population policies' in his opening speech at the 1972 Stockholm Conference.[654] As Strong reportedly stated at the 1992 Earth Summit: 'Either we reduce the world's population voluntarily or nature will do this for us, but brutally.'[655] At the 2009 Copenhagen Summit, he declared: 'The climate change issue and the economic issue come from the same roots. And that is the gross inequity and the inadequacy of our economic model. We now know that we have to change that model. We cannot do all of this in one stroke. But we have to design a process that would produce agreement at a much more radical level.'[656] In one of his last extended interviews, Strong stated that 'growth in the world population has increased the pressures on the Earth's resources and life-support systems.' He added that 'China's one-child policy is not a perfect policy by any means, but, on the other hand, how do you control growth in your population?' Strong viewed widespread aspirations for a better life as problematic, for if everyone 'enjoyed the same patterns of consumption that we in the West do, then we would have an unsustainable situation, and we're actually on the way to that now. We are in a situation that is unsustainable.' Interestingly, Strong had similar reservations about the rapid development of cities such as Singapore and Hong Kong, as they could only prosper 'by reaching out to the rest of the world for supplies and support. So they are financially successful, but they require a disproportionate share of the world's resources. On a global basis, that would inevitably create an unsustainable world.'[657]

As part of his work on 'globalizing the environmental movement,'[658] Strong tasked the British economist and writer, Barbara Ward, and René Dubos, a French-born American microbiologist, to craft *Only One Earth: The Care and Maintenance of a Small Planet*.[659] As historical climatologist Tim Ball put it, this book-length publication 'essentially became the first state of the environment report. It reinforced the shrinking planet perspective provided by the Apollo 8'[660] mission, while driving home the idea of ecological and physical limits for a growing global population. As such, their views can certainly be considered mainstream among environmental policy makers and activists at the time carbon dioxide emissions became a significant policy concern. The gifted popularisers and wordsmiths engaged by Strong created unforgettable environmental slogans and images that have been burned into our memory. The phrase 'think globally, act locally,' for example, is a staple of the classroom and farmers' markets around the developed world even now, and René Dubos is one of those often credited with conceiving it, although it is more likely he publicized it.[661] Ward and Dubos expressed the kind of outlook that has ever since characterized much environmentalist thinking: 'If all man can offer to the decades ahead is the same combination of scientific drive, economic cupidity and national arrogance, then we cannot rate very highly the chances of reaching the year 2000 with our planet still functioning and our humanity securely preserved.'[662]

Ward's 'only one earth' motto lent itself to powerful pessimist imagery as well, as pictured on the 1973 cover of the *UNESCO Courier*, reproduced below as Figure 5.4. The image showing planet Earth as a wax candle being consumed by intense flames at both 'ends' communicated, in both graphic and metaphorical terms, that humanity was burning through earth's resources at an alarming and unsustainable rate, and it was going to face a catastrophic 'burn-out.'

The accompanying text warned about the ideological bankruptcy of rallying to the optimist solution of technological innovation: 'Proud of his technological mastery and eager to grasp its benefits, man has been burning the candle at both ends and despoiling the biosphere on which his existence depends. Careless technology has polluted the oceans, land and atmosphere to such an extent that the quality of life is rapidly depreciating.'[663] In this issue Ward wrote that 'one point is surely clear. There are limits. The biosphere is not infinite. Populations must become stable. So must the demands they make.'[664]

As hinted earlier, under the direction of UNEP and with the UNFCCC articles approved at the 1992 Earth Summit as the ideological guidelines, the IPCC started gathering and weighing scientific information in earnest in 1988. It thus closed the loop that influential environmental activist elites opened in 1967 when they sought out focused global leadership 'on the extremely complex problems related to the human environment.'[665] The IPCC message certainly came from the top. Its first chairman (1988–1997) was the Swedish meteorologist Bert Bolin, the lone dissenting voice in the 1974 sensationalistic pro-cooling documentary *The Weather Machine*.[666] Bolin stated then that carbon dioxide emissions might warm up the world by a few degrees in the coming decades. Interestingly, Bolin is also on the record as stating in 1959 that the increase in carbon dioxide atmospheric concentrations 'caused by the burning of fuels by industry and transport' could have an 'effect on climate' that 'might be radical.'[667] Bolin would also play a crucial role through his 'involvement in global environmental issues' in creating 'an early interest in Sweden' in carbon dioxide emissions and global warming.[668] In 1975 he was asked by the Swedish Government to summarise the available knowledge on the subject. Later that year the conclusion of a government bill on future Swedish energy policy was that '[i]t is likely that climatic concerns will limit the burning of fossil fuels rather than the size of the natural resources.' As the journalist Donna Laframboise commented, although Bolin 'doesn't tell us what that opinion was,' one can infer that had the Swedish government 'misunderstood Bolin's position – or had egregiously exaggerated its import...he'd have said so in his [history of the IPCC].' Laframboise thus concludes that we are left 'with the uneasy feeling that a full 13 years before the IPCC was even born, its first chairman had already decided that fossil fuels didn't merely affect the climate, but that the affect was so adverse their use would need to be curtailed.'[669] Whether or not Bolin reached this conclusion a decade and a half or three decades before the creation of the IPCC, it seems fair to say that, in the words of Canadian academic Michael Hart: 'As often happens in science, when a scientist has decided to dedicate his career to discovering the

Figure 5.4: One Earth cover, *UNESCO Courier*, January 1973.

Robertson, Mary. 1973. 'Only One Earth' [Cover image]. The UNESCO Courier (January). Retrieved from http://unesdoc.unesco.org/images/0007/000748/074879eo.pdf. Information about the artist and the image found on the bottom of [p. 3], number inferred from the pagination of the articles in the issue.

role of a particular factor, he finds it and focuses on it to the exclusion of all others. Bolin *was* such a scientist.'[670]

Not surprisingly, Bolin was also a pessimist on population and resources issues, as evidenced in his stance on the controversy surrounding the 2001 publication of *The Skeptical Environmentalist* by Danish political scientist Bjørn Lomborg. Bolin stated he 'largely share[d] the gist of the...analyses' of Lomborg's critics John Holdren and John Bongaarts.[671] Bongaarts, a demographer long associated with the Population Council and a former chair of the Panel on Population Projections of the National Academy of Sciences, had then opined: 'Population is not the main cause of the world's social, economic and environmental problems, but it contributes substantially to many of them. If population had grown less rapidly in the past, we would be better off now. And if future growth can be slowed, future generations will be better off.'[672] For his part, John Holdren contradicted some of his earlier writings and argued that while the word was not 'running out of energy,' it was 'running out of environment,' by which he meant 'running out of the capacity of air, water, soil and biota to absorb, without intolerable consequences for human well-being, the effects of energy extraction, transport, transformation and use.'[673]

The second chairman of the IPCC (1997–2002), Robert Watson, would later go on the record as stating: 'The more people we have on the Earth and the richer they are, the more they can demand resources. There's more demand for food, more demand for water, more demand for energy...So, there's no question the threats on the Earth today are far more than, say, 50 years ago and in 50 years' time, there will even be more threats.'[674] The third chairman of the IPCC, Rajendra K. Pachauri (2002–2015), was even more explicit when he stated in 2007 that humanity has 'been so drunk with this desire to produce and consume more and more whatever the cost to the environment that we're on a totally unsustainable path.' He was 'not going to rest easy until [he has] articulated in every possible forum the need to bring about major structural changes in economic growth and development. That's the real issue. Climate change is just a part of it.' When asked why Indians shouldn't aspire to the same standard of living as westerners, Pachauri answered: 'Gandhi was asked if he wanted India to reach the same level of prosperity as the United Kingdom. He replied: "It took Britain half the resources of the planet to reach its level of prosperity. How many planets would India require?"'[675] In his resignation letter Pachauri admitted that for him, 'the protection of Planet Earth, the survival of all species and sustainability of our ecosystems is more than a mission. It is my religion and my dharma.'[676]

Another important figure is former American senator Timothy E. Wirth, who 'focused on environmental issues, particularly global climate change and population stabilization,'[677] during his Washington tenure. Senator Wirth was also the main organizer of the 1988 'historic [James] Hansen hearings on climate change.'[678] From 1998 to 2013, he served as president of the Ted Turner-funded United Nations Foundation. Wirth is on the record as stating in 1993: 'We've got to ride this global warming issue. Even if the theory of global warming is wrong, we will be doing the right thing in terms of economic and environmental policy.'[679] Similar comments were made in 1998 by Christine Stewart, then Canadian Minister of the Environment, who when speaking before editors and reporters of the *Calgary Herald* said: 'No matter if the science of global warming is all phony... climate change [provides] the greatest opportunity to bring about justice and equality in the world.'[680]

Connie Hedegaard, European Commissioner for Climate Action (2010–2014), argued that the European Union policy on climate change was right even if the science was wrong. As she put it:

> Say that 30 years from now, science came back and said, 'wow, we were mistaken then; now we have some new information so we think it is something else'. In a world with nine billion people, even 10 billion at the middle of this century, where literally billions of global citizens will still have to get out of poverty and enter the consuming middle classes, don't you think that anyway it makes a lot of sense to get more energy and resource efficient...
>
> Let's say that science, some decades from now, said 'we were wrong, it was not about climate', would it not in any case have been good to do many of things you have to do in order to combat climate change?
>
> I believe that in a world with still more people, wanting still more growth for good reasons, the demand for energy, raw materials and resources will increase and so, over time, will the prices... I think we have to realise that in the world of the 21st century for us to have the cheapest possible energy is not the answer.[681]

Executive Secretary of the United Nations Framework Convention on Climate Change, Christiana Figueres, once said 'We should make every effort to change the numbers... obviously less [sic] people would exert less pressure on the natural resources,' and humanity is 'already exceeding the planet's planetary carrying capacity, today.'[682] She added that population control was not enough and that fundamental changes need to be made to our current economic system.[683] A dominant figure in popular debates and in the IPCC process, the late climatologist Stephen Schneider was a leading advocate for major reductions of greenhouse gas emissions. Schneider was sometimes derided by his critics for having switched, almost overnight, from being a major proponent of global cooling to becoming one of the most prominent supporters of global warming. What is less well known about him, however, is that he never changed his Ehrlich-inspired belief in the existence of a 'wide consensus that exponential growth, for both economies and human populations, cannot continue indefinitely,'[684] and that 'population growth must *ultimately* be controlled.'[685] As Schneider wrote in a 1977 popular book mainly devoted to the perils of global cooling, the 'obvious point about population growth [that] must be stated and restated' is that 'population increases will only dilute the effectiveness' of achieving 'rapid improvements in per capita living standards for the present 4 billion people on earth.'[686] Twenty years later, having become a major proponent of global warming, he still believed that 'control of population growth has the potential to make a major contribution to raising living standards and to easing environmental problems like greenhouse warming.' Not surprisingly, he urged the United States government to 'resume full participation in international programs to slow population growth' and to 'contribute its share to their financial and other support.'[687]

A decade later, Professor Hans Joachim Schellnhuber, the director of the influential Potsdam Institute for Climate Impact Research and adviser in the writing of the encyclical *Laudato Si*, estimated the carrying capacity of the planet at 'below 1 billion people.'[688] More recently, researchers associated with the Population Reference Bureau and the Worldwatch Institute stated:

> Human population influences and is influenced by climate change and deserves consideration in climate compatible development strategies. Achieving universal access to family planning throughout the world would result in fewer unintended pregnancies, improve the health and well-being of women and their families, and slow population growth – all benefits to climate compatible development.[689]

The spirit of these scientists, activists and bureaucrats was arguably best captured by a now iconic 2009 cartoon published just before the Copenhagen Climate Change Conference, where it quickly became an attendees' favorite (Figure 5.5):

In summary, over the last several decades, numerous like-minded individuals developed a significant institutional infrastructure that, building on earlier efforts, promoted a pessimistic discourse on ecological limits, first centered around overpopulation and later climate policy, and the creation of various top-down solutions, the ultimate aim of which was to restrict economic and population growth. The confluence of the environmental and pessimist discourses, facilitated by influential and widely read articles, reports and books, was thus much more than a groundswell of popular and grassroots sentiments, which, of course, also contributed their share to the growing momentum.

Figure 5.5: Climate summit: What if it's a big hoax?

Originally published in USA Today in December 2009. For a broader history of the origins and impact of this cartoon, see Pett (2012).

From climate change back to population growth

To anyone familiar with the history of the population control movement, the view of people as being essentially nothing more than carbon dioxide emitters is reminiscent of older perspectives in which people were viewed as nothing more than mouths to feed.[690] In this context it is more politically expedient, as climate change activist Bill McKibben observed in 1998, to promote population control than measures designed to lower standards of living, for, as he put it, 'it's easier to change fertility than lifestyle.'[691]

It is interesting to give a few additional, recent illustrations on top of those already listed in the introduction to this book. In their discussion of the key interactions between human population, food production and biodiversity protection, sociologist Eileen Crist, biogeographer Camilo Mora and science journalist Robert Engelman invoked climate change as justifying actions to 'slow and eventually reverse' population growth and the emergence of a 'global middle class' with a fondness for meat, automobiles and other consumer products.[692] In Mora's words, this cannot be avoided if 'one accepts the overwhelming body of evidence linking ongoing climate change to burning fossil fuels and agricultural practices, then one can safely argue that climate change is a by-product of supplying human demands; thus, overpopulation is a key component of projections in carbon emissions.'[693] In a recent viewpoint article signed by over 15,000 scientists, the 'current trajectory of potentially catastrophic climate change due to rising [greenhouse gases] from burning fossil fuels' was deemed especially troubling. Humanity, it was argued, was jeopardizing its future by not 'reining in [its] intense but geographically and demographically uneven material consumption and by not perceiving continued rapid population growth as a primary driver behind many ecological and even societal threats.'[694] As could be expected, a few years ago the Ehrlichs warned us yet again about impending climate Armaggedon as a result of our numbers and lifestyle:

> The likelihood of such a collapse is, of course, the result of the perfect storm of environmental problems that now threaten all nations. Those problems are all related to Earth's severe overpopulation, continuing population growth, and associated vast overconsumption, especially by the rich. Climate disruption alone, closely tied to human population size, could end the society we know. If the planet warms by, say, five degrees Celsius (as seems ever more possible), the impacts on the global food supply would be catastrophic. Additional threats from global toxification, loss of biodiversity, a decaying epidemiological environment, severe resource depletion, and the prospect of increasing resource or geoengineering wars (possibly going nuclear) are all very real and escalating, as are the classic signs of impending civilizational collapse (e.g. diminishing returns to complexity).[695]

In short, while much has been written of late – and many calculations made – on the link between population growth and dangerous climate change, most of these read like new iterations of long-debunked rhetoric and arguments. If one nonetheless feels compelled to single out a few key points that were given less emphasis in the past, the following issues are probably the most significant:[696]

In terms of carbon dioxide emissions, nothing is worse than having a child

> In a world where people are viewed as carbon dioxide emitters rather than creative contributors to the human experience, the greenest thing to do is to reduce population growth and overall number, ideally by not having children.

Many studies have shown that, in line with pessimist assumptions, population control is the most effective way to reduced greenhouse gas emissions.[697] For instance, some researchers have calculated that having one less child (an average for developed countries of 58.6 tonnes CO_2-equivalent (tCO_2e) emission reductions per year), living car-free (2.4 tCO_2e saved per year), avoiding airplane travel (1.6 tCO_2e saved per roundtrip transatlantic flight) and eating a plant-based diet (0.8 tCO_2e saved per year) are much more effective than comprehensive recycling (four times less effective than a plant-based diet) or changing household lightbulbs (eight times less).[698]

Population growth versus consumption

> Per capita consumption is now increasing much more rapidly than in the past. As a result, despite a slowdown in the rates of population increases, the world is witnessing rapidly growing carbon dioxide emissions.

Carbon dioxide emissions are obviously related to levels of economic development. There are marked differences between countries in this metric and it is therefore too simplistic to link greenhouse gas emissions to population growth rates. As population analyst David Satterthwaite observed: 'it is not the growth in (urban or rural) populations that drives the growth in greenhouse gas (GHG) emissions but rather, the growth in consumers and in their levels of consumption.'[699] Interestingly, while advanced economies have per-capita carbon dioxide emissions that are 4–50 times those of least- and less-developed countries, carbon dioxide emissions are now growing up to 10 times faster in less developed countries.[700] The discrepancy between more and less developed countries nonetheless remains significant, as can be seen in Figure 5.6.

As in the past, many calls have been made to the world's wealthiest people to scale back or adopt 'radical transformation of damaging material consumption and emissions' in the 'most developed and the emerging economies.'[701]

As pessimist analysts point out, however, this 'artificial distinction is unhelpful as it can lead to argument over whether policy should focus on reducing population growth or on improving the sustainability of consumption, while both are clearly important.'[702]

Regrets expressed at the abandonment of China's one-child policy

> For all its flaws, China's one-child policy exemplified the type of bold action required to fight dangerous climate change.

At the 2009 Copenhagen summit, Chinese officials publicly argued that their three decade-old 'one-child' family policy should have been given more recognition in the context of climate change negotiations. According to their calculations, the policy resulted in 400 million fewer people than would otherwise have been born, a significant effort in terms of climate mitigation (a reduction of approximately 1.83 billion tons of CO_2 emissions in China per annum at the

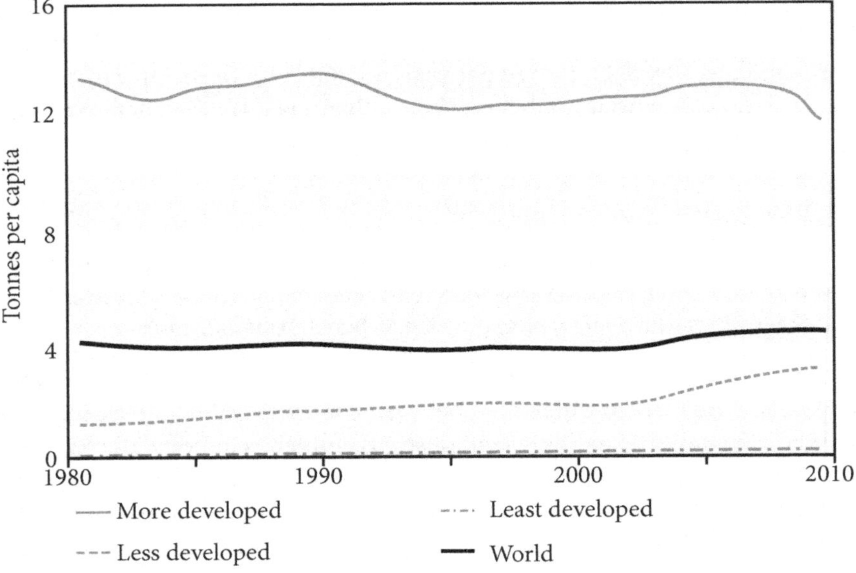

Figure 5.6: Per capita carbon dioxide emissions in least-, less- and more-developed countries.

Source: Royal Society (2012, p. 55).

time).[703] Whether or not these numbers are plausible,[704] many population control activists and academics have lamented its phasing out at the end of 2015 and the beginning of 2016.[705]

5.5 The case for carbon fuels and economic development

In public letters written to prominent politicians, climatologist James Hansen argued in no uncertain terms that 'coal is the single greatest threat to civilisation and all life on our planet,' that the 'trains carrying coal to power plants are death trains' and that coal-fired power plants 'are factories of death.'[706] More recently, Canadian author and columnist Murray Dobbin wrote about 'the slow motion apocalypse of global climate change' and 'the ever-increasing production and use of fossil fuels [that] will, over time, kill billions of us and irreversibly change all life on the planet.'[707] Yet one cannot help but wonder if Hansen and Dobbin have ever considered that there would not be much of a modern civilization and billions of us to save, to say nothing of current levels of flora and fauna in many parts of the world, without the historical development and large-scale use of carbon fuels, nor that poverty – especially the absence of affordable, reliable and scalable coal-powered electricity production – is a much more significant public health threat than the alleged consequences of global warming.[708]

Indeed, it seems fair to say that the predicted catastrophic impacts of climate change remain largely theoretical and uncertain, often ignore the benefits that come with increased atmospheric concentrations of carbon dioxide (both in terms of wealth creation and on flora), typically depend on people failing to adapt to obvious problems, or have simply not materialized in the timeline predicted by their proponents. It is also certain that humanity going off or preventing the development of carbon fuels in the absence of less problematic alternatives guarantees several negative outcomes, such as a large death toll in poor economies, a growing number of economically vulnerable individuals being pushed into energy poverty in advanced economies, and significantly higher extractive pressures on all of our planet's ecosystems.[709]

As the physicist Robert Zubrin eloquently put it:

> Since 1950, humanity has utilized a great deal of carbon. Simultaneously, three major changes have occurred worldwide:
>
> 1. The standard of living, as measured by average global gross domestic product per capita, has increased by 400%;
> 2. The rate of plant growth on Earth has increased by 15%;
> 3. The average global temperature has increased by 0.2%.[710]

Zubrin labels 'carbon-benefit deniers' people who ignore tangible positive outcomes and focus instead on hypothetical worst-case scenarios. After all, as psychologist Steven Pinker put it, industrialization has been good to humanity as it 'has fed billions, doubled lifespans, slashed extreme poverty, and, by replacing muscle with machinery, made it easier to end slavery, emancipate women, and educate children. It has allowed people to read at night, live where they want, stay warm in winter, see the world, and multiply human contact. Any costs in pollution and habitat loss have to be weighed against these gifts.'[711] Independent scientist and father of the 'Gaia hypothesis' James Lovelock, who once worried about anthropogenic climate change, now similarly believes that while carbon dioxide is going up, albeit not as fast as once predicted, the 'computer models just weren't reliable. In fact I'm not sure the whole thing isn't crazy, this climate change. You've only got to look at Singapore. It's two-and-a-half times higher than the worst-case scenario for climate change, and it's one of the most desirable cities in the world to live in.'[712]

In other words, while environmental activists invoke the vulnerability of poor individuals to climate-change-caused hunger, disease and poverty, they remain oblivious to the facts that affordable and reliable energy, which can only be provided on the necessary scale by carbon fuels, is essential for economic development and that wealthier people can adapt to local conditions and trends. To echo Lovelock's arguments, wealthy people can live well in climates as different as those found in the cities of Edmonton and Singapore and humanity's best insurance policy against unavoidable bad weather events – to say nothing of other unavoidable natural challenges such as earthquakes, diseases and agricultural pests – is the better infrastructure, advanced warning systems and long-distance transportation that accompany economic development. Indeed, if our planet saw an end to the current 'climate pause' and a resumption of warming, the problems it would create would simply be exacerbations of challenges that have always plagued humanity. We should also keep in mind that, despite some global warming over the twentieth century, 'aggregate mortality attributed to all extreme weather events globally has declined by more than 90% since the 1920s, in spite of a four-fold rise in population and much more complete reporting of such events.'[713] In philosopher Alex Epstein's words: 'We do not take a safe climate and make it dangerous; we take a dangerous climate and make it safe'[714] through carbon-fuel-powered economic development.

Other considerations that warrant a questioning (and in our opinion disregarding) of the calls for population reduction and a move away from carbon fuels in the absence of superior substitutes include the following:

Farmers are adaptable Over the last two centuries, commercial agricultural producers have had to switch to new crops and livestock or go out of business, for reasons such as the emergence of lower-cost competitors in other locations or a drop in demand for their output.[715]

Predictions of calamity have already failed The 350 parts per million (ppm) threshold for the 'safe' level of carbon dioxide ultimately rests on the work of one scientist and his collaborators.[716] This threshold was passed more than 25 years ago and is now exceeded by a significant margin, yet no climate calamity has ensued.[717] The notion of a threshold or a tipping point in the context of climate change is also questionable, at least inasmuch as the Earth has been both much warmer and much colder in the past than is presently the case, yet neither extreme proved irreversible.

The cure is worse than the ailment The only proven ways to reduce substantially carbon dioxide emissions are either economic collapse (as occurred in Eastern Europe after the fall of the Berlin Wall) or the large-scale substitution of coal by nuclear, hydroelectric and (fracked) natural gas technologies. Activists who oppose these substitutions and recommend instead unreliable technological or bureaucratic alternatives with no actual proven track record of reducing carbon dioxide emissions do not take their own climate alarmist rhetoric seriously.

The precautionary principle is flawed The population control activists' take on the precautionary principle is that, in the absence of certainty that global warming is not happening or that greenhouse gas emissions do not exacerbate it substantially, humanity should stop emitting greenhouse gases through the burning of carbon fuels. Yet, stopping carbon fuel-based economic development will arguably cause far more harm than any predicted climate change scenarios ever will. As Julian Simon observed over two decades ago, while it might superficially make sense 'to control population growth if the issue were simply the increased risk of catastrophe due to population growth, and if only the number of deaths mattered, rather than the number of healthy lives lived. A flaw in this line of reasoning is revealed, however, by pushing it to its absurd endpoint: One may reduce the risk of pollution catastrophe to zero by reducing to zero the number of persons who are alive. And this policy obviously is unacceptable to all except a few. Therefore we must dig deeper to learn how pollution ought to influence our views about population size and growth.'[718]

Historically, technology has made things better A more useful guiding principle should be based on the historically true claim that, in the context of a market economy, technological advances create fewer and smaller problems than those that existed before. Had our ancestors adopted a strong version of the precautionary principle, humans would still be dwelling in caves without (dangerous and likely to cause much damage) fire and living a more solitary, poorer, nastier, more brutish and shorter existence. Had resistance to change and unwillingness to bear some risks been more significant in the last two centuries, real income, life expectancy and food consumption would be much lower than they currently are, while infant mortality, food prices and hours worked, among other things, would be much higher.

In the end, as energy journalist Robert Bryce put it, humans have had to cope with the climate for millennia and 'every sensible 'no-regrets' climate policy recognizes the need to prepare for future storms and droughts,' fears of carbon dioxide emissions-induced climate change or not. 'The hard reality,' Bryce argues, 'is that we must make our cities and systems more resilient' and that what truly matters is 'our preparedness with early-warning systems, flood-control measures, and evacuation plans.'[719]

6 Blind, blinkered, or bought: why do pessimists resist reality?

Regardless of the predictive power, or alignment with evidence, of the arguments from the optimist side, most pessimist thinkers have stuck to their original forecasts. Paul Ehrlich's numerous failed predictions were recently described as not wrong, merely not intended for public consumption due to their scientific complexity: '[t]imetables for disaster like those he once offered have no significance... because to someone in his field they mean something 'very, very different' from what they do to the average person.'[720] And yet, it seems disingenuous to insist that Ehrlich did not mean massive starvation on a global scale by 2100,[721] a clear and understandable 'timetable for disaster,' as the answer to his own question 'Is it likely humanity will satisfactorily feed 11 billion people around the end of this century?'[722] Even though some recent analyses of the world's remaining food problems have characterized them as declining, and predominantly on the distribution end,[723] Ehrlich and long-time collaborator John Harte stated in an opinion piece published in April 2018:[724]

> What would make us more optimistic that massive starvation can be avoided? First and foremost would be bringing the issues of climate change and the many dimensions of the food security situation... to the top of the policy agenda everywhere... Above all, a most hopeful sign would be more nations providing more access to modern contraception and backup abortion and truly equal rights for women. Those steps could move the world toward population *reduction*, the sine qua non of sustainability, and without which none of the other environmental goals are likely to be reached. [italics in the original]

To Ehrlich and other individuals sharing his outlook, a growing, fed, wealthier and healthier population coexisting with resource abundance and environmental remediation may be an oxymoron characterizing the confused thinking of those who must, indeed, be firmly led by the able few. Perhaps, as science journalist Ronald Bailey has suggested, pessimist activists and thinkers see themselves as priestly prophets: 'Soothsayers once sought the portents of doom in the livers of sheep, in the flight of geese across the sky, and in the patterns of juggled bones. Modern seers examine the entrails of equations, measure molecules in the air, or conjure with computer models looking for signs of the impending apocalypse.'[725]

As compelling as such explanations are, we find that most solutions tend to be messy and complex. Thus, in the spirit of embracing messiness and complexity, we will present a number of hypotheses generated by psychologists, political scientists, and other researchers that each explain a subset of behaviours and tendencies behind entrenched intellectual positions such as environmental pessimism. As we stated at the outset of this book, our aim is to add to a balanced discussion, not to a rigidly balanced book, so the goal of this chapter is to arrive at an evidence-based model of entrenched pessimism given that, as we showed in earlier chapters, data appear to favour a long-term optimist outlook.

6.1 The iron triangle

The penchant for undemocratic solutions that subordinate the agency of individuals to policy outcomes such as population control has long been an avowed goal of many pessimist theorists and activists.[726] We choose to believe that this is a function of their deeply held beliefs and sincere concerns. However, more cynical, if not downright uncharitable interpretations of such political action may be found in, among others, the writings of the controversial essayist H.L. Mencken:

> Civilization, in fact, grows more maudlin and hysterical; especially under democracy it tends to degenerate into a mere combat of crazes; the whole aim of practical politics is to keep the populace alarmed (and hence clamorous to be led to safety) by an endless series of hobgoblins, most of them imaginary.[727]

If the cynics were correct, an important driver for much doomsday rhetoric would thus be the self-preservation alarmism of various institutions: 'There are more than 450 national [US] organizations, and countless ones at the local levels, promoting environmentalism... they all share an institutional imperative to find and publicize an endless series of crises and disasters, since without calamities to combat, they have no reason to exist.'[728]

While we will encounter reasons to tread softly, if always with an open mind, through the terrain of published science research[729] in the next section, the consequences of the competitive drive of scientists vying for limited funding also caution us against an uncritical reception of all published research:

> Another disturbing and disheartening aspect of the rise of radical environmentalism is the growing pressure on scientists to manipulate research findings in order to attract funding. 'It is well known that Congress has short attention span – so short that it often appears capable of dealing only with crises. Because everyone else is crying 'crisis,' responsible scientists are forced to join the chorus or risk losing their research programs,' avers Harvard University researcher Peter Rogers. He adds that the phony crisis atmosphere engendered by this dismal process causes environmentalists, politicians, and citizen's groups to demand immediate action, which is not what most scientists had in mind at all.[730]

Thus, it appears that the competitive edge in modern high-stakes science does not necessarily come from presenting empirical results that address non-trivial hypotheses, but from successfully framing such hypotheses in terms of a politically active 'crisis.' If experimental science cannot be carried out without funding, and if funding is driven by crises, moreover, if crises are for the most part political, it follows that science will become politicized under these conditions, tracking the narratives with the most political impact. Unfortunately, according to some critics, 'the sciences surrounding environmental issues have been politicized from top to bottom.'[731]

One more element tends to add itself to this cynical, negative and crisis-driven model for the prevalence of pessimism: 'if it bleeds, it leads.' When, over two decades ago, science journalist Ronald Bailey presented the proposal for an optimistic outlook on environmental issues to his editor at St. Martin's Press, Thomas Dunne, he was told: 'Ron, we'll publish your book and we'll both make some money. But I want to tell you that if you'd brought me a book predicting the end of the world, I could have made you a rich man.' Human beings do have a psychological bias toward believing bad news and discounting good news.[732] Harvard University psychology professor Steven Pinker pointed out the same negativity bias in his massive work *Enlightenment Now*.[733]

Perhaps as a survival strategy that rewards the speed and effectiveness of engaging in 'fight or flight' behaviours, people tend to focus on threats, but are not conditioned to spend valuable energy examining the reasons for, or the consequences of, such a selective focus. 'Our modern skulls house a stone age mind,'[734] wrote the University of California, Santa Barbara, psychology professor Leda Cosmides and her anthropologist colleague John Tooby. In their text on evolutionary psychology, they assured their students that a stone-age mind is an exceedingly complex and refined instrument, but 'its circuits were not designed to solve the day-to-day problems of a modern American – they were designed to solve the day-to-day problems of our hunter-gatherer ancestors. These stone age priorities produced a brain far better at solving some problems than others.'[735] On the evolutionary scale, even the last 10,000 years of agriculture have barely registered, let alone affected human mental circuitry.[736] When faced with the evolutionarily unprecedented problems of modern life, such as rapid-fire, conflicting, and complex information, we react like the threatened stone-age hunter-gatherers our brains evolved to serve.

The innate negative bias in human perception may thus become reinforced by the crisis mentality in politics and in the media, and the appearance of one even in the research community. This unholy trinity has been characterized by Ronald Bailey as: 'an iron triangle of scientists pleading for research funds, interest groups who need crises to justify their existence, and a press that needs to sell papers. It's no wonder people are frightened.'[737] In science, as in the media or in politics, there are people with sincere beliefs and the best of intentions, in addition to the need for a paycheque. Thus, we are interested in finding reasons for entrenched pessimism beyond the feedback loop of the iron triangle's financially driven fear mongering. What other biases or behaviours may help explain the unwillingness, or perhaps the inability, of avowed pessimists to consider optimist views as even worthy of discussion, let alone potentially correct?

Psychologists, political scientists, economists and writers[738] have considered this question because the dynamics of socially-based decision-making – decision-making influenced by societal norms and issues as well as directly reflected back onto politics and policy – are important in societies with democratically-run institutions. We will start with psychological mechanisms that affect cognitive biases of individuals and groups. We will follow with how these biases may spread to the wider society. After laying the groundwork, we will consider mechanisms that rely on disciplinary assumptions, moving on to mechanisms that affect disciplinary experts and other intellectual elites. Finally, we will integrate some of these psychologically verified behaviours and professional tendencies into complex 'syndromes.' These syndromes combine motivations, goals and actions into ethically grounded systems, identified by Jane Jacobs as work-centered 'systems of survival.'[739] The goal of this section is to show how particular issues or viewpoints become cornerstones of systems of belief, which, in turn, are woven into the fabric of work and life. Far beyond being simply intellectual positions regarding social or economic issues, the pessimist and the optimist positions become the foundations for individual and group narratives.

6.2 The psychology of intellectual entrenchment

The Cornell University developmental psychologists Stephen Ceci and Wendy Williams have developed a synthesis of 'concepts from psychological science that help explain the entrenched arguments'[740] characteristic of emotion-laden clashes of ideas and ideals, showing that participants learn arguments and arrive at judgements in specific ways. Ceci and Williams noted that 'participants prefer to learn information from in-group sources and agree more with in-group members on moral and political issues, and this preference can be found even among preschoolers.'[741] This insight appears to be compatible with the developmental basis for the iron triangle negative bias: a stone-age brain would certainly prioritize information from the immediate hunter-gatherer in-group, particularly in new situations where uncertainty and danger were almost guaranteed.

Ceci and Williams added significant depth to the discussion of group cognitive biases by collating other previously published cognitive bias effects that take over when individuals retreat into entrenched arguments.[742] The best known of these is the Dunning-Kruger effect,[743] which, in this context, translates into a lack of awareness, or the underestimation, of the individuals' ignorance of issues or facts that are objectively part of the debate. In addition to underestimating their ignorance, group members 'overestimate their understanding of controversial issues, known as the *illusion of understanding bias.*'[744] According to the authors of the 2013 study on that subject, 'evidence suggests that people's mistaken sense that they understand the causal processes underlying policies contributes to political polarization.'[745] The more the participants of the study were asked to offer in-depth physical or factual explanations of the underlying causes of the policies they were embracing, the more their attitudes adjusted to a middle or conciliatory stance, away from their previous extremes.[746] The more they dwelt on their own preferences or other subjective aspects of the issue, the more polarized their positions became.

There are other cognitive effects that shape perception. One of them is the effect of prior beliefs on the evaluation of new information, which may result in both confirmation bias and motivated reasoning, also known as motivated scepticism.[747] Confirmation bias occurs when one selectively focuses on evidence supporting one's prior beliefs while disregarding opposing evidence.[748] Motivated scepticism is the behaviour one may adopt when presented with evidence contradicting prior beliefs: A motivated sceptic will carry out repeated attempts to 'fit' or 'rework' the non-conforming data into the framework before beginning to think of questioning the framework.[749]

In 2006, Stony Brook University political scientists Charles Taber and Milton Lodge[750] set out to study the existence of confirmation bias and motivated scepticism among ordinary citizens. Taber and Lodge's model predicted that prior beliefs would 'anchor' new information appraisal and integration at some known departure point in the cognitive space, then lead the participants of the study to assess the evidence based on its relevance, authority and overall credibility, and either upgrade or downgrade the information 'independent of one's prior judgment.'[751] However, what the social scientists found overturned this model in favour of selective information processing infused with confirmation bias. Instead of assessing each new piece of evidence on its merits, 'citizens are prone to overly accommodate supportive evidence while dismissing out-of-hand evidence that challenges their prior attitudes… [W]e find that rather than moderating or simply maintaining their original attitudes, citizens – especially those who feel the strongest about the issue and are the most sophisticated – strengthen their attitudes in ways not warranted by the evidence.'[752] The degree and prevalence of such selective information acquisition led Taber and Lodge to expect attitude polarization 'whereby attitudes will become more extreme, even when people have been exposed to a balanced set of pro and con arguments.'[753] Indeed, they found exactly that those participants who had the most sophisticated prior knowledge and arguments polarized significantly by the end of the experiment. 'By contrast, unsophisticates and those with weak priors did not polarize[.]'[754] Thus, a motivated reasoning effect in processing new data led to a strong attitude polarization, particularly among those who claimed both expertise and engagement with the issue, a discouraging result if one wishes to engage in an evidence-informed debate.

It is important to note that researchers such as Taber and Lodge insist that people do not approach these studies with a closed mind and a desire to stick to their prior beliefs at all costs. Study participants do not lie to the experimenters and themselves about their desire to give all ideas a chance. 'Rather, they try hard to be fair-minded or at least preserve the 'illusion of objectivity'…but they are frequently unable to do so.'[755] It takes a concerted effort of consistent, evidence-based persuasion for crystallized attitudes to start crumbling, and the shift towards change is not guaranteed. The onset of motivated or asymmetrical scepticism 'deposits in mind all the evidence needed to justify and bolster our priors with a clear conscience.'[756] As Taber and Lodge concluded:

> Our studies show that people are often unable to escape the pull of their prior attitudes and beliefs, which guide the processing of new information in predictable and sometimes insidious ways… In the extreme, if one distorts new information so that it always supports one's priors, one cannot be rationally responsive to the environment; similarly, manipulating the information stream to avoid any threat to one's priors is no more rational than the proverbial ostrich. For many citizens, perhaps, the bias may be less extreme, but there are certainly ideologues and bigots who fit both of these descriptions. Luker (1984), for example, found that attitudes among abortion activists are so linked to their beliefs and feelings about sexuality, gender, religion, and family, that they have become completely incapable of entertaining points of view that challenge their own.'[757]

The troubling legacy of these models of selective information processing is their strong stamp on the sophisticated and expert participants. As we saw with Taber and Lodge's work, the stronger the prior intellectual engagement with the issue, the stronger the attitude polarization after exposure to new information. We will come back to these results when we discuss how experts carry out scientific work and how they exert influence on others.

In addition to highlighting the selective perception biases we have just studied, Ceci and Williams also brought up a cognitive attitude called 'naïve realism.'[758] Psychologists Lee Ross and Andrew Ward[759] have proposed a model of naïve realism resting on three assumptions about the mental states of individuals:

- What individuals see is the world 'as it is,' unbiased, unmediated and objective.
- Given the same information, physical settings, and a rational attitude, others will necessarily come to the same conclusions, views and behaviours about and towards the world as the original individuals.
- If others do not come to the same conclusions despite sharing the same starting points and reasoning processes, it is those others that lack knowledge, objectivity, rationality, or exhibit bias.[760]

Ross and Ward's construction of naïve realism goes back to the roots of subjectivist psychology in the 1940s and 1950s when pioneers such as Jean Piaget and Gustav Ichheiser built the field on the foundation of Gestalt and other theories.[761] Naïve realism rests on two key assertions: 'that differences in subjective interpretation or construal *matter*, that they have a profound impact in the conduct of everyday social affairs. The second assertion is that social perceivers characteristically make insufficient allowance for such impact in the inferences and predictions they make about others.'[762] Thus, the construction of arguments about an issue, let alone any facts about that issue, is key in directing the formation of individual interpretations of the issue. According to the tenets of naïve realism, however, every individual interpreting this constructed information will assume that he or she is completely unbiased and fully rational in his or her perception of the issue, and creates an inner construct of that issue in a completely fact-based way. Moreover, a naïve relativist will expect others to arrive at the same inner construct and conclusions as his or her own, and will judge those who did not do so as ignorant and biased.

Ross and Ward extended their findings from the naïve realist bias to the false consensus effect. This effect is observed when 'people who make a given choice...see that choice as more common and more "normative" (i.e. less revealing of personal attributes or idiosyncrasies) than do people who make the opposite choice.'[763] Thus, under the false consensus effect, people who choose as we do are immediately judged to be more 'normal,' 'rational,' and unbiased than those who do not. In the words of Ross and Ward: 'even adults persist in feeling that their own perceptions and interpretations are essentially free of distortion, and that other people in general and their adversaries in particular see the world through the distorting lenses of ideology and self-interest.'[764] These findings have by now been corroborated by two decades of research. Taken together, they indicate that even those adults who are open-minded find it difficult to learn new facts without succumbing to either confirmation bias or motivated reasoning. In addition, many rational adults persist in operating from a naïve realist standpoint, often acting according to the false consensus effect to disparage others who do not conform to the consensus viewpoint. In other words, it is difficult to overcome psychological biases when attempting to learn new information.

What we have so far, thanks to decades of experimental work by psychologists and political scientists, is a picture of how individuals acquire and process information, and how they construct a mental model of others as information agents. What about the mechanisms for social transmission of ideas? Journalist Christopher Booker[765] has investigated two such mechanisms. What is key about social transmission of ideas is their contingency on an aspect of construal we have not studied: the construction of authority.

Modern scholarship on perception bias dates back to the 1950s.[766] Yale research psychologist Irving L. Janis[767] made a significant contribution to the field in the 1970s by describing the phenomenon of groupthink. Christopher Booker studied Janis's work and found that there were three rules 'implicit in his analysis throughout the book, and form the core of his theory as to how groupthink operates:'[768]

- Members of a group develop a belief that is not testable empirically.
- Because the shared belief cannot be fully tested, group members 'feel the need to reinforce its authority by elevating it into a "consensus".'[769]
- The views of those who do not agree with the consensus challenge the authority of the belief and become unacceptable; they are excluded from further discussion since '[d]issent cannot be tolerated.'[770]

Thus groupthink allows people to insulate themselves from the diversity of views, opinions, and, ultimately, facts concerning a shared belief. Group members use consensus in place of dogma to control the membership of the in-group and the degree of variance from the orthodoxy permitted to them.[771]

In essence, groupthink seems to encourage both the Dunning-Kruger effect and the illusion of understanding bias by restricting access to external triangulating facts and viewpoints: in-group members cut off from outside input do not increase their expertise and tend to both underestimate their ignorance and overestimate their knowledge of the various elements of their belief. Moreover, consensus seems to work like the central tenet of a naïve realist's universe; failure to accept the consensus as a self-evident corollary of the reality of the in-group world automatically excludes the non-conformists as 'heretics.' Any ideas that do get through to the in-group are processed via confirmation bias and motivated reasoning, hence they rarely have a chance to change the consensus. At the groupthink level, rules of construal still hold, and, as Ross and Ward observed, 'the manipulation of labels and language can be used effectively to disengage normal mechanisms of moral evaluation, that is, to promote and justify individual or collective actions that might otherwise be constrained by moral or ethical standards'[772] Groupthink thus certainly appears to be the necessary ingredient to the success of any cult.

Booker noted that the successful popular uptake of a new idea also depends on 'how much authority could be attributed to those putting it forward.'[773] His source for this observation was the French medical doctor turned writer and explorer Gustave Le Bon, whose 1895 work *The Crowd: A Study of the Popular Mind* is still seen as a classic of social psychology.[774] Booker wrote that Le Bon's 'shrewdest observation was the crucial part played in changing the opinions of huge numbers of people by 'prestige:' the particular deference paid to those who are taking the lead in putting them forward.'[775] Prestige plays well with the cognitive biases we have studied: accepting an idea based on prestige of the proponent, particularly if the idea already fits in, or confirms, prior knowledge, aligns not only with confirmation bias but also with the false consensus bias. Combined with the coercive pressure of groupthink, if it is brought to bear in its favour, an idea with an authoritative pedigree is a strong contender for a deeply held group belief. Arguing against such an idea involves mustering evidence not only against the factual manifestations of the idea, but also against the construed prestige of the proponents. We will see how such appeals to authority work when we examine the influence of experts, and the unwillingness of popular opinion, or groupthink, to discredit those proven wrong by the facts but still in possession of an authoritative narrative.

6.3 The blinders of disciplinary knowledge

The scientific method versus rampant bias

The scientific method, at least as framed by the philosopher of science Karl Popper, appears to limit confirmation bias by specifying that scientists first seek to falsify or disprove their hypotheses, and only then attempt to corroborate (but never verify) them through a different set of experiments.[776] However, few real scientists seem to follow this Popperian prescription.[777] University of Virginia psychologist Brian Nosek, who has studied bias in scientific research for years, pointed out a common violation of the falsification method: 'One basic fact that is always getting forgotten is that you can't generate hypotheses *and* test them with the same data... At present we mix up exploratory and confirmatory research.'[778] Such practices open the door to a variety of biases[779] that have been documented in many fields of academia, ranging from physics to political science, where they have been shaping research landscapes for decades.[780]

John P.A. Ioannidis, an epidemiologist who has made some of the more ground-breaking contributions to studying biased science, defined bias as 'the combination of various design, data, analysis, and presentation factors that tend to produce research findings when they should not be produced.'[781] Nosek, who, on top of his psychology research work has co-founded and directs the Open Science Framework,[782] which facilitates transparent design and full data use throughout the research process, pointed out that, in fact, the most pervasive and most problematic bias in science is one we have met before: motivated reasoning.[783] With motivated reasoning 'we have already made the decision about what to do or to think, and our 'explanation' of our reasoning is really a justification for doing what we wanted to do – or to believe – anyway.'[784] With motivated reasoning '[w]e interpret observations to fit a particular idea,'[785] not a big departure from our typical reasoning since 'most of our reasoning is in fact rationalization.'[786]

These frank admissions of serious limitations in scientific thinking should worry us as we investigate the effects of scientific practice on the entrenched position of pessimism. These reasoning biases, in fact, sound like steps towards entrenchment. They also invite some caution towards accepting any single result – even in peer-reviewed science – unquestioningly, steering us rather to seek the outcomes of a prolonged debate giving the floor to multiple perspectives.[787] With time and sufficient effort '[s]cience as a communal activity is self-correcting.'[788] But that correction may often be too little, too late: not arriving 'quickly or smoothly as we might like to believe.'[789]

In addition to design, analysis and presentation biases, there is also rampant publication bias.[790] NYU professor and *Retraction Watch* editor Ivan Oransky,[791] interviewed by science writer Philip Ball along with Brian Nosek, described positive result publication bias as a greater threat to science's integrity than even motivated reasoning or confirmation bias:

> '... while all of the incentives in science reinforce confirmation biases, the

> exigencies of publication are among the most problematic.'
>
> 'To get tenure, grants, and recognition, scientists need to publish frequently in major journals...'
>
> 'That encourages positive and "breakthrough" findings, since the latter are what earn citations and impact factor.'[792]

Sadly, the work of Oransky, Ioannidis and Nosek seems to corroborate rather than refute Bailey's iron triangle, the primal feedback loop of career, monetary and political drivers tethered to the lowest common denominator of stone-age brain's fight or flight heuristic. 'Not only can poor data and wrong ideas survive, but good ideas can be suppressed through motivated reasoning and career pressures.'[793]

As dispiriting as the situation appears to be, one may perhaps hope that it is still not universal. This may, unfortunately, not be the case: Ioannidis' work suggested that the validity of results from most empirical studies is at best questionable: 'Most research findings are false for most research designs and for most fields.'[794] Ioannidis' analysis was published in 2005 and has been much discussed since in both the peer-reviewed literature, with critiques of overly restrictive statistical modeling and exaggerated claims,[795] and in the more popular media.[796] Ioannidis listed six corollaries 'about the probability that a research finding is indeed true.'[797] The first four are paraphrased and compiled in a footnote.[798] The last two are paraphrased below:[799]

- The greater the financial and other interests and prejudices in a scientific field, the less likely the research findings are to be true.
- The 'hotter' a scientific field (with many competing scientific teams involved, and a quick accumulation of papers), the less likely the research findings are to be true.

When examining these corollaries, Ioannidis elaborated on each one, but he wrote the most incisive lines about the proliferation of bias because of researcher prestige or career interests:

> Scientists in a given field may be prejudiced purely because of their belief in a scientific theory or commitment to their own findings... Prestigious investigators may suppress via the peer review process the appearance and dissemination of findings that refute their findings, thus condemning their field to perpetuate false dogma. Empirical evidence on expert opinion shows that it is extremely unreliable.[800]

Of course, science's self-correcting mechanisms of verification, refutation, and discussion did engage with Ioannidis' work, and researchers such as Steven Goodman and Sander Greenland were able to affirm many, but dispute some, of his claims.[801] Important for us, Goodman and Greenland strove to show why Ioannidis' claim was too dramatic, with our italics for emphasis: 'So the model employed [by Ioannidis] *cannot be considered a proof that most published claims are untrue*, but is rather a claim that no study or combination of studies can ever provide convincing evidence.'[802] In this form, the insight is still powerful in its implications: appealing to peer-reviewed empirical research will provide evidence for a claim, just not enough to call it 'settled' or beyond any further discussion.

Goodman and Greenland had further points to add to Ioannidis' work regarding his sixth corollary. They wrote, with our italics, again:

> [T]he paper claims to have proven something it describes as paradoxical; that the 'hotter' an area is (i.e., the more studies published), the more likely studies in that area are to make false claims. We have shown this claim to be erroneous[[803]]. The mathematical proof offered for this in [Ioannidis' 2005 paper] shows merely that *the more studies published on any subject, the higher the absolute number of false positive* (and false negative) studies. It does not show what the papers' graphs and text claim, viz, that the number of false claims will be a higher proportion of the total number of studies published (i.e., that the positive predictive value of each study decreases with increasing number of studies).[804]

In other words, Goodman and Greenland ensured we understood research in the 'hot' field was not disproportionately accruing false results, merely accruing a high number of poorly done studies *faster* due to the greater rate of activity in the field. Thus Goodman and Greenland's critique made Ioannidis' work easier to understand and interpret, the way virtually any form of human intellectual output[805] will benefit from thoughtful engagement and feedback.

What we have presented regarding the pervasive biases in scientific research, and the efforts to combat them, appears to address the state of the larger debate, not just the experimental research, on both climate change and population growth. Both fields are undoubtedly 'hot' and rife with financial and political interests as well as with the deep-seated prejudices we have spent several chapters describing. Given Ioannidis' analysis and its elucidation by Goodman and Greenland, it is unlikely that much of what is widely hailed as settled science regarding the catastrophe of population growth and its ongoing negative effects on climate change describes real, or fully convincing effects. Indeed, it may simply be, in Ioannidis' words, an 'accurate measure[s] of the prevailing bias.'[806] And yet, because of the confirmation bias consensus model whose effects inform Ioannidis' fifth corollary,[807] there is very little 'negative' or non-conforming research published on both climate and population growth. This missing research, which rarely gets to the peer review stage, let alone to publication, makes it more difficult to discuss and understand these issues in light of all possible evidence. Instead, we only hear one side and one message, very loudly. As Ioannidis concluded: 'Too large and too highly significant effects may actually be more likely to be signs of large bias in most fields of modern research.'[808]

What does this mean with respect to the views of avowed pessimists? From our previous section we have learned that naïve realism combined with selective perception biases and the in-group preferences driving the conformity of groupthink all but guarantee that those who had strong prior opinions will most likely become more entrenched and less likely to want to examine new evidence. We also know that evidence from experimental science will be prone to biases and manipulation, particularly in politically contested fields. Pessimists will thus carry on doing science and using the 'consensus' model without engaging in an open debate. Several mechanisms we have studied will maintain the pessimists' in-groups hermetically sealed from any outside influences. In some cases, as in that of Paul Ehrlich and his associates, the highly regarded patrician pessimist experts will continue wielding global influence while spreading dogma instead of disseminating science. In the next section we will learn about the disciplinary variables that most likely contributed to the shaping of many pessimists' strong prior beliefs.

Disciplines shape minds

Why are disciplinary affiliations important? Sociologists of science have been studying them since the 1940s, focusing in particular on disciplinary differences.[809] The normative or Mertonian regime of sociological inquiry,[810] in which both the disciplines and the scientists populating them were studied in isolation from their social substrates, was thoroughly replaced, starting in the mid-1960s, by the constructivist model, which followed the publication of, and the subsequent paradigm-shifting reaction to, Thomas Kuhn's *The Structure of Scientific Revolutions*.[811] Sociologists, historians and philosophers of science have since been focusing on the study of specific disciplinary practices such as laboratory research, emphasizing the nature of the sciences as community-based belief systems.[812]

Since the 1990s, scholars have been looking at disciplines increasingly as epistemic cultures:[813] cognitive and social contexts that shape the ways in which members of a group come to know what they know, ways that are influenced, if not determined, by the history and social interactions of the group through time. For us, the overwhelming importance of this is the insight that disciplinary milieus truly do shape their members' cognitive reflexes and beliefs through a process of acculturation that could be likened to indoctrination.

Ludwik Fleck, the pioneering Polish-Jewish microbiologist who contributed key insights to the sociology of science in the 1930s,[814] captured these disciplinary epistemic processes lucidly. Fleck characterized disciplinary epistemic cultures as closed systems of opinion,[815] socio-cognitive[816] structures that give meaning and consistency to observations and actions, and that reinforce themselves via a feedback process. 'Once a structurally complete and closed system of opinion consisting of many details and relations has been formed, it offers enduring resistance to anything that contradicts it.'[817] In fact, these systems' apparent agency was their essential feature to Fleck, who saw 'tenacity'[818] at work in a closed system of opinion: 'What we are faced with here is not so much simple passivity or mistrust of new ideas as an active approach... A contradiction to the system appears unthinkable... What does not fit into the system remains unseen.'[819] These insights will help us understand disciplinary background effects evident in the creation of pessimist elites' strong prior beliefs.

The epistemic culture of biology

For over two decades, the optimist economist Julian Simon made many attempts to engage intellectually with the pessimist star Paul Ehrlich. Ehrlich, however, always refused to debate Simon face-to-face and regularly disparaged him in both academic and popular outlets.[820] While trying to engage with Ehrlich, Simon was perplexed by the propensity of trained scientists to not only formulate models disconnected from empirical facts, but also to neglect addressing their repeated failures. After years of analyzing the pessimist arguments put forward by Ehrlich and his fellow scientific travelers, Simon finally hypothesized that Ehrlich's shortcomings were corollaries of his scientific training as an entomologist.[821] In fact, Simon identified a strong disciplinary trend among pessimists, including both his contemporaries and some earlier figures we have mentioned in Chapters 2 and 3:

> [T]he most strident prophets of doom about environment, resources, and population have been biologists, with some handmaidens among physicists and chemists. The bestsellers among the book-length warnings of disaster due to population growth have been William Vogt's *Road to Survival* (1948), Fairfield Osborn's *Limits of the Earth* (1953), Karl Sax's *Standing Room Only* (1960), and Paul Ehrlich's *The Population Bomb* (1968), all biologists, and there are literally scores more by biologists that are little known; *The Limits to Growth* is a rare exception in this genre that was produced by MIT engineers.[822]

In his reflection on the biological science origins of many deeply rooted cognitive habits of the pessimists, Simon certainly anticipated the epistemic culture approach to understanding ingrained thought patterns, also showing a strong alignment with Fleck's ideas on the tenacity of closed systems of opinion. According to Simon, Ehrlich and other biologists[823] came to study complex social problems with the wrong set of 'cognitive elements':[824]

> Over the years I have wondered about the modes of thought involved in the thinking of people at large that lead them to consistently-erroneous judgments and prophecies about materials and environment. Others and I have identified a long list of cognitive elements. Causes of the wide dissemination of these judgments without scientific foundation have also been discussed – for example, the penchant of the newspapers for bad news. But the specific characteristics of the thinking of biologists – I speak about the category for convenience, though of course there are important exceptions – have not previously been discussed, to my knowledge.... And in light of the importance of biologists in this movement, the topic calls for special treatment.[825]

Simon identified the following common cognitive problems in the reasoning of biologists who made forays into the social sciences.

Misuse of time-scales and lack of historical awareness: 'The non-historical character of most biological work, except for the study of evolution.'[826] The key problem with assuming humanity to be invariant within millennial (non-evolutionary) time scales is the neglect of the vast cultural, social, intellectual and technological changes always occurring within human civilizations. The adoption of animal husbandry and agriculture, for example, revolutionized the human relationship with the Earth and accelerated the human divergence from the animal population and consumption models. 'Applying the assumption of constancy in society's responses to a food or fuel shortage, or to a change in climate, since (say) 5000 BC until now, leads to grave (sic) mistakes...The causes of starvation no longer include the physical inability of society to transfer food to starving people, or the incapacity of cultivators to plant, harvest, and store enough for their needs.'[827] Another consequence of hard scientists' lack of sophistication when dealing with research on people and societies is their reluctance to work with much longer time scales than in biology. Human trends may need centuries to emerge.[828]

Misunderstanding sample variability: 'The characteristic use of experimentation with individuals rather than survey of the aggregate universe, epidemiologists constituting an exception.'[829]

Misunderstanding what is a representative population: 'Working with individuals as representative rather than with a sample as representative.'[830]

Misuse of biological concepts: 'The subject of biological study is usually either a non-human organism or is at a level of organization below the organism. Concepts that are appropriate for non-human organisms – niche, carrying capacity, etc. – are inappropriate for the creative aspect of human beings which is the central element in long-run economic activity. Biologists then consider the human to be 'just' an animal.'[831]

Adducting biological mechanisms to complex human behaviour: 'Knowing too much about certain mechanisms may damage biologists' reasoning by causing these mechanisms to be adduced when they are inappropriate. An ecological example is the mechanism that pushes animal species toward equilibrium in population size.'[832]

Disciplinary overconfidence and presumption of expertise: 'Many biologists make astonishingly brave assertions about subjects that are wholly outside their fields of research, assertions intended to be understood as expertise rather than as mere lay opinion.'[833]

Simon was working with a sample of several scientists, but we can add at least two biologists of a more recent vintage who produced pessimistic material exhibiting the above characteristics on both population and the environment. One is the Canadian geneticist and science popularizer David Suzuki who starred in an influential bacterial growth short film. In his video, a test tube full of food was presented as an analog to economic growth in human societies. Suzuki's main lesson was threefold:

- the capacity of the biosphere, like that of the test tube, is fixed/finite;
- the solution is not to be found in other test tubes, nor on other planets;
- growth cannot be equated with progress.[834]

Another was the Nobel laureate, John Sulston, who was the chair of the People and the Planet Working Group at the Royal Society that delivered the pessimistic report of the same name discussed in previous sections.[835]

Interestingly, some of the cognitive habits of biologists Simon had identified may be interpreted as aligning with elements of high modernist ideology described by the anthropologist and political scientist James C. Scott.[836] Whereas certain aspects of high modernist ideology may be seen as more closely allied with Simon's optimism, for example 'self-confidence about scientific and technical progress, the expansion of production, the growing satisfaction of human needs,[837] the underlying assumption that 'rational design of social order [is] commensurate with the scientific understanding of natural laws'[838] characterized what Simon had observed about the biologists' cognitive biases. Simon implied but did not quite spell out what this master assumption may have led to, in terms of becoming a lens through which further observations would be viewed. Yet Simon's intuition may be assembled from the list of biases we have studied: the false identity of scientific understanding of nature equalling rational design of human society may lead to dangerous simplifications in the name of science. As Scott had put it: 'High modernism must not be confused with scientific practice. It was fundamentally, as the term "ideology" implies, a faith that borrowed, as it were, the legitimacy of science and technology.'[839] When we study Thomas Sowell's anointed elite, we will examine to what extremes ideological rigidity may push an expert when combined with high social and cultural status.

Simon's analysis thus revealed how a number of specific misconceptions based on disciplinary, cognitive and epistemic habits have long doomed to failure the biologists' analysis of the interactions between human population, natural resource availability and environmental impact. Indeed, for reasons we do not quite understand, biologists seem unable to account for the fact that, unique among all other species, modern humans developed strong propensities to trade and to innovate by combining existing things in new ways, to say nothing of their ability to culturally transmit information between individuals and across generations, thus making irrelevant standard biological analysis of the impact of their activities. As demographer Nicholas Eberstadt deplored a generation ago: 'One of the reasons that Ehrlich's been so wrong is that he has no understanding of or sympathy for the economic process that human beings engage in.'[840]

Let us now explore the expertise-based, elite status and moral syndrome explanations for the intellectual inflexibility and entrenched beliefs of pessimists.

6.4 Foxes and hedgehogs

While investigating the issue of the typically poor track record of expert predictions, writer and journalist Dan Gardner proposed a hypothesis based on the cognitive style of expertise consolidation to address the question of why experts such as Paul Ehrlich cannot seem to realign their compass in the face of the evidence. Gardner studied the work of the psychologist Philip Tetlock, who researched the variables impacting the severity and quality of predictions by a large sample of experts from different fields and with both academic and non-academic backgrounds.[841] Gardner reported that '[w]hat made a big difference is *how* they think. Experts who did particularly badly – meaning they would have improved their results if they had flipped a coin through the whole exercise – were not comfortable with complexity and uncertainty.'[842] Gardner quoted Tetlock's insight that these experts tended to translate each problem into one 'core theoretical theme'[843] they used repeatedly to inform their opinions and to formulate their responses. This core theme became 'like a template, to stamp out predictions...They were sure their One Big Idea was right and so the predictions they stamped out with that idea must be, too.'[844]

Along with the cognitive complexity model, Gardner also adopted Tetlock's classification of experts into 'foxes' and 'hedgehogs', depending on how they responded to new evidence and uncertainty.[845] The foxes are nimble and subtle, capable of integrating new knowledge dynamically and adapting to circumstances; they are, however, skittish and not likely to assert that anything is certain. What they say does not make for good headlines or convincing media sound bites. Ehrlich, thus, did not act like a fox but like a hedgehog: Hedgehogs know one thing, but they know it to the core of their being and they are always willing to stand up to defend it, even in the face of contradiction and potential ridicule, which they tend to sidestep or ignore.

Factual evidence, like the Simon–Ehrlich wager's demonstration of a ten-year decrease in the price of five apparently scarce commodities,[846] might have suggested, to a more open-minded individual than Paul Ehrlich, that a different system than the one he subscribed to was governing reality. Accepting Gardner's insights into Tetlock's cognitive model of the dogmatic intellectual stance of hedgehogs, it may be fair to say that the default position of pessimist analysts like Ehrlich must be a steadfast refusal to see the evidence that does not support their core insight and viewpoint. In Ehrlich's case, the core viewpoint is, arguably, that infinite growth cannot be sustained in a finite system. Since every problem ultimately reduces to the paradigm hedgehogs understand and embrace, new evidence can only introduce confusion and uncertainty. It must be ignored, not even considered seriously or debunked, as that would give it legitimacy or attract attention. In light of what we have described in the section on the psychology of intellectual entrenchment, hedgehogs elevate confirmation bias and motivated reasoning to an art. Their expert cognitive stance is, to borrow Fleck's terminology, tenaciously closed.

6.5 The anointed elite

Disciplinary experts may or may not belong to the intellectual and cultural elite. Experts like Paul Ehrlich appear to ensure that they do and that they control the prevailing vision through the significance of their public profile; Ehrlich appeared over 20 times on Johnny Carson's *The Tonight Show*, for example. Economist and political theorist Thomas Sowell studied the social dynamics of prevailing visions, particularly the behaviour of their champions in the face of new evidence or uncertainty. Sowell, who provided us with the intellectual basis for the term 'anointed elite' in our section title, wrote [original italics]:

> The focus here will be on one particular vision – the vision prevailing among the intellectual and political elite of our time. What is important about that vision are not only its particular assumptions and their corollaries, but also the fact that it is a *prevailing* vision – which means that its assumptions are so much taken for granted by so many people, including so-called 'thinking people,' that neither those assumptions nor their corollaries are generally confronted with demands for empirical evidence. Indeed, empirical evidence itself may be viewed as suspect, insofar as it is inconsistent with that vision. Discordant evidence may be dismissed as isolated anomalies, or as something tendentiously selected by opponents, or it may be explained away ad hoc by a theory having no empirical support whatever – except that this ad hoc theory is able to sustain itself and gain acceptance because it is consistent with the overall vision... [W]hy it is so necessary to believe in a particular vision that evidence of its incorrectness is ignored, suppressed or discredited – ultimately, why one's quest is not for reality but for a vision. What does the vision offer that reality does not offer? [847]

Sowell's analysis presents a complementary, yet deeper, perspective to the hedgehog and fox model. Experts adopting hedgehog or fox behaviours towards new evidence supposedly displayed those behaviours consistently because of internal factors such as their temperament coupled with rigid disciplinary blinders and other biases we have discussed. Tetlock's experts, let's remember, were not necessarily all household names or stars of their academic disciplines. They were simply experienced professionals and academics, although a subset was certainly in the media. The fox and hedgehog behavioural complexes were perhaps somewhat independent of the social context in which the experts found themselves. Foxes were thus, typically, thoughtful and open-minded, if neurotic, whereas hedgehogs always stuck to their One Big Idea regardless of their social milieu or exposure.

Sowell, on the other hand, looked at a different subset of 'experts.' He investigated the behaviour of social and political elites: people who already possessed a certain amount of power, visibility and media name recognition. These people had a different incentive than Tetlock's experts: the preservation of that insider elite status. In Tetlock's case, status, if it was achieved, may have been dependent on the quality or outcome of expert prediction. In Sowell's case, elite status was pre-existing. Since we saw that foxes often made for poor headlines with their nuanced and uncertain views, we may hypothesize that Sowell's elites would, in fact, display hedgehog behaviour with respect to that prevailing social vision he identified. Sowell, however, showed them engaged in a more incentive-driven and strongly emotional pattern of behaviour [italics in the original]:

> What a vision may offer, and what the prevailing vision of our time emphatically *does* offer, is a special state of grace for those who believe in it. Those who accept this vision are deemed to be not merely factually correct but morally on a higher plane. Put differently, those who disagree with the prevailing vision are seen as being not merely in error, but in sin.[848]
>
> The contemporary anointed and those who follow them make much of their 'compassion' for the less fortunate, their 'concern' for the environment,...for example, as if these were characteristics which distinguish them from people with opposite views on public policy...One reason for the preservation and insulation of a vision is that it has become inextricably intertwined with the egos of those who believe it...[T]he vision of the anointed is not simply a vision of the world and its functioning in a causal sense, but is also a vision of themselves and of their moral role in that world. *It is a vision of differential rectitude.* It is not a vision of the tragedy of the human condition: Problems exist because others are not as wise or as virtuous as the anointed.[849]

Thus, Sowell's elites adhere to the prevailing vision not just because that vision aligns with their disciplinary prejudices and biases, or because cognitively they are hedgehogs, or further still because adherence will keep them in power, although all these motivations may likely be right to some extent. Sowell's elites seem to cling to the prevailing vision because the vision gives them power and meaning, and defines their existence on a higher plane than that of the non-adherents, for all to see, much like the exercise of a high religious office would. Sowell's anointed elites appear to be both moralistic and narcissistic.

Living as a high priest 'in and of' the vision redeems the adherents morally while giving their life the stamp of a more evolved and rarefied being with the power to make others recognize it. While working on behalf of the vision, the anointed cannot but be right, both factually and morally. The anointed are Tetlock's hedgehogs on steroids and in full body armour, convinced of their right to lead, their infallibility, and their invincibility. They are, in fact, fanatics. As such, they may be formidable opponents but also unfair adversaries in an intellectual argument: as the anointed, they may appeal to the white-hot emotional core sustained by belief and revealed 'truth,' not to empirical fact and logic. In fact, the anointed don't seem to want to conduct experiments or to have a dialogue: they want to annihilate their moral enemies.

If having absorbed the many biases inherent in human behaviour heuristics and organized science, having been trained as a biologist or having the cognitive temperament of a hedgehog does not begin to explain the intellectual enigma that is Paul Ehrlich, perhaps Sowell's dissection of Ehrlich as one of the anointed does. 'Paul Ehrlich is perhaps pre-eminent for having been wrong by the widest margins, on the most varied subjects – and for maintaining his reputation untarnished through it all.'[850] How could that be? Perhaps, Sowell suggests, it is because Ehrlich is the elite enforcer, the hedgehog with the best One Big Idea, the most authoritative-sounding mouthpiece of misapplied biological method. '[T]here is, as the bottom line, a power agenda by which the vision of the anointed is to be imposed on the masses. According to Ehrlich, we must 'take immediate action' for 'population control' – 'hopefully through changes in our value system, but by compulsion if voluntary methods fail.'[851] Perhaps Paul Ehrlich has sold the pessimist package with the most flair; perhaps, also, he has paid for his right to do so with the pure gold of fanatical devotion.

6.6 The guardians versus the agents of commerce

Throughout this intellectual journey, we have not yet attempted to ask how it is that some individuals became naïve realists and succumbed to confirmation bias while others fought the easy answers and gave up in-group acceptance for a mangle of conflicting opinions. How is it that some experts were able to set up trading zones across disciplinary boundaries[852] and fruitfully integrate concepts from many fields of study while others remained embedded in the disciplinary matrix of their first epistemic culture? Finally, how is it that some experts, such as Julian Simon and Bjørn Lomborg, started out on the pessimist side but broke out of their crystallized opinions and became active optimists, whereas many others, including Paul Ehrlich, remained among the pessimists? While theories of personality may provide many clues, we will presently take a different approach to this problem by adopting a set of constructs based on how individuals understand the goals of their working lives.

Let us consider the following view of human nature: 'Like the other animals, we find and pick up what we can use, and appropriate territories. But unlike the other animals, we also trade and produce for trade. Because we possess these two radically different ways of dealing with our needs, we also have two radically different systems of morals and values – both systems valid and necessary.'[853] Jane Jacobs opened her unusual work *Systems of Survival*,[854] an exploration of the ethical foundations of work, with this very reflection on humanity. Her book is singular not only because of the insightful and complex questions she attempts to answer, but also because of its format, that of a Socratic dialogue. Her characters struggle to understand and reconcile the functions of these two different systems of thinking, much like the readers who, as Jacobs cautioned, may 'have taken on casts of mind so skewed toward one set of morals and values that we have little understanding of the other, and little if any appreciation of its integrity too.'[855] Why is it necessary to understand and appreciate the differences between the two systems? Because the interplay between these two modes of being makes us human: It is what has allowed us to survive and prosper materially both as a species and as a succession of cultures.[856]

It follows from these arguments that failure to come to terms with both of these modes may deprive many prescriptive moral arguments of their depth. As the economic geographer Peter J. Taylor pointed out:

> [A]ll animal species have access to locally available means of reproduction but humans also have access to non-local means of reproduction. Evidence abounds for trading in early human settlements because, for instance, the geological origins of exotic stones such as amber and obsidian can be traced. Archaeologists call this 'the release from proximity'... extending human social ties for at least the last 60,000 years.[857]

Thus, the freedom from relying solely on the resources of our immediate surroundings is part and parcel of humanity, and is as important as the biological markers of our species. In fact, Taylor posited that the tension between locality and release from proximity is key to 'generic ideas for understanding human behaviour.'[858]

Jacobs' methodology for arriving at the two systems, which she called 'syndromes' – from the Greek meaning 'things that run together'[859] – was what we would call a content analysis of literature ranging from news articles and detailed academic case studies to business ads and ancient texts.[860] Jacobs arranged behavioural precepts that she extracted from the literature into groups of related qualities that emerged as 'the ethical foundations for these different ways of making a living.'[861] The two syndromes were the Commercial syndrome[862] and the Guardian syndrome,[863] each consisting of fifteen precepts arranged in the order of increasing cognitive and moral complexity and further subdivided into functional clusters.[864] Table 6.1 shows a summary of both syndromes by cluster. Taylor noted that none of the precepts could be violated without endangering the integrity of the system; all precepts had to be observed in order for individuals to succeed within a syndrome.[865] The Commercial syndrome encompasses work in 'making and trading commodities'[866] in the manufacturing, information, farming, mining, wholesaling, retailing, logistics and transport sectors, to name a few; the Guardian syndrome includes administrative, governmental, and legal work such as police and law enforcement, elected political office, state-run education, and all state services.

Table 6.1: Peter J. Taylor's analysis of Jane Jacobs' Commercial and Guardian syndromes by clusters of moral precepts.

Commercial syndrome		Guardian syndrome	
Cluster	Precept	Cluster	Precept
Key virtue	Be honest	Key virtue	Be loyal
The rest of basic cluster	Shun force	The rest of basic cluster	Shun trading
	Come to voluntary agreements		Exert prowess
Operating cluster	Collaborate with strangers and aliens	Action cluster	Be exclusive
	Compete		Take vengeance
	Respect contracts		Respect hierarchy
	Dissent for the sake of the task		Deceive for the sake of the task
Enterprise cluster	Be open to inventiveness and novelty	Lifestyle cluster	Be obedient and disciplined
	Be efficient		Adhere to tradition
	Use initiative and enterprise		Make rich use of leisure
	Invest for productive purposes		Dispense largesse
	Be industrious		Treasure honour
	Be thrifty		Be ostentatious
Life cluster	Promote comfort and convenience	Life cluster	Show fortitude
	Be optimistic		Be fatalistic

Source: Taylor (2013, based on table on p. 37.)

While the key virtue of the Commercial syndrome is 'Be honest,' with supporting values in the basic cluster being 'Shun force' and 'Come to voluntary agreements,' the corresponding key value of the Guardian syndrome is 'Be loyal,' complemented by 'Shun trading' and 'Exert prowess.'[867] Just those top values alone demonstrate how thoroughly each syndrome differs from the other, and how correct action in one becomes incongruous and inappropriate in the other. While the Commercial syndrome prizes honesty, openness and a willingness to come to an unforced understanding between participants, the Guardian syndrome abhors any sort of dealing and bribery, shuns absolute honesty in favour of unquestioned loyalty, and approves of coercion through the use of force. The Commercial syndrome celebrates Taylor's release from proximity in supporting collaboration with strangers, innovative and enterprising solutions, and 'dissent for the sake of the task;'[868] the Guardian syndrome settles for locality in its respect for hierarchy, tradition, obedience, and the need for vengeance against transgressors.

So far, we have seen how mutually exclusive the two syndromes are, yet their most significant difference is in their so-called Life clusters, which consist of comfort, convenience and optimism on the Commercial side, and fortitude and fatalism on the Guardian side. According to Taylor:

> These define two very different mindsets. The commercial syndrome is ultimately premised on assuming a better future – why else would you invest? Every freely agreed contract benefits both sides – this is a Win–Win world. But for guardians, change is a matter of life and death (literally in battle, career-wise in elections) – this is a Win–Lose world, a zero-sum game.[869]

Jacobs' and Taylor's subsequent analysis of the long-term life outlook of both syndromes gives us much to reflect upon. A tendency towards fatalism and a zero-sum mentality characterize the pessimists, as we demonstrated in Chapter 1. An emphasis on human creativity, agency, collaboration, efficiency, and a win–win spirit characterize the optimists and their attitude to both their work and the world as a whole. In fact, Jacobs herself described the final precept of the Commercial syndrome as 'Be optimistic.' By defining the two different and contradictory approaches to making a living in human society, Jacobs fully characterized the pessimist and the optimist perspectives described in this book. Thus, Jacobs' and Taylor's analyses of the irreconcilable attitudes towards the goals of work apply to the stances that the pessimists and the optimists take towards the intellectual labour of understanding the relationship between climate change and population growth. Jane Jacobs' model of the two moral syndromes, in fact, appears to illuminate the fatalism, catastrophism, and the adherence to the neo-Malthusian intellectual traditions of the pessimists. It also predicts the efficiency-driven and change-focused outlook anticipating the release from proximity characteristic of the optimists.

What value is there in this analysis? To us, Jacobs' syndromes appear to encapsulate the philosophical, psychological and ethical cores of the pessimist and the optimist positions, as well as their extremes. The Guardians, at their most pessimistic, predict extinction, but at their most positive, engage in responsible stewardship of local resources. The Commercial agents, at their most optimistic, are agents of change transforming the Earth and pushing the limits of humanity; at their most disorderly, however, they may perhaps become agents of chaos. The syndromes, moreover, allow us to gain insights into the goals and motivations of an avowed pessimist like Paul Ehrlich. We understand his inability to change his opinions more clearly in light of his Guardian ethos: he must refrain from 'wheeling and dealing' with those who don't share his views, he must adhere to his intellectual tradition, he must show fortitude in the face of opposition, and, of course, he must always be fatalistic about the coming apocalypse. As a Guardian, even more than as Tetlock's hedgehog, Paul Ehrlich makes sense. His behaviour over his long career has been aligned with his goal of preserving the Earth from being overrun by greedy masses placing Earth's limited resources under commercial exploitation.

7 Conclusion

In a scathing critique of the romantic poet Robert Southey's negative assessment of the industrial economy of his time, the British historian and Whig politician Thomas Babington Macaulay famously observed in 1830:

> To almost all men the state of things under which they have been used to live seems to be the necessary state of things... Hence it is that, though in every age everybody knows that up to his own time progressive improvement has been taking place, nobody seems to reckon on any improvement during the next generation.

Macaulay added that while no one can definitely prove that 'those are in error who tell us that society has reached a turning point, that we have seen our best days. But so said all who came before us, and with just as much apparent reason.' 'On what principle is it that,' he then asked, 'when we see nothing but improvement behind us, we are to expect nothing but deterioration before us?'[870]

Apparently not much has changed since Macaulay's day, especially when it comes to the conflict of visions between the pessimists and the optimists, the Guardians and the Commercial Agents. Much of the public discussion is still dominated by erroneous ideas such as the 'Malthusian trap', according to which population growth is absolutely limited by finite resources; that because there is only so much to share, a smaller population will be inherently better off; that technological or social innovations can at best delay the unsustainable character of population growth; and that because of projected future ills, a range of – sometimes drastic – preventive policy interventions is justified in the present. This perspective was repeatedly brought to the fore over the last two centuries under the feather, pen, typewriter or keyboard of some (often highly credentialed) concerned individuals. And almost invariably, each time scores of public intellectuals, activists, bureaucrats, politicians, academic journal editors, private foundation and grant agency officials echoed, promoted, funded or implemented restrictive policies in the name of preventing the careless lemmings from jumping off the cliff.

In keeping with the pessimist outlook of the Guardians, a group of sustainability scientists recently reported that it would be impossible, without an ecological catastrophe, to provide for more than the minimal survival needs of more than seven billion people on Earth given that the universal achievement of those needs 'would require a level of resource use that is 2–6 times the sustainable level, based on current relationships.'[871] According to these scientists, the Earth is, once again, hopelessly overrun by the plague of humanity. But perhaps the grip of the Guardians has loosened somewhat, as new voices are being heard on different frequencies. The environmental policy expert and left-leaning (albeit not Marxist) Breakthrough Institute director Ted Nordhaus[872] found the article just quoted worthy of challenging because of its standard population-linked view of ecological sustainability and its use of numerous sophisticated analytic frameworks[873] with the trappings of scientific precision. Remarkably, Nordhaus was able to reach a mainstream audience in a left-wing outlet despite questioning such 'nebulous'[874] and 'pseudo-scientific limits'[875] associated with carrying capacity.

What many pessimists truly object to, however, is often not so much just population growth, which is now nearing its peak, but the alleged chaos and environmental destruction created by unrestrained capitalistic commerce.[876] Nordhaus noticed this too, and brought up this shifting of the goalposts by the pessimists to everyone's attention, pointing out that, in parallel with population growth, the growth in consumption will also eventually saturate and decline. While many critics still claim capitalism functions like protozoa and 'cannot survive without endless growth of material consumption,' he observed that there is:

> no particularly well-established basis for this claim and plenty of evidence to the contrary. The long-term trend in market economies has been towards slower and less resource-intensive growth. Growth in per-capita consumption rises dramatically as people transition from rural agrarian economies to modern industrial economies. But then it tails off.[877]

In fact, environmental policy experts such as Nordhaus who originally came from and are still somewhat closer to a more pessimistic tradition are slowly catching up with the insights of optimists like Julian Simon, who long ago observed that, overall, 'human creation is greater than human destruction, in the sense that our environment is becoming progressively more hospitable to humankind... The movement away from equilibrium is a movement toward safety and sustenance. This progress carries with it some undesirable features for a while, but eventually we get around to fixing them.'[878]

It is, of course, true that environmental degradation and resource depletion can be observed in various locations at different points in time – such as in present day Venezuela and Zimbabwe – but optimistic analysts can explain most of them as temporary and attributable to factors such as bad governance, poor incentive structures, insufficient respect for private property rights and lack of voluntary exchange structures rather than to population growth, resulting scarcity of physical materials, and ecological overshoot.[879]

Rather than emulating the growth pattern of bacteria in a test tube, human population is stabilizing. Rather than being static and constrained, our environment is dynamic. Rather than passively awaiting catastrophe, 'we have been engineering our environments to more productively serve human needs for tens of millennia... It took six times as much farmland to feed a single person 9,000 years ago, at the dawn of the Neolithic revolution, than it does today, even as almost all of us eat much richer diets. What the palaeoarchaeolgical record strongly suggests is that carrying capacity is not fixed.'[880] In other words, now more than ever, pessimists are on the wrong side of the limits to growth debate and must resort to bending the facts and invoking theoretical catastrophes to fit their narrative.

Astrophysicist and astrobiologist Adam Frank[881] has gone further along this line of reasoning: 'The Earth and its inhabitants have been evolving together for eons, and we are just the most recent in a long line of its experiments.'[882] Frank, a firm believer in anthropogenic climate change,[883] also knows this: 'We are not the first time a species has changed a planet's climate through its own success.'[884] And he is not panicking, nor is he a pessimist. His perspective is exciting, fresh, and very much in need of being shared. Frank admitted that the story humans tell themselves about their activity on Earth may be summarized in two discouraging words: 'We suck.'[885] Of course, a guilt-trip follows this statement in a typical pessimist narrative: 'Human beings are greedy and selfish. We are nothing but a plague on the planet.'[886] Frank has rejected this viewpoint categorically:

> That story is not only unhelpful and impoverished, it's also entirely wrong from the perspective of the new understanding of life and planets we've recently gained. People often cast the climate crisis in terms of 'saving the planet.'... It's not the Earth that needs saving. Instead, it's us and our project of civilization that need a new direction. If we fail to make it across the difficult terrain we face, the planet will just move on without us, generating new species in the novel climate it evolves. The 'we suck' narrative makes us villains in a story that, ultimately, has none. What the story does have are experiments – the ones that failed and the ones that succeeded.[887]

In effect, what Frank wanted us to derive from this is what he told the podcaster Joe Rogan: 'we are what the biosphere is making right now.'[888]

When one adopts Frank's radical but lucid and self-consistent perspective, many assumptions of the pessimists suddenly lose their force and appear insignificant, if not petty and – well – blinkered. Frank's strong belief in anthropogenic climate change coupled with an uncharacteristic lack of guilt allows him to come to terms with the notion that the dominant species of the biosphere is about to completely transform the planet. It has happened before, as he has stated, and it is a mark of species success, not catastrophe. As an optimist, he would like to see technological change and boundless innovation to take over the transformation so that the earth could become even safer and more hospitable to humanity while preserving as much of the rest of the biosphere as can be done, given both our needs and the ability of other life-forms to adapt.[889] His vision is one of an earth where people have learned to project the best of both of Jacobs' syndromes by tweaking Guardianship towards dynamic stewardship and adjusting the Commercial syndrome to its creative, adaptive best.

Nordhaus, similarly, rejected the guilt of the pessimist 'we suck' narrative:

> Viewing humans in the same way that we view single-celled organisms or insects risks treating them that way. Malthus argued against Poor Laws, in the belief that they only incentivised the poor to reproduce. Ehrlich argued against food aid for poor countries for similar reasons, and inspired population control measures of enormous cruelty.[890]

Both Nordhaus and Frank, although likely diverging on many ideological points, share a fundamentally optimist belief that people belong on Earth and bring value to life, to the planet, and to one another. In fact, Nordhaus concluded his article with a sentiment echoing some of Frank's arguments:

> ...threats of societal collapse, claims that carrying capacity is fixed, and demands for sweeping restrictions on human aspiration are neither scientific nor just. We are not fruit flies, programmed to reproduce until our population collapses. Nor are we cattle, whose numbers must be managed. To understand the human experience on the planet is to understand that we have remade the planet again and again to serve our needs and our dreams. Today, the aspirations of billions depend upon continuing to do just that.[891]

Most optimist thinkers would obviously concur.

Still, what about our pessimist colleagues and neighbours? How can we help them while ensuring we don't become them? Professor of creative writing Robert Grant Price has suggested the practice of 'methodological belief'[892] as a way of opening one's mind to arguments one abhors. The key is to select some of the best quality writings from the rival perspective 'to engage a writer as a friend, rather than as an enemy, and to see the text as a gift, not a grenade. If you approach a text as a diehard skeptic, you won't hear what the other person is saying or let yourself change your mind.'[893] If that fails, perhaps reading history is the next best thing. Dare we suggest Macaulay?

Julian Simon noted that the 'doomsayers believe we are in period of greater destruction than creation – that is, headed toward a reduction in the safety and hospitableness of our environment. They speak about the planet being in a worsening 'crisis'. But if this were true, it would be a complete break with all past trends.'[894] Of course, he added, this is logically possible. But it is helpful 'to remember that there have always been plausible-sounding theories of approaching doom, always statements that this moment is different than any that has gone before; the making and believing of such ideas seems to be psychologically irresistible for many. But to succumb to such unfounded beliefs is to court disaster – as groups that have sold all their belongings and gone to mountain tops to await the end of the world have found out.'[895]

In the end, population growth and the development and growing use of carbon fuels liberated human labour and brains from subsistence agriculture while simultaneously reducing pressures on both wild flora and fauna. As a result, not only has much marginal agricultural land been rewilded in many parts of the world over the last several decades, but an increasingly large number of human brains and hands were given the opportunity to purse an ever-wider range of occupations through ever-more diverse, useful and powerful means. Trade, the division of labour, more people and more carbon fuels are what allowed humanity to simultaneously bake and enjoy an ever-larger number of economic and environmental cakes, while in the process making human societies ever more resilient against extreme weather events and any climate change trend they might be confronted with. One can also rest assured that, provided human creativity is allowed to flourish in the context of market economies, future energy transitions will deliver both economic and environmental benefits. As hopefully an ever-larger number of individuals will come to appreciate, the sustainable way forward is paved with innovative ideas and ever more brainpower rather than stagnation, degrowth and despair. And the best way to achieve this outcome is to make sure there are more of us around who enjoy the benefits of ever-freer societies...

Notes

1. Address of the retiring Vice-President, Section Q, American Association for the Advancement of Science, Washington DC, December 31. Excerpts reproduced in *The Bulletin of the American Association of University Professors*, 11 (5), 271–276. We would like to thank Phil Magness for drawing our attention to this quote. Henry Wyman Holmes (1880–1960) was the inaugural dean at the Harvard Graduate School of Education. For a brief overview of the history of eugenics at Harvard, see Cohen (2016).
2. Latour (2017).
3. Bookchin (1994).

Chapter 1 Introduction

4. Petroni (2009, p. 275).
5. Harte and Harte (2008).
6. The analogy that the atmosphere acts like a greenhouse is misleading, but we will nonetheless use it throughout this paper because of its importance in shaping the understanding of the main issues discussed among policy makers and the general public. For a more concise discussion of the problems involved, see ACS (Undated).
7. Scientific American (2009).
8. Cafaro (2016, pp. 60–61). For links to Cafaro's output on the topic, see http://www.philipcafaro.com/.
9. See, among others, Pearce (2014); Sulston *et al.* (2013).
10. Easterbrook (2003, p. xviii).
11. Astor (2018).
12. Population Matters (2018).
13. Conceivable Future (ND).
14. Negative Population Growth (2017).
15. Stanberry (2017).
16. Rieder (2016, p. vii).
17. Rieder (2016). Rieder's website can be found at http://www.bioethicsinstitute.org/people/travis-n-rieder. Quote taken from the summary of the book available on the publisher's webpage at http://www.springer.com/us/book/9783319338699.
18. Ehrlich and Harte (2015, pp. 904–905).

19. While the VHEMT webmaster's *nom de guerre* of Les U. Knight, as well as some of the material, might suggest the website may be a parody or hoax, Dryzek considered VHEMT a genuine, if tiny, organization. See Dryzek (2005, p. 41).
20. Knight (ND).
21. Knight (ND). This is, of course, an understatement, as VHEMT is interested in a final solution, not in a temporary easing of congestion. Here is a section of the VHEMT website presenting the movement's position on the question: 'Will new viruses, wars, famine, and toxic waste help the cause of human extinction?' The (somewhat regretful in tone) answer is: 'No. Epidemics actually strengthen a species if enough of them are living to have an adequate survival rate. With seven billion of us, there is no virus that could get us all. A 99.99% die off would still leave more than 700,000 naturally-immune survivors to replicate, and in less than 50,000 years we could be right back where we are now.' See Knight (ND) section on mortality.
22. PBS (2008). A partial transcript of the relevant passages is in Graham (2008).
23. Plautz (2014).
24. Hoff and Robertson (2016, p. 267).
25. Cox (2014).
26. Podesta and Wirth (2018).
27. The quote is from Podesta and Wirth (2018). The research they link to is Casey and Galor (2016). These authors summarize their contribution in Casey and Galor (2017a). See also Casey and Galor (2017b).
28. Podesta and Wirth (2018).
29. For several anti-population growth quotes from once or still prominent individuals, see, among others, the websites of Population Matters https://www.populationmatters.org/resources/agreements-quotes-polls/quotations/; Population Elephant http://populationelephant.com/populationelephant.com/PEQuotes.html and Growth Busters https://www.growthbusters.org/population-growth/. For a detailed overview of the stance of the British elite on these issues over the last century and a half, see, among others, Drysdale (1889); Bashford (2014). For a recent re-statement of these ideas in modern academic parlance, see Royal Society (2012). Other broad historical perspectives on the population control movement include Chase (1977); Connelly (2008); Hoff (2012); Robertson (2012). For more spirited denunciations of the population control movement that cover much historical ground, see Zubrin (2012a) and Kay (2018).
30. Whitehead (1917).

Chapter 2 Conflicting perspectives

31. For more detailed intellectual histories on the analysis of the relationship between population growth, resource availability and environmental impact, see, among others, Nitti (1894); Stangeland (1904); Ryan (1911); Ogden (1917); Gonnard (1923); UN (1973/1953); Schumpeter (1954); Barnett and Morse (1963); Hutchinson (1967); Peron (1995); Simon (1998); Kelley (1999); Tobin (2004); de Sherbinin *et al.* (2007); Bradley Jr (2009); Bashford (2014); Higgs (2014); Lane (2015); Desrochers and Geloso (2016a).
32. See, among others, Nisbet (1980); De Steiguer (2006); Ben-Ami (2016).

33. Epstein (2014).
34. Dryzek (2005, pp. 16–22).
35. Dryzek (2005, p. 17).
36. Dryzek (2005, p. 51).
37. Mann (2018c, p. 6).
38. Mann (2018c, pp. 6–7).
39. Rees (1985, Section is on pp. 31–39).
40. These terms are more commonly used by optimistic analysts. See, among others, Moore and White (2016). Other variations include 'doomsdayer' (see Maddox (1972)) and 'eco-doomster' (see Beckerman (1974)).
41. Rees (2002, p. 31).
42. Mann (2018c, p. 8).
43. These terms have obviously been used by many other authors. The adjective 'cornucopian' was initially meant to be pejorative and was profoundly disliked by, among others, optimistic economist Julian Simon. See Desrochers and Hoffbauer (2009) and Dryzek (2005).
44. The nature and significance of the Simon–Ehrlich wager on the future price of some non-renewable commodities is discussed in more detail in Sabin (2013) and Desrochers and Geloso (2016a).
45. Luten (1980, p. 125).
46. Marshall (1890, p. 223).
47. Barnett and Morse (1963, p. 1).
48. Kelley (1949, p. 17).
49. Robert (1798).
50. See, among others, Beck and Kolankiewicz (2000); Kay (2018). A recent attempt to revive immigration restrictions in the name of environmental preservation is Cafaro (2014). For a summary of his argumentation, see Cafaro (2016).
51. See, among others, Chase (1977); Connelly (2008); Bashford (2014).
52. For a concise literary and video introduction to the mindset of the time, see Haberman (2015). For more detailed discussions, see, among others, Kasun (1999/1988); Desrochers and Geloso (2016a,b).
53. Gimenez (1973). Quotes taken from the translation.
54. See, among others, Bailey (1994); De Steiguer (2006).
55. Dryzek (2005).
56. Hardin (1968).
57. Ehrlich (1968).
58. Meadows *et al.* (1972).
59. Dryzek (2005, p. 30). Energy problems were made worse by various policies (e.g. price control, windfall profit taxes) meant to address these issues. See, among others, Anonymous (2006).
60. Dryzek (2005, p. 30).
61. This issue is discussed in greater detail in Sec. 3.3. For a concise and freely available presentation on the subject of declining birthrates in various parts of the world, see Smith (2018).

62. While this was generally true in advanced economies, many visible minority groups maintained a higher fertility rate, thus making population control seem inherently racist at the time. See, among others, Ehrlich and Ehrlich (1970), and its reprint, Holdren and Ehrlich (1971a, pp. 157–159) as well as Beck and Kolankiewicz (2000).
63. For an account of environmentalist NGOs' struggles and loss of interest in the issue in the 1990s written by two long-time members and supporters of population control policies, see Beck and Kolankiewicz (2000). Preston (1996) suggests that in the 1990s Malthusian thinking had returned to land scarcity and degradation as a major constraint to development. Chapter 4 provides a brief discussion and additional references as to how concerns about global warming came to dominate the environmentalist agenda.
64. Boulding (1955).
65. Dryzek (2005, p. 33).
66. O'Barney (1980).
67. Simon and Kahn (1984, pp. 1–2).
68. Simon (2001, p. 4).
69. Simon (2001, p. 4).
70. Martine (2009, p. 12).
71. Martine (2009, p. 14).
72. Anonymous (2017a).
73. Ashmead (1997, p. 77).
74. Dryzek (2005, pp. 28–29).
75. Cohen (1995, p. 6). For a more detailed treatment, see Draffkorn Kilmer (1972).
76. Chen (1911).
77. Hutchinson (1967, p. 9).
78. Plato (Approximately 380 BC).
79. Tertullian (Quintus Septimius Florens Tertullianus) (Approximately 203 AD, Ch. 30).
80. Saint Jerome (1893, p. 345).
81. Botero (1606); Ortes (1775). Both Botero (a Jesuit) and Ortes (a Dominican) quit their respective Catholic order at some point in their lives. The original (1798) edition of Thomas Robert Malthus' influential tract was entitled *An Essay on the Principle of Population as it Effects the Future Improvement of Society; with Remarks on the Speculations of Mr. Godwin, M. Condorcet and Other Writers*. He subsequently reworked his text, added much new information and reached more nuanced conclusions. See Malthus (1826).
82. Robert (1798). Malthus would essentially abandon this argument in later editions and emphasize instead the role of diminishing returns to scale.
83. Dryzek (2005, p. 29).
84. Dryzek (2005, p. 29).
85. Dryzek (2005, p. 30).
86. Dryzek (2005, p. 30).
87. Dryzek (2005, p. 31).
88. Dryzek (2005, p. 31).
89. Dryzek (2005, pp. 32–33).
90. Dryzek (2005, p. 33).

91. Røpke (2004).
92. Dryzek (2005, p. 34).
93. Dryzek (2005, p. 34). For a history and discussion of the limits of the concept of carrying capacity, see Sayre (2008).
94. Mill's original stance is in Chapter 6 of his 1848 Principles of Political Economy (Mill, 1920/1848). Interestingly, Mill believed that the 'density of population necessary to enable mankind to obtain, in the greatest degree, all the advantages both of co-operation and of social intercourse, has, in all the most populous countries, been attained.' Unlike later writers on the topic, however, Mill theorized the stationary state as an outcome of spontaneous market processes.
95. Hardin (1968).
96. Mill (1869, Ch. 5).
97. Dryzek (2005, p. 37).
98. A current list of such organizations can be found at https://en.m.wikipedia.org/wiki/List_of_population_concern_organizations.
99. Kasun (1999/1988, p. 217). For an online publication that summarizes some of Kasun's research, see Peron (1995). For other discussions of the legacy of eugenics among later population control activists, see Chase (1977); Connelly (2008); Desrochers and Hoffbauer (2009); Pearce (2010); Zubrin (2012a); Bashford (2014); Kay (2018).
100. Kasun (1999/1988, p. 217).
101. Chase (1977, p. 406).
102. See, among others, Connelly (2008); Zubrin (2012b); UN (ND). For some additional academic references on this subject, see Kelley (1999).
103. Zubrin (2012b).
104. Machiavelli (1517, Ch. 5).
105. Quoted by Saether (1993, p. 511).
106. Symes (1886, p. 47). The 'raft in space' metaphor was used a few years earlier by economist Henry George in his 1879 *Progress and Poverty. An Inquiry into the Cause of Industrial Depressions and of Increase of Want with Increase of Wealth: The Remedy*. (George, 1879, Book IV, Ch. 2). It would later be used by other authors, perhaps most prominently George Orwell in his 1937 book, *The Road to Wigan Pier*.
107. Isaacson (1912, pp. xxvi and xxvii).
108. Isaacson (1912, p. xxvii).
109. Isaacson (1912, p. xxvii).
110. Holdren and Ehrlich (1971b, pp. 7–10, quote on p. 7).
111. Quoted in United States Congress (1973).
112. Boulding (1966, pp. 3–14).
113. Negative Population Growth, 'About us' http://www.npg.org/about-us.html.
114. Malthus (1826, Book III, Ch. XIV).
115. Caplan (2007). The comment was made in the context of an online debate with economist Bryan Caplan's discussion of Clark (2007).
116. Anonymous (1879, p. 6).
117. Vogt (1948, p. 285).
118. Ehrlich (1968, p. 198).
119. Rockefeller Commission (1972).

120. Bryson (1976, p. xii). He also believed in a finite supply of economically valuable resources.
121. Ashmead (1997, pp. 16–17).
122. Ashmead (1997, p. 83).
123. BBC News (2009).
124. Population Matters. 'Jane Goodall speaks about population.' https://www.populationmatters.org/goodall-population/.
125. Porritt (2015).
126. McKie (2012).
127. Most pessimistic writers rarely – if ever – extended the argument to manufacturing activities.
128. Malthus (1826, Ch. 1).
129. Mill (1920/1848, Book I, Ch. XIII, Sec. 2).
130. Wrigley (1988, p. 34). A short – and freely accessible – introduction to this author's thought is Wrigley (2011).
131. Cook (1951, p. 321).
132. Bongaarts (2002, p. 68).
133. Jevons (1866/1865, Ch. 1).
134. Patzek cited in Inman (2010). The original study is Patzek and Croft (2010).
135. Ehrlich and Holdren (1969, p. 1069).
136. Ehrlich and Ehrlich (1975/1974, p. 100).
137. Ehrlich and Ehrlich (1975/1974, p. 44).
138. Heilbroner (1974, p. 19).
139. Ehrlich and Harte (2015, p. 904).
140. Ehrlich and Harte (2015, p. 904).
141. For a more nuanced take on this issue that explores arguments both for and against this stance, see Fitter (2013).
142. Osborn Jr (1948, p. 201). There is a more detailed discussion of Osborn's book in Desrochers and Hoffbauer (2009). For a more complete history of his environmental activism, see Connelly (2008).
143. Osborn Jr (1948, p. 199).
144. Osborn Jr (1948, p. 68).
145. Vogt (1948, p. 147). For a more detailed discussion of Vogt's book, see Desrochers and Hoffbauer (2009). For a more detailed history of his life and environmental activism, see Connelly (2008); Mann (2018c).
146. Heilbroner (1974, p. 49).
147. Ehrlich (1968, p. 11).
148. Ehrlich and Holdren (1969, p. 1065).
149. Ehrlich and Holdren (1969, pp. 1065, 1070–1071).
150. Ehrlich and Holdren (1969, pp. 1066).
151. Ehrlich and Holdren (1970).
152. Easterbrook (2003, pp. 288–289).
153. Tobias (2013).
154. Holdren *et al.* (1980, p. 1301).
155. Ehrlich and Ehrlich (2008).

156. Jevons (1866/1865, Ch. 2).
157. Marshall (1890, p. 180).
158. Marshall (1890, p. 180).
159. Cook (1951, p. 319).
160. Cook (1951, p. 295).
161. Brown (1954, p. 6).
162. East (1928/1923, p. viii).
163. East (1928/1923, pp. 8–9).
164. East (1928/1923, p. 345).
165. Vogt (1948, p. 56).
166. Ehrlich (1968, p. xi).
167. Dobbs *et al.* (2011, p. ii).
168. UN (1973/1953).
169. Aristotle (b).
170. Devas (1919/1907).
171. Proudhon (1886/1848).
172. Historically, this group has included those labeled as feebleminded, infirm, criminal, morally defective, poorer, lower caste or of the wrong race or ethnicity.
173. Vogt (1948, p. 257).
174. Vogt (1948, p. 13).
175. See Bates (1962/1955, pp. 1–2). Additional background on this internal debate can be found in Mann (2018c).
176. Quoted in Hillaby (1952).
177. Huxley (1958).
178. Hardin (1974).
179. In short, population growth focuses investments on children rather than activities that might generate more economic development.
180. See, among others, Sabin (2013); Desrochers and Geloso (2016a).
181. Ehrlich (1968, p. 1).
182. Ashmead (1997, p. 40).
183. Ashmead (1997, p. 85).
184. Dryzek (2005, p. 40).
185. Dryzek (2005, p. 42).
186. Dryzek (2005, p. 41).
187. Vogt (1948, p. 265).
188. Ehrlich and Ehrlich (1997).
189. Translated quote in Spengler (1966/1942), p. 32. Vauban, however, insisted that 'a ruler's subjects, to be of maximum worth, must be employed, comfortable and happy' (idem). Original quote in Le Prestre Vauban (1707).
190. Hume (1742/1777).
191. Quoted by Nitti (1894).
192. Baudeau (1910 (1771, p. 13); translation from Hutchinson (1967, p. 98).
193. Heilbroner (1974, p. 19), further distinguishes the fondness for growth expressed by 'Victorians, traditional Marxists, and managerialists.'
194. Godwin (1820, Ch. 3).

195. Blaug (2000).
196. George (1879, Book II, Ch. 2).
197. George (1879, Book II, Ch. 4).
198. Barnett and Morse (1963).
199. Simon (1981, 1996). His more scholarly book on the topic is Simon (1977).
200. Dryzek (2005, p. 53).
201. Dryzek (2005, p. 59).
202. Simon (1996, p. 589).
203. Dryzek (2005, p. 47). More recent Marxism-inspired debates on Malthusianism and environmental issues are discussed in, among other places, the left-wing academic journal *Organization & Environment* (vol. 11 (4), 1998) and Saito (2016). For left-wing and pro-growth critique of such writings, see Boisvert (2014); Phillips (2015).
204. Chase (1991, pp. 57–58).
205. Fong (2017).
206. Dryzek (2005, p. 48). See also Beck and Kolankiewicz (2000); Mock (2013).
207. See, among others, Hartmann (1999).
208. Dryzek (2005, p. 47).
209. The traditional theoretical opposition to Malthusianism by Catholic intellectuals was arguably more sophisticated than many recent writings would suggest. See, among others, Ryan (1911).
210. Anonymous (2017b). Interestingly, many prominent Catholic writers expressed nuanced positions on the subject in the early nineteenth century. See Vallin (1983).
211. See Bowden (1985); Priest (2014). McKelvey spent thirty-seven years at the USGS before being fired by the Carter administration because of his optimistic stance on the availability of natural resources.
212. RFF's (http://www.rff.org/) stance was often not optimistic when discussing the polluting impact of economic activities. The think tank's output became more pessimistic regarding resource availability in the mid-1970s and was later re-oriented towards policy solutions to climate change. See, among others, Bradley Jr (2016).
213. For a critical perspective that attempts to quantify their impact, see Jacques *et al.* (2008).
214. These organizations are generally affiliated with the Atlas Network which maintains a directory of links to their websites https://www.atlasnetwork.org/partners/global-directory.
215. For a longer list that includes religious, distributive and international trade arguments, see Spengler (1933, p. 439).
216. Cannan (1922/1914, Ch. IV)
217. Say (1821).
218. George (1879, Book II, Ch. 4).
219. Anonymous (1889, p. 287). A rebuttal was later published by a prominent Malthusian in the same outlet. See Drysdale (1889).
220. Bauer (1991, p. 26).
221. Ridley (2010, p. 193).
222. Jacobs (1969, pp. 118–9).
223. Hutchinson (1967, pp. 100–104) discusses several past writings on this subject.

224. Barnett and Morse (1963, pp. 7–8).
225. Jacobs (1969, p. 117). Among the other technological optimists at the time was the RAND Corporation, whose authors advocated widespread ocean farming and human settlement. See Gardner (2010, pp. 10–11).
226. See Spencer (1857) and its reprint Spencer (1891, pp. 8–62).
227. George (1879, Book II, Ch. 4).
228. Atkinson (1890/1889, p. 160).
229. Atkinson (1890/1889, p. 8).
230. Atkinson (1890/1889, p. 158). Of course, nitrogen synthesis from the atmosphere would soon be a reality. For a more detailed history, see Smil (2001).
231. Anderson (1803, pp. 127–137, 290–299, 368–382, 465–473).
232. Engels (1844).
233. See, among others, Grigg (1979).
234. Lenin (1901).
235. Cannan (1922/1914, Ch. IV).
236. Brandt (1945, citation on pp. 135–136).
237. Petty (1888/1682, p. 49)
238. Cannan (1922/1914, Ch. IV).
239. Zubrin (2012a, p. 24).
240. Machlup (1962, 143–167).
241. Everett (1823, p. 26).
242. Everett (1823, p. 28).
243. Engels (1844).
244. Barnett and Morse (1963, p. 236).
245. Ridley (2010, p. 270).
246. Ridley (2010, p. 271).
247. Johnson (2010).
248. Johnson (2010, p. 52).
249. Johnson (2010, pp. 30–31).
250. Johnson (2010, pp. 30–31).
251. For a more detailed historical perspective on the limits of the concept, see Sayre (2008).
252. George (1879, Book II, Ch. 3).
253. Modern research has since established that indigenous populations in the Americas were once much more numerous than George believed to be the case at the time. For example, O'Fallon and Fehren-Schmitz established that stable pre-contact populations of several tens of millions suffered a bottleneck that reduced the maternal gene pool by at least 50%. See O'Fallon and Fehren-Schmit (2011). This new information does not affect the validity of George's argument.
254. George (1879, Book II, Ch. 3).
255. George (1879, Book II, Ch. 3).
256. Jacobs (1969, p. 118).
257. Kropotkin (1912/1898, Ch. II).
258. Kropotkin (1912/1898, Ch. II).
259. Zimmermann (1933, p. 3).

260. Zimmermann (1933, pp. 814–815).
261. Clark (1973, p. 7).
262. Simon and Kahn (1984, p. 45). For more on the neglected work of Herman Kahn on this topic, see Dragos Aligica (2007).
263. Kasun (1999/1988, p. 31).
264. Taylor (2013, p. 34).
265. Cannan (1922/1914, Ch. IV).
266. Landsberg (1964, pp. 11–12).
267. Simon (1996, Epilogue).
268. Simon (1996, Ch. 1).
269. Simon (2001, p. 6).
270. Heilbroner (1974, p. 77).
271. For a more detailed introduction to the topic, see, among others, Meek (1971/1953); Perelman (1979); Holden and Levy (1993). For a more concise overview, see Gimenez, Martha E. 1973. 'Befolkningsproblemet: Marx kontra Malthus.' Den Ny Verden (December): 74–88. ('The population issue: Marx vs Malthus,' Journal of the Institute of Development Research; Copenhagen, Denmark) Non-paginated English translation available at https://www.colorado.edu/Sociology/gimenez/work/popissue.html.
272. Sanger (1922, Ch. VII).
273. Weissman (1971, p. ix). See also, among others, Canadian Party of Labour (1973).
274. Simon (1996, Introduction).
275. Simon (1990, pp. 169–170).
276. Bauer (1998, p. 67).
277. Kaysen (1972, p. 663).
278. Simon (1995, pp. 24–25).
279. Barnett and Morse (1963, pp. 247–248).
280. Jacobs (1969, p. 120).

Chapter 3 Contradictory forecasts: an assessment

281. For both pessimistic and optimistic predictions made in the last few decades, see, among others, the Julian Simon-inspired blog Master Resource (masterresource.org). On past predictions and forecasts on crude oil production, see, among others, Bowden (1985); Porter (1995); Smil (1998); Priest (2014).
282. Simon (2001, p. 6).
283. Jevons (1866/1865, Ch. 8).
284. Jevons (1866/1865, Ch. 1).
285. Lardner (1840, p. 4).
286. Lardner (1840, p. 8).
287. Lardner (1840, p. 8).
288. Lardner (1840, pp. 8–9).
289. Lardner (1840, p. 9).
290. Isaacson (1912, p. xxiii).
291. Isaacson (1912, p. xxvi).

292. East (1928/1923, pp. 346–7).
293. East (1928/1923, pp. 346–7).
294. Burch and Pendell (1947, p. 2).
295. Osborn Jr (1948, p. vii).
296. Osborn Jr (1948, p. 201).
297. Osborn Jr (1948, p. 5).
298. Osborn Jr (1948, p. ix).
299. Osborn Jr (1948, p. 43).
300. Vogt (1948, p. xiii).
301. Vogt (1948, p. 72).
302. Vogt (1948, p. 68).
303. PWFS (1967, p. 44).
304. Ehrlich (1968, p. xi).
305. Ehrlich (1969).
306. Ehrlich and Ehrlich (1997).
307. See especially Ehrlich and Ehrlich (2013).
308. Haberman (2015).
309. Huffington Post (2014).
310. Editors of The Ecologist (1972, p. 3).
311. Editors of The Ecologist (1972, p. 3).
312. For compilations of catastrophic energy and environmental predictions from the 1960s to the 1980s, see, among others, Epstein (2014, Ch. 1), Gardner (2010, pp. 7–57, 118–143, 161–190, 222–236) and Bradley Jr (2017). For a contemporary view of the calamity industry between 1962 (the year Silent Spring was published) and the early 1970s see Maddox (1972).
313. Heilbroner (1974, pp. 19–20).
314. Everett (1823, p. 40).
315. Atkinson (1890/1889, p. 160).
316. Anonymous (1889, p. 287).
317. Wright (1904, pp. 808–809).
318. Mather (1944, p. 12).
319. Mather (1944, p. 15).
320. Mather (1944, p. 18).
321. Mather (1944, p. 18).
322. Mather (1944, p. 29).
323. Mather (1944, quote from the book dust-jacket cover).
324. Simon (1994).
325. Simon (1995, p. 642). Simon was right, as Easterbrook (2003) showed.
326. For much more comprehensive reviews of the available data, see

- World Bank, World Development Indicators http://databank.worldbank.org/data/reports.aspx?source=world-development-indicators;
- Gapminder https://www.gapminder.org/;
- Our World in Data https://ourworldindata.org/;
- Human Progress http://humanprogress.org/.

Recent optimistic books build around this type of data include Norberg (2016); Pinker (2018c); Rosling *et al.* (2018); Easterbrook (2018). Pinker's environmental chapter is for the most part available in Pinker (2018a). For earlier synthesis that shared the perspective presented in this section, see Simon (1996); Lomborg (2001); Goklany (2007); Ridley (2010). More cautious recent additions include Dobbs *et al.* (2011, p. 26) and Blomqvist (2015b). For a pessimistic perspective, see the various *State of the World* reports published by the WorldWatch Institute http://www.worldwatch.org/bookstore/state-of-the-world. We address our main misgivings with alleged threats to sustainability blamed on economic development in Chapter 5.
327. Floud *et al.* (2011, p. 5).
328. Easterbrook (2003, p. 46).
329. Easterbrook (2003, pp. 46–47).
330. Roser and Ortiz-Ospina (2017/2013).
331. Roser and Ortiz-Ospina (2018). See also Human Progress, http://humanprogress.org/.
332. Roser (2017).
333. Ellis (2012). For a more detailed analysis, see Ellis *et al.* (2013).
334. For a synthesis of recent developments, see, among others, Tupy (2018a).
335. Hajkowicz (2015, pp. 43–44).
336. Hajkowicz (2015, p. 59).
337. Rosling (2013).
338. Ausubel (2015).
339. Hajkowicz (2015, p. 178).
340. Bailey (2018a).
341. Mann (2018b).
342. Pinker (2018b).
343. Epstein (2014, p. 25).
344. Toynbee (1913/1884, pp. 89–90). Toynbee is frequently mistaken for his nephew, the universal historian Arnold Joseph Toynbee (1889–1975).
345. Atkinson (1890/1889, p. 156).
346. Wolfe (1928, pp. 530–531).
347. Brown (1954, p. 5).
348. Bates (1962/1955, pp. xi-xii).
349. Heilbroner (1974, pp. 20–21).
350. McKibben (1998a, pp. 74–75).

Chapter 4 Market processes

351. Clark (1973, p. 63).
352. Ritchie (2017).
353. Mann (2018a).
354. For a short description of the problem, see Bonniel (2016). For a short essay on the benefits of the transition from horse power to horsepower (cars, trucks), see Desrochers (2015).

355. Goklany (2007).
356. This is not to say, of course, that the total share of employment or value creation of the manufacturing sector has not diminished. For a brief introduction to the issue in the United States and several related papers, see the Cato Institute webpage 'Manufacturing and industrial policy' https://www.cato.org/research/manufacturing-industrial. For recent numbers on manufacturing output in the USA, see US Bureau of Labor Statistics, Manufacturing Sector: Real Output [OUTMS], retrieved from FRED, Federal Reserve Bank of St. Louis, February 21, 2018 https://fred.stlouisfed.org/series/OUTMS.
357. For an accessible introduction and several links to the topic, see Bühner (2012).
358. For an overview and different perspectives on the topic, see, among others, UNEP IRP (2011); Blomqvist (2015b); Ward *et al.* (2016).
359. Blomqvist (2015b).
360. Petroski (1992, p. 22).
361. Carter (1939, p. 143).
362. See, among others, Ausubel (1998) and Desrochers (2010). Many other illustrations can also be found in Bryce (2014) and Smil (2017). For a brief historical overview of modern work and controversies surrounding dematerialization, see, among others, Magee and Devezas (2017).
363. Blomqvist (2016).
364. Roser and Ritchie (2017, 2018b).
365. Ausubel (2015).
366. Ausubel (1998).
367. BTI (2016).
368. Barnett and Morse (1963, p. 10).
369. Barnett and Morse (1963, p. 10).
370. Ward *et al.* (2016).
371. Bernstam (1990, p. 334).
372. Bernstam's argument is actually more complex and builds on the theory of market socialism of the Hungarian economist Janos Kornai who argued that socialist planners regularly and routinely plowed resources into failing enterprises even when they exceeded their budgets. This 'soft budget constraint' stood in sharp contrast to the 'hard' constraint of bankruptcy in market economies.
373. Bernstam (1990, p. 333).
374. See Desrochers and Leppälä (2010), Desrochers (2012) and Desrochers and Szurmak (2017), among others. For a critical look at the overall significance of the phenomenon, see Haas *et al.* (2015). We disagree with their assessment as we do not consider fuel inputs for the production of energy (e.g. clean-burning natural gas; properly handled ash from coal combustion) and high-volume and low-value residuals that are disposed of properly (e.g. waste rock, tailings, fluids injected deep into the ground between impermeable layers of rocks) as environmentally problematic.
375. Anonymous (1887).
376. Price (1886, p. 464).
377. Lamborn (1904, p. 16).
378. Talbot (1920, pp. 17–18).
379. Kershaw (1928, p. vii).

380. Miall (1931, p. iii).
381. Grimshaw (1889, pp. 192–193). For a compilation of some of his writings, see http://onlinebooks.library.upenn.edu/webbin/book/lookupname?key=Grimshaw%2c%20Robert%2c%201850-.
382. For a much more detailed discussion of this case, see Desrochers and Szurmak (2017).
383. Desrochers and Haight (2014).
384. Desrochers (2010, 2012).
385. Marx (1906/1894, pp. 95–96 and pp. 120–121).
386. Smil (2017). There is an in-depth treatment in Ch. 5: 'Fossil fuels, primary electricity, and renewables' (pp. 225–293) and Ch. 6: 'Fossil-fueled civilization' (pp. 295–384).
387. Smil (2017, p. 225).
388. Smil (2017, p. 226).
389. Smil (2017, p. 230). Also see the renewables section on pp. 284–289.
390. See, among others, BP (2017).
391. Simon (1995, p. 27).
392. See, among others, Smil (2014a) and Ausubel (2000).
393. In the same basic way that charcoal is made out of wood, (metallurgical) coke is a solid fuel made by heating coal in the absence of air so that the volatile components are driven off.
394. For a thorough and up-to-date discussion see Smil (2017, Ch. 5).
395. Jevons (1866/1865, Ch. Vlll).
396. Wrigley (1988, p. 5).
397. Wayland (1870/1838, pp. 66–67).
398. Hawke (1988, p. 195).
399. Jones (1859, pp. 70–71).
400. Wayland (1870/1838, p. 67).
401. Keir (1926, p. 123).
402. Jevons (1866/1865, Ch. Vlll).
403. Jevons (1866/1865, Ch. Vlll).
404. Desrochers and Shimizu (2012a).
405. Smil (2017, p. 230).
406. Detailed – but still incomplete, due to a lack of lifecycle data – calculations of the (rising) costs of establishing wind turbine electrical generation are presented by Blanco (2009). Blanco noted: 'Wind energy is a capital-intensive technology', with the need for various materials such as specific metal alloys driving the costs and the fabrication complexities.
407. A calculation of the manufacture energetics for standard solar cells is given in 'Solar panels: a true carbon-free source of energy?' 2012. Energy, Technology & Policy. https://webberenergyblog.wordpress.com/2012/04/15/solar-panels-a-true-carbon-free-source-of-energy/. Also see Smil (2017, pp. 286–288) for current peak power and capacity factor figures for photovoltaics.
408. Adapted from Voosen (2018).

409. More detailed yet accessible discussions of the topic of the historical rise of fossil fuels, written in the spirit of this book, can be found in Epstein (2014); and Moore and White (2016).

410. Smil (2014c).

411. Smil (2014c).

412. Sterman *et al.* (2018).

413. Smil (2014c).

414. Google.org, RE<C Initiative, https://www.google.org/rec.html. See also Koningstein and Fork (2014).

415. See, among others, Ausubel (2007); Bryce (2010); Morriss *et al.* (2011).

416. Smil (2008, p. 84).

417. For more detailed discussions, see Desrochers and Shimizu (2016), BP (2017) and Ritchie and Roser (2018a).

418. Smil (2014b, p. 55).

419. Huber and Mills (2005, pp. 173–174).

420. For an accessible introduction to the topic, see, among others, Moore and White (2016).

421. Adelman (1993, p. xi).

422. For a concise introduction to the concept, see Hanania *et al.* (2015).

423. Fieldner (1925, p. 14).

424. Ausubel (1998).

425. For relevant analysis of Standard Oil see Chandler (1994/1990), especially pp. 24–25 for the rationale behind the creation of the Standard Oil Trust. A more critical collection of papers is in the special issue 'The centennial of the Standard Oil of New Jersey decision.' Review of Industrial Organization 38 (3) (May 2011).

426. Bacon and Hamor (1916, p. 260).

427. The first significant popular indictment of Standard Oil came from Lloyd (1881). The better known one is Tarbell (1904). A detailed government report rather hostile to the claims of Standard Oil is USBC (1907). See also Scherer (2011).

428. See, among others, McGee (1958); Armentano (1972); Reed (1980) and Epstein (2011).

429. USIC (1899, pp. 379–380).

430. USIC (1899, p. 372).

431. Armentano (1972, p. 70) and Epstein (2011, Part III) .

432. Spitz (1988).

433. Wrigley (1969, pp. 57–58).

434. McCollough and Check Jr (2010).

435. For a more detailed discussion and some additional references on these products, see Desrochers and Shimizu (2012a).

436. This section was based on Desrochers (2009), to where the reader is referred for additional technical details and references.

437. Coal gasification products varied greatly, both in terms of substance and volume, depending on the types of coal and technology used, with an increased quantity of gas obtained at the expense of its (and other residuals') quality.

438. Clegg (1841, p. 5).

439. Playfair (1852).
440. Talbot (1920, pp. 14–15).
441. Talbot (1920, p. 15).
442. Findlay (1917, pp. 26–29); see also Barger (1951, pp. 100–111).
443. Olson (1971, p. 132).
444. A rubbery substance derived from the latex of various tropical trees. It was used as an electrical insulator, waterproofing compound, and for making golf balls.
445. Meldola (1905, p. 71).
446. Lunge (1887, p. 12).
447. Desrochers (2008).
448. Although the process only became economically successful a decade later, following the award of another patent in 1842.
449. Meldola (1905).
450. Dodd (1852).
451. Crory (1876, p. 38).
452. For more detailed discussion of the development of by-products in the early days of the American petroleum industry, see Williamson and Daum (1959, Ch. 10). Despite some advantages (most notably its lower price), kerosene was more dangerous to use than whale oil, an issue first made worse by the (arguably widespread) adulteration of kerosene with naphtha and benzene, residual products of distillation for which there were originally no lucrative markets. It was these problems that inspired John Rockefeller to call his company Standard Oil.
453. Estall and Buchanan (1973, p. 221).
454. Estall and Buchanan (1973, pp. 221–222).
455. Leffler (2008, p. 1).
456. Copp and Zanella (1993, p. 147).
457. In this context, air–gas machines refer to gas machines used to illuminate mills, factories, public institutions of all kinds and large mansions. Crude naphtha also found a market for gas illumination at the time.
458. Chernow (1998, p. 181).
459. Copp and Zanella (1993, p. 156).
460. Perry (1908, pp. 73–74). Paraffin wax was originally created from Scottish shale and later on was made from coal oil. Arguably the key figure in the development of paraffin out of petroleum residuals was the chemical engineer and inventor Herman Frasch (1851–1914) who would then go on to, among other things, the development of processes to remove sulphur from low-quality crudes in Ohio and Ontario (Canada), turning them into much more valuable commodities. For short biographical treatments see 'Frasch, Herman.' Encyclopedia of Cleveland History https://case.edu/ech/articles/f/frasch-herman/ and 'Frasch, Herman (1851–1914)' World of Earth Science http://www.encyclopedia.com. For a more detailed discussion of Frasch's contribution to petroleum refining, see Scherer (2011). A detailed biographical treatment of Frasch's life is Sutton (1984).
461. For additional details, see Williamson and Daum (1959, pp. 249–250).
462. Williamson and Daum (1959, p. 249).
463. Williamson and Daum (1959, p. 250).

464. This analysis of by-product development at the Standard Oil Company first appeared as Montague (1903, pp. 323–324). It was later reprinted as part of Montague (1904).
465. Carlson (1956, p. 64).
466. Talbot (1920, pp. 16–17). More detail can be found in Copp and Zanella (1993), Ch. 6: 'Gasoline: From waste product to fuel.'
467. Talbot (1920, pp. 15–16).
468. Estall and Buchanan (1973, p. 222).
469. Lox (1992).
470. Smith *et al.* (1961, p. 309).
471. For other concise discussions of this issue with additional references, see Goklany (2015); Bast and Ferrara (2018).
472. For detailed discussion of these benefits, see Desrochers and Shimizu (2012b).
473. Wrigley (1969, p. 58).
474. See Desrochers (2015); and Morris (2007).
475. Roser and Ritchie (2018a).
476. Ritchie and Roser (2018b).
477. Coal was the first significant feedstock but was later displaced by petroleum and natural gas.
478. Idso (2013). See also Goklany (2015). Another line of evidence supporting this perspective can be found in NASA/Goddard Space Flight Center (2016).
479. Zaichun *et al.* (2016).
480. For recent work on and interesting visual illustrations of past deforestation in Europe, see Kauppi *et al.* (2018) and the results of the 'Deforesting Europe: A pollen-based reconstruction of Holocene land cover change' project https://www.plymouth.ac.uk/research/centre-for-research-in-environment-society/deforesting-europe-a-pollen-based-reconstruction-of-holocene-land-cover-change. For a broader outlook, see World Bank – Forests http://www.worldbank.org/en/topic/forests and UN FAO – Forestry http://www.fao.org/forestry/en/.

Chapter 5 Carbon dioxide emissions as the environmental crisis of last resort

481. Jacobs (2012).
482. Jarrett (2011, Introduction; pp. viii–ix).
483. Boulding (1970, pp. 157–170).
484. Spengler (1966, p. 10). Interestingly, by this time he did not believe that resource scarcity would ever be a meaningful economic issue.
485. Kneese (1970).
486. Shelesnyak (1969, p. 141).
487. Ehrlich *et al.* (1977, p. 955). For an accessible summary of the Ehrlichs' stance on this issue, written two decades ago, see Ehrlich and Ehrlich (1997).
488. McKibben (1998b).
489. Caradonna *et al.* (2015).
490. Caradonna *et al.* (2015).

491. UNEP IRP (2016, p. 14).
492. Including ammonia, formaldehyde, polyester fibre, and styrene, along with hardware and energy technologies such as transistors, laser diodes, crude oil, photovoltaics, and wind energy.
493. Chu (2017). The published version of the study is Magee and Devezas (2017). The original formulation of Jevons was as follows: 'It is wholly a confusion of ideas to suppose that the economical use of fuel is equivalent to a diminished consumption. The very contrary is the truth.' Jevons (1866/1865, Ch. 7). Jevons derived his insight from economic reasoning that explained how labour-saving technologies always end up creating more employment in other lines of work. For a more detailed discussion of Jevons' paradox from an environmentalist perspective, see Polimeni *et al.* (2008).
494. See, for instance, Ward *et al.* (2016).
495. UNEP (2016, p. 20).
496. UNEP (2016, p. 35).
497. Curran and de Sherbinin (2004).
498. UNEP (2016, p. 5).
499. Ehrlich (1968).
500. Ehrlich and Ehrlich (1970). Reprint in Holdren and Ehrlich (1971a, pp. 157–159; quote on pp. 157–158).
501. Holdren *et al.* (1973, p. 279).
502. Tinbergen *et al.* (1976, p. 90). Quotes taken from Laframboise (2009).
503. Ehrlich *et al.* (1977, p. 954).
504. Daily and Ehrlich (1992, pp. 762–763).
505. Ehrlich and Ehrlich (2008).
506. Gore (1992, p. xxi).
507. Ehrlich and Ehrlich (2008).
508. Ehrlich and Harte (2015, pp. 904 and 905).
509. UNEP (2016, p. 20).
510. Royal Society (2012, p. 75).
511. Vogt (1948, p. 14).
512. Malin (1949, p. 243).
513. Broader histories of the concept, its problems, current status and uses in academia, along with more general discussions of the impact of population growth on environmental quality, can be found in, among others, Preston (1996); Chertow (2001); Cohen (2010); Grossman (2012); UNEP (2016, p. 14).
514. Ehrlich and Holdren (1971).
515. Ehrlich and Holdren (1971, p. 1212).
516. Ehrlich and Ehrlich (2008).
517. Ward *et al.* (2016).
518. Angus and Butler (2011, p. 48).
519. Angus and Butler (2011). Discussion of IPAT limitations on pp. 47–49.
520. Hynes (1993, p. 23).
521. Hynes (1993, p. 23).
522. Meadows (1995).

523. Angus and Butler (2011, p. 38). Angus and Butler give a more detailed illustration of their argument by invoking the 'two accounts' model of Allan Schnaiberg in which one set of figures is given as the explanation for another. The work they use for their analysis is Schnaiberg (1980). Schnaiberg, Angus and Butler observe that the causes for these 'expansions' and 'degradations' of economic activities and environmental assets exist, but they are complex, nuanced and socio-economic in nature.
524. Angus and Butler (2011, pp. 47–48).
525. Angus and Butler (2011, pp. 40–41), from Satterthwaite (2009). The latter article offers tables showing the lack of alignment between population growth in various parts of the world and those areas' carbon emissions.
526. Satterthwaite (2009, p. 550).
527. Satterthwaite (2009, p. 550).
528. See, among others, Chertow (2001); Waggoner and Ausubel (2002).
529. For more detailed critiques of the ecological footprint framework – from various theoretical perspectives – see Gordon and Richardson (1998); van den Bergh and Verbruggen (1999); Deutsch *et al.* (2000); Jørgensen *et al.* (2002); Fiala (2008); Wiedmann and Barrett (2010); Blomqvist *et al.* (2013); Blomqvist (2015a).
530. The EF consists of six land categories: cropland, grazing land, forest land, fishing ground, energy footprint and built-up land.
531. Wackernagel and Rees (1996).
532. See the website of the Footprint Network www.footprintnetwork.org.
533. See the relevant WWF webpage at http://wwf.panda.org/about_our_earth/all_publications/living_planet_report_timeline/.
534. See the Overshoot Day website https://www.overshootday.org/.
535. From the Overshoot Day website https://www.overshootday.org/.
536. McDonald (2015).
537. WWF (2016).
538. Rees (2002).
539. WWF (2016).
540. Blomqvist *et al.* (2013).
541. Eschenbach (2010).
542. For quantitative estimates and rankings demonstrating the poor state of the environment in less advanced economies, see the results of the Environmental Performance Index https://epi.envirocenter.yale.edu/ based on 24 performance indicators across ten issue categories covering environmental health and ecosystem vitality, including the quality of air, water, forest cover, fisheries, agricultural lands, and natural habitats in 180 countries.
543. For a more detailed presentation of the framework, later revisions and updates along with responses to critics, see the website of the Stockholm Resilience Centre http://www.stockholmresilience.org/research/planetary-boundaries.html. An influential popularization of the PBF with additional social justice considerations is Oxfam senior researcher Kate Raworth's 'Doughnut Economics' https://www.kateraworth.com/doughnut/.
544. Rockström *et al.* (2009a). A shorter version was published as Rockström *et al.* (2009b).

545. Steffen *et al.* (2015).
546. Rockström *et al.* (2009b).
547. Rockström *et al.* (2009a).
548. Rockström *et al.* (2009a).
549. Steffen *et al.* (2015).
550. A 'safe minimum standards' approach to environmental protection supplements traditional cost–benefit analysis by placing greater emphasis on the protection of the environment wherever thresholds of irreversible damage are said to be threatening. See, among others, Crowards (1998). The precautionary principle is discussed in more detail in Section 5.5. The 'tolerable windows approach' is a scheme for integrated assessment of climate change that is based on a set of guardrails which refer to various climate-related attributes. See Petschel-Held *et al.* (1999).
551. O'Neill *et al.* (2018).
552. Steffen *et al.* (2011).
553. See, among others, DeFries *et al.* (2012). For a more detailed critical analysis, see Nordhaus *et al.* (2012b); Ellis (2012); Brook *et al.* (2013). For broad introductions to the PBF debate and additional web links, see Heffernan (2009); Nordhaus *et al.* (2012a); Lalasz (2013); Revkin (2015); and Rockström and his colleagues' replies and rejoinders at http://www.stockholmresilience.org/research/research-news/2012--07--02-addressing-some-key-misconceptions.html.
554. Nordhaus *et al.* (2012a).
555. Ellis (2012).
556. Nordhaus *et al.* (2012a).
557. Nordhaus *et al.* (2012a).
558. Brook *et al.* (2013, p. 396).
559. Nordhaus *et al.* (2012a).
560. Bailey (2018b). See the Environmental Performance Index https://epi.envirocenter.yale.edu/ for a ranking of these countries.
561. Angus and Butler (2011, pp. 66–67).
562. For more detailed yet accessible introductions to – and critical perspectives on – climate modeling, see Ball (2014, pp. 82–131); Curry (2017).
563. Stott (2007).
564. See, among others, Weart (2018), Bailey (1994), Simon (1996, Ch. 18), Watts (2014), and Lewin (2017).
565. For an accessible and more detailed overview of many historical and technical issues discussed in this section, see Mann (2018c, Ch. 7). Another scare that would warrant further attention, but is not discussed in this book, is acid rain. See Darwall (2017b). Bernie Lewin discusses this and other issues, such as supersonic transportation and the ozone hole controversy, that also shaped greenhouse gas control initiatives Lewin (2017). Our editorial choice was based on a desire to focus on past controversies with a more direct Malthusian angle.
566. 'Climate' refers to the average pattern of weather for a particular place over a significant period of time, at a minimum several decades. See, among others, IPCC (2017, Sec. 1.2.2).

567. 'Weather' describes atmospheric conditions (rainfall, temperature, wind speed, for example) at a particular place and time.
568. Aristotle (a). For a broader historical perspective, see, among others, Le Roy Ladurie (1971).
569. Extreme weather is part of weather, with or without the effects of climate change. These events include torrential rains and the resulting floods, droughts, hurricanes, tornadoes, unseasonable warmth and cold.
570. von Storch and Stehr (2006); Lewin (2017).
571. Laframboise (2013).
572. Ruddiman (2003).
573. Ferrill (2011).
574. See, among others, Butt *et al.* (2011).
575. See Williams (2003).
576. For an overview of the most influential texts on both sides of the debate published between the 1860s and the 1930s, see Whitaker (1940).
577. Avery (2000, p. 201).
578. Oosthoek (1998).
579. The quote is from 'Atrahasis and Cypria (1).' The Melammu Project. The Heritage of Mesopotamia and the Ancient Near East http://www.aakkl.helsinki.fi/melammu/database/gen_html/a0001154.php.
580. Plato (Approximately 360 BC).
581. For concise discussions of the issue and additional references, see Cunfer (2004) and Buonanduci (2009).
582. Jacks and Whyte (1939).
583. Jacks and Whyte (1939, p. 21).
584. Vogt (1948, pp. 110 and 284).
585. Vogt (1948, p. 33).
586. Chandrasekhar (1956/1954, p. 215).
587. Brandt (1950, pp. 88–90).
588. Hanson (1949, p. 369).
589. Hanson (1949, p. 14).
590. Hanson (1949, p. 135).
591. Hanson (1949, p. 12).
592. Hanson (1949, p. 12).
593. Hanson (1949, p. 13).
594. Hanson (1949, p. 370).
595. Hanson (1949, p. 14).
596. Hanson (1949, p. 371).
597. Hanson (1949, p. 372).
598. Hanson (1949, p. 272).
599. Hanson (2003, pp. 44–49).
600. Kelley (1949, p. 19).
601. Kelley (1949, p. 19).
602. For a more detailed discussion of Bennett's article refer to Desrochers and Geloso (2016b).

603. Kelley (1949, p. 19).
604. Parts of this section are adapted from Desrochers and Hoffbauer (2009).
605. See, among others, USGARP (1975); Lewin (2017). For a more detailed discussion of how cooling came to dominate the climate policy agenda in the 1970s, see Lewin (2017). An attempt to downplay the importance of global cooling in the scientific literature is Peterson *et al.* (2008). As detailed below, other writers and more recently sceptical bloggers have compiled various lists of pro-cooling academic and popular pieces published at the time. In our assessment there was indeed more debate in the 1970s over the factors that might influence climate change and future climate trends than was the case in later decades. Whether or not this owes more to later 'certainties' about catastrophic warming or to organized bureaucratic and political efforts to promote this perspective remains open to debate in our opinion.
606. Bryson (1968). Reprint in Holdren and Ehrlich (1971a, pp. 78–84).
607. Clark Jr (1974, p. 117).
608. Compilations of academic articles and quotations from climate scientists in the popular press can be found in Bray (1991), Goddard (2013), Watts (2013), and Bradley Jr (2008, 2015). The CIA report is CIA (1974).
609. Apart from the links listed in the previous note, see also PopularTechnology.net (2013).
610. Ponte (1976, p. xiv).
611. Ponte (1976, p. xvi).
612. Dando (1980, p. 104).
613. Ehrlich *et al.* (1977, p. 686).
614. Ehrlich and Ehrlich (1996, p. 34).
615. Simon (1995, p. 646).
616. For a balanced introduction to some of the key events and main American actors involved in this debate, see Allitt (2014).
617. Lindzen (2016). For instance, CO_2 emissions were relegated to a minor appendix in the Report of the Environmental Pollution Panel (EPP, 1965). For an alarmist's take on the significance of this report, see Nuccitelli (2015).
618. Bryson (1968).
619. Clark (1973, pp. 10–11).
620. Plimer (2015, p. 12).
621. Lindzen (2016, p. 1).
622. Lindzen (2016, p. 1).
623. Boehmer-Christiansen (1997). See also Hart (2015, Ch. 5).
624. Weart (2018, The public and climate change).
625. Weart (2018, The public and climate change).
626. Weart (2018, The public and climate change).
627. For a broader perspective on how the environmentalist and radical leftist agenda merged long ago, see Bailey (1994, Ch. 1).
628. Klein (2014, p. 4).
629. From IPCC, Working Group II: Impacts, Adaptation and Vulnerability http://www.ipcc.ch/ipccreports/tar/wg2/index.php?idp=22. Official or mainstream accounts

of how carbon dioxide emissions and global warming concerns came to dominate environmental policymaking and popular debate can be found in 'IPCC – History' http://www.ipcc.ch/organization/organization_history.shtml; Bolin (2007). Critical histories include Darwall (2014); Lindzen (2016); Darwall (2017c); Lewin (2017); Booker (2018).

630. For a debunking of this claim, see, among others, Reiter (2008). For a discussion of this and other such cases, see Booker (2018).

631. See, among countless others, Relman *et al.* (2008); Harte and Harte (2008).

632. See, among others, the various publications of the IPCC http://www.ipcc.ch/publications_and_data/publications_and_data_reports.shtml and NASA's Global Climate Change webpage https://climate.nasa.gov/.

633. Royal Society (2012, p. 78).

634. See, among others, Mann (2013).

635. Royal Society (2012, p. 78).

636. Hughes (2017). On the magnitude of the challenge, see Smil (2006, p. 21).

637. See, among others, the various publications of the Nongovernmental International Panel on Climate Change http://climatechangereconsidered.org/about-the-nipcc/ and of the Global Warming Policy Foundation https://www.thegwpf.org/, Moran (2015) and Hart (2015).

638. Plimer (2015, pp. 10–25).

639. Curry (2015). See also Curry (2017).

640. For the mainstream view, see the reports prepared by the IPCC http://www.ipcc.ch/ and Weart (2018). For critical discussions of topics such as the nature of the scientific consensus on the issue, questionable climate modeling assumptions, the recent pause in global warming, the interglacial nature of our current climate along with the facts that contradictory evidence (for example, both dry and wet winters) is used to back climate alarmism, that carbon dioxide was once 20 times today's concentration and that numerous great ice ages began with much higher atmospheric concentrations of carbon dioxide than exist at present, see, among others, the various publications of the Nongovernmental International Panel on Climate Change http://climatechangereconsidered.org/about-the-nipcc/, Moran (2015); and Curry (2017). As energy analyst Vaclav Smil observes, the 'phenomenon itself is complex (the relation between the atmospheric concentration of greenhouse gases and the mean tropospheric temperature is nonlinear, and it is subject to many interferences and feedbacks), and any appraisals of future impacts are immensely complicated by two key uncertainties: because the future rate of greenhouse gas emissions is a function of many economic, social, and political variables, we can do no better than posit an uncomfortably wide range of plausible outcomes. And because the biospheric and economic impacts of higher temperatures will be both counteracted and potentiated by numerous natural and anthropogenic feedbacks, we cannot reliably quantify either the extent or the intensity of likely consequences.' Smil (2008, p. 175).

641. A history of the IUSIPP (now IUSSP) can be found on the organization's website at http://iussp.org/en/about/history.

642. Simon (1996, Ch. 30). Simon expanded on his view of global warming in Myers and Simon (1994, Ch. 5).

643. Simon (1996, Ch. 30).
644. Kasun (1999/1988, p. 49).
645. Ball (2014, p. 17). Ball explicitly states that targeting CO_2 emissions was done with the goal of achieving the pessimists' vision. As he put it: 'The claim of anthropogenic global warming (AGW) was the final strategy used to bully the world into accepting that the world was on a path of self-destruction.' Ball also describes global warming as a 'contrived problem,' but adds '[h]owever, most of those who know it is contrived still believe overpopulation is a problem.' In Ball (2018).
646. For a brief overview of UN activities in the areas of population growth and the environment at the time, see UN (2001).
647. For different takes on Strong's life and work, see Manitou Foundation (2017) and Foster (2015).
648. Foster (2015).
649. Grieger (2012).
650. UNEP.
651. UNEP.
652. Ball (2014, p. 45).
653. Hickman (2010). Strong discussed this incident, along with his position on economic development and population control, in a 1972 BBC interview https://www.youtube.com/watch?v=cwNJQiOnqay.
654. Strong (1972).
655. PMC (2011).
656. Strong (2009).
657. All quotes from Hickman (2010).
658. UNEP. This quote is found twice, in the phrase 'critical role in globalizing the environmental movement,' in the first paragraph of this UNEP webpage devoted to Strong.
659. Ward and Dubos (1972). This description highlighting the report's apparent consultative, consensual, global and authoritative nature is found on its title page: '[a]n unofficial report commissioned by the Secretary-General of the United Nations Conference on the Human Environment, prepared with the assistance of a 152-member committee of corresponding consultants in 58 countries.' For more detail as to how the manuscript came to be written and the contribution of each author, see Satterthwaite (2006).
660. Ball (2014, p. 41).
661. This memorable phrase appears to have had many creators. See Ball (2014, p. 42). Apart from Dubos, another claimant is David Brower, the founder of Friends of the Earth, sponsor of Paul Ehrlich's *Population Bomb* and the enthusiastic organizer of the first Earth Day. See Anonymous (2000) and Mann (2018a). The most likely originators of this phrase are the French sociologist and scholar Jacques Ellul and his friend Bernard Charbonneau, who reportedly invented it in the 1930s while working with local environmental associations in France. See the original quote from the publisher's summary of Ellul's collected environmental works entitled 'Penser globalement, agir localement.' The quote states: 'Précurseur, avec son ami Bernard Charbonneau, du mouvement écologique et initiateur des associations locales de défense

de l'environnement en Aquitaine, Jacques Ellul inventa, dans les années 1930, la formule: "Penser globalement, agir localement"." Source: Renaud-Bray Livres Numériques Divers. 2007. Publisher's summary, in Penser globalement, agir localement by Jacques Ellul http://www.renaud-bray.com/Livre_Numerique_Produit.aspx?id=1633426.
662. Ward and Dubos (1972, p. 66).
663. Anonymous (1973). 'Only One Earth' [Cover image text]. The UNESCO Courier (January). Retrieved from http://unesdoc.unesco.org/images/0007/000748/074879eo .pdf. Information about the image found on the bottom of [p. 3], number inferred from the pagination of the articles in the issue.
664. Ward (1973, p. 10).
665. The 1967 Swedish delegation to the UN was headed by Sverker Astrom and Borje Billner. See Grieger (2012).
666. The Weather Machine (1974) http://genome.ch.bbc.co.uk/0271db1075b544c299 6ebb81b38b9096. See also Booker (2018, pp. 6–7).
667. The account of Bolin's 1959 statement is in New York Times (1959).
668. Bolin (2007, p. 33).
669. Laframboise (2011).
670. Hart (2015). Italics in original.
671. Bolin (2007, pp. 183–185); Lomborg (2001); Holdren (2002); Bongaarts (2002). The replies were published as part of a broader set of pessimistic responses to Lomborg in the January 2002 issue of *Scientific American*. While not all links in this controversy are freely accessible, some are at https://www.scientificamerican.com/article/a-respons e-to-lomborgs-re/. A more detailed account of this controversy is by Ridley (2002)
672. Bongaarts (2002, p. 69).
673. Holdren (2002, p. 65).
674. Robert Watson interview in Wernick (2018).
675. Walker (2007).
676. Pachauri (2015).
677. UN.
678. UN. For more detail on Hansen's testimony and its significance, see the three-part series published in *Grist* twenty years later: Block (2008).
679. Fumento (1993, p. 362).
680. Quoted by Bell (2012). Original quote in the *Calgary Herald*, December 14, 1998.
681. Waterfield (2013).
682. Adams (2015).
683. Adams (2015).
684. Schneider and Mesirow (1977, p. 318). Ehrlich's influence on both Schneider and Mesirow (1977) was major. Ehrlich was the first expert thanked in their acknowledgements and the most cited author in their list of suggested readings. Interestingly, while Schneider and Mesirow's text was arguably more balanced than those of many other catastrophists at the time, their list of suggested readings is heavily skewed towards the pessimistic perspective.
685. Schneider and Mesirow (1977, p. 25). Italics in original.
686. Schneider and Mesirow (1977, p. 318).
687. Schneider and Mesirow (1977, p. 150).

688. Kanter (2009).
689. PRB (2014).
690. Influential studies and essays not discussed in this section include Murtaugh and Schlax (2009) and Cohen (2010). Although she would undoubtedly disagree with much of our take on the issue, sociologist Louise Carver admits: 'Proponents offer evidence both for and against the claim that current rates of population growth will make emissions abatement harder to achieve. The voices from either side of the debate are related to the well-trodden ground of Malthusian theory, around which each camp seems to be recasting their boundary lines.' In Carver (2010, p. 103).
691. McKibben (1998a, p. 118).
692. Crist *et al.* (2017, pp. 260 and 261). The authors further suggest that the preservation of Earth's genetic heritage and natural ecosystems be used as an economic development constraint.
693. Mora (2014).
694. Ripple *et al.* (2017).
695. Ehrlich and Ehrlich (2013).
696. One recent issue we did not address is the 'social cost of carbon'. This is because, while significant in terms of climate change policy, it is rarely discussed in the context of population growth and emission mitigations. One exception is Scovronicka *et al.* (2017).
697. Murtaugh and Schlax (2009); O'Neill *et al.* (2010).
698. Wynes and Nicholas (2017).
699. Satterthwaite (2009).
700. Royal Society (2012, p. 56).
701. Royal Society (2012, p. 8). See also Wilson (2013).
702. Royal Society (2012, p. 60).
703. Reuters (2009).
704. The effectiveness of China's one-child policy has been challenged by Whyte *et al.* (2015).
705. Conly (2015); Prystupa (2015).
706. Hansen (2009).
707. Dobbin (2014).
708. Goklany (2012); Darwall (2017a).
709. See, among others, Goklany (2014, 2015); Lomborg (2014).
710. Zubrin (2014).
711. Pinker (2018a).
712. Aitkenhead (2016).
713. Goklany and Morris (2011). The primary data are from The International Disaster Database: Centre for Research on the Epidemiology of Disasters, http://www.emdat.be.
714. Epstein (2014, p. 126).
715. Desrochers and Shimizu (2012b).
716. Hansen *et al.* (2008).
717. Because of technical issues and recalibrations by researchers, some satellite data show no rise in global average temperature while others do. Surface temperature data is also problematic for a number of reasons, ranging from the elimination of many

weather stations, to the effects of urban heat islands – localized warming around weather stations in cities. It is nonetheless fair to say that nothing suggests a major climate calamity since the 350 ppm mark was exceeded over a generation ago. See, among others, Driessen and Skates (2014); Knappenberger and Michaels (2014); Whitehouse (2015).
718. Simon (1996, Ch. 30).
719. Bryce (2014, p. 240).

Chapter 6 Blind, blinkered or bought?

720. Haberman (2015). Since Ehrlich is an entomologist by training, one would be tempted to assume that Haberman was implying Ehrlich defined his 'timetables for disaster' in caterpillar-equivalent years, or some similar absurdity, instead of giving him the courtesy of taking his plain words at face value.
721. Ehrlich and Harte (2018, expression and time scale on p. 1).
722. Ehrlich and Harte (2018, p. 1 of 5).
723. For a recent example, see Hajkowicz (2015, pp. 43–44).
724. Ehrlich and Harte (2018, p. 3 of 5).
725. Bailey (1994, p. 1).
726. As discussed in Chapters 2 and 3 of this book.
727. Mencken (1918, II: The war between the sexes – 13. Women and the emotions).
728. Bailey (1994, p. 16).
729. Since we know of no better alternative to science as far as a systematic and open method of building knowledge about the world is concerned, we are in no way advocating abandoning it. We are merely suggesting it is, as most things human, perfectible and flawed. Understanding its flaws may make it seem more limited, but perhaps more truly useful. For a thoughtful discussion of the human dimensions of such facets of science as objectivity see: Daston and Galison (2007).
730. Bailey (1994, p. 19).
731. Bailey (2015, p. xvii).
732. Bailey (2015, p. xvii).
733. Pinker (2018c).
734. Cosmides and Tooby (1997, Principle 5).
735. Cosmides and Tooby (1997, Principle 5).
736. Cosmides and Tooby (1997).
737. Bailey (1994, p. 22).
738. Among others mentioned in the upcoming sections are Irving L. Janis, as analyzed in Booker (2018); a 2018 synthesis of psychology research in Ceci and Williams (2018); original work on selective information processing in Taber and Lodge (2006); Gardner (2010) summarizing Philip Tetlock's findings; Simon (1999a) and Sowell (1995).
739. Jacobs (1992).
740. Ceci and Williams (2018, p. 299). Ceci and Williams have analyzed the free speech versus safe space clash, offering a number of psychological insights on the entrenchment of arguments. We have adapted these insights to our parallel conflict.

741. Ceci and Williams (2018, p. 300).
742. Ceci and Williams (2018). Ceci and Williams discuss the various cognitive biases on p. 300.
743. Originally presented in Kruger and Dunning (1999). This effect describes the fact that people who are unskilled at a task perceive their ability to be higher than it is because they are unable to recognize and put in perspective their lack of skill.
744. Ceci and Williams (2018, p. 300), describing the work of Fernbach *et al.* (2013).
745. Fernbach *et al.* (2013, p. 939).
746. Fernbach *et al.* (2013).
747. Several recent studies and popular articles summarize the situation with cognitive biases in the sciences. A good starting point is Ball (2015). Ball interviewed the University of Virginia psychologist Brian Nosek who founded the Open Science Framework (OSF) to combat biased research. Another good summary is Banta (2015).
748. First studied, among others, by Lord *et al.* (1979).
749. See Ziva Kunda's work on motivated scepticism in Kunda (1990).
750. Taber and Lodge (2006).
751. Taber and Lodge (2006, p. 755).
752. Taber and Lodge (2006, p. 756).
753. Taber and Lodge (2006, p. 757).
754. Taber and Lodge (2006, p. 765).
755. Taber and Lodge (2006, p. 757).
756. Taber and Lodge (2006, p. 757).
757. Taber and Lodge (2006, p. 767). The reference mentioned by Taber and Lodge is Luker (1984).
758. Ceci and Williams (2018, p. 300).
759. Ross and Ward (1996).
760. Ross and Ward (1996). Tenets expounded on pp. 110–111.
761. Ross and Ward (1996, p. 104).
762. Ross and Ward (1996, p. 104. Italics in the original).
763. Ross and Ward (1996, p. 111).
764. Ross and Ward (1996, p. 117).
765. Booker (2018, Sec. 5).
766. See, for instance, Hastorf and Cantril (1954). Cantril and Hastorf were Princeton psychology researchers. Cantril, in particular, is regarded as having made significant contributions to the psychology of perception and to public opinion research.
767. Janis (1972).
768. Booker (2018, p. 3 (17 of 123)).
769. Booker (2018, p. 3 (17 of 123)).
770. Booker (2018, p. 4 (18 of 123)).
771. Booker (2018). Booker started discussing climate change rhetoric as groupthink on p. 6 (20 of 123) in Section 5. He found that all principles of groupthink applied to the quality of reasoning within communities invested in the idea of anthropogenic climate change.
772. Ross and Ward (1996, p. 105).
773. Booker (2018, Sec. 5).

774. Le Bon has been maligned for his work's influence on autocratic figures over several decades, including Lenin, Hitler, and, most recently and perhaps less justifiably, given this figure's predilection for 280 characters as opposed to 280 pages, Donald Trump. See Zaretsky (2016).
775. Booker (2018, Sec. 5).
776. The falsification of theories as part of the scientific method goes back to the philosopher Karl Popper, his problem of demarcation, and his *Logic of Scientific Discovery* (1959), in which he specified a deductive procedure to falsify or corroborate theories. '[U]nlike traditional empiricists, Popper holds that experience cannot determine theory (i.e., we do not argue or infer from observation to theory), it rather delimits it: it shows which theories are false, not which theories are true.' Quote is from an excellent synopsis of Popper's work on scientific discovery in Thornton (2017). An overview of the scientific method contrasting the hypothetico-deductive verification method with Popper's falsification is Andersen and Hepburn (2016).
777. See, for example, Giere *et al.* (2006). The authors state, somewhat crossly: 'It is often said that science is distinguished by the use of something called the 'scientific method.' This claim is doubtful, at best, because the methods scientists actually use are as varied as the subjects they study.' Quote on p. 19.
778. Ball (2015, para 25), Ball's italics.
779. Ioannidis (2005).
780. Taber and Lodge (2006). See the Introduction for this discussion.
781. Ioannidis (2005, p. 697).
782. Nosek (2017).
783. Ball (2015, para. 3).
784. Ball (2015, para. 3).
785. Ball (2015, para. 3).
786. Ball (2015, para. 3).
787. Ioannidis (2005, discussion on pp. 700–701).
788. Ball (2015, para. 7). Also see Ioannidis *et al.* (2014).
789. Ball (2015, para. 7).
790. Ioannidis *et al.* (2014).
791. Oransky (2015).
792. Ball (2015, para. 12).
793. Ball (2015, para. 14).
794. Ioannidis (2005, p. 699).
795. An excellent source showing that Ioannidis' analysis was too statistically restrictive and made some exaggerated claims is Goodman and Greenland (2007). The bulk of the scientific community's discussion of Ioannidis' 2005 paper can be found on the first page of the online (not the PDF) version of Ioannidis (2005) at https://www.ncbi.nlm.nih.gov/pmc/articles/PMC1182327/?tool=pmcentrez&report=abstract.
796. A good example of the careful attention of the scholarly community to Ioannidis' claims is the curation of related work around his science bias research by the Hoover Institution economist and podcaster Dr. Russ Roberts: Roberts (2018). Look, in particular, at the 'Delve deeper' section.
797. Ioannidis (2005, p. 697).

798. Ioannidis (2005). The corollaries are found on pp. 697–698. The first four are: 1. The smaller the sample size of the studies conducted in scientific field, the less likely the research findings are to be true. 2. The smaller the effect sizes in a given field, the less likely the research findings are to be true. 3. The greater the number of tested relationships and the lesser their selection in a field, the less likely the research findings are to be true. 4. The greater the flexibility of study design, definitions, outcomes and analytical methods in a scientific field, the less likely the findings are to be true.
799. Ioannidis (2005, p. 698).
800. Ioannidis (2005, p. 698).
801. Goodman and Greenland (2007).
802. Goodman and Greenland (2007).
803. A reference to this paper, no longer available at BePress site, is Steven and Greenland (2007).
804. Goodman and Greenland (2007).
805. We reserve judgment on original art, merely noting that feedback on art, if it can be incorporated, will almost definitely transform it, and along with it the participants' experiences. With research and science writing, our concern is the content of its intellectual arguments and the facts it presents, much less any subjective experience. Fact checking and attention to the logic of an argument can, and should, be transformative, with net benefit for both authors and readers.
806. Ioannidis (2005, p. 700).
807. Ioannidis (2005, p. 698).
808. Ioannidis (2005, p. 700).
809. For a selection of authors and themes see Garfield (1955); Merton (1968/1957); Barber (1952); De Solla Price (1965).
810. Wyatt *et al.* (2017, pp. 87–112).
811. Kuhn (1962).
812. See, for example, the work of Barnes and Edge (1982); Collins and Pinch (1982); Latour and Woolgar (1979); Knorr-Cetina (1999).
813. See Knorr-Cetina (1999) and Vinck (2010, discussion on p. 184).
814. Most of the insights from Fleck's work in this book come from Fleck (1981/1935). See also the translation of Fleck's book Entstehung und Entwicklung einer wissenschaftlichen Tatsache: Einfhrung in die Lehre vom Denkstil und Denkkolektiv (The Genesis and Development of a Scientific Fact: An Introduction to the Theory of Thought Style and Thought Collective). Please note the almost half a century between Fleck's original publication date and the publication of his English translation in 1981, twenty years after his death. The delay due to translation partly explains why Fleck's insights did not influence English-language sociology of science before the constructivist revolution. Intellectually, Fleck's contributions predated the constructivists and appear to complement the English-language epistemic culture tradition dating to the 1990s. For more on Fleck's life and contributions see Sady (2017). Depending on the source and translator, Fleck's first name is spelled either Ludwig (German sources) or Ludwik (non-German sources).
815. Fleck (1981).
816. Fleck's translators wrote 'socio-cogitative' in Fleck (1981, p. 25).

817. Fleck (1981, p. 27).
818. Fleck (1981, p. 27).
819. Fleck (1981, p. 27).
820. For a list of the non-academic epithets Ehrlich hurled at Simon and other people who disagreed with him, see Desrochers and Geloso (2016a, pp. 43–44).
821. Simon (1999a, Ch. 11).
822. Simon (1999a, Ch. 11, para. 3).
823. Simon (1999a, Ch. 11).
824. Simon (1999b).
825. Simon (1999a, Ch. 11, para. 12).
826. Simon (1999a, Ch. 11, para. 13).
827. Simon (1999a, Ch. 11, para. 14).
828. Simon (1999a, Ch. 11, paras 15–16).
829. Simon (1999a, Ch. 11, para. 17).
830. Simon (1999a, Ch. 11, para. 19).
831. Simon (1999a, Ch. 11, para. 23).
832. Simon (1999a, Ch. 11, para. 25).
833. Simon (1999a, Ch. 11, para. 27).
834. Suzuki's video was produced by the National Film Board of Canada http://testtube.nfb.ca/. As of this writing, this video could also be accessed at https://www.youtube.com/watch?v=8x98KFcMJeo&t=2s.
835. See the Royal Society's website for a link to various components of the report and a video summary by Sulston https://royalsociety.org/topics-policy/projects/people-planet/report/.
836. Scott (1998).
837. Scott (1998, p. 4).
838. Scott (1998, p. 4).
839. Scott (1998, p. 4). Scott's analysis of high modernist ideology also observed that '[h]igh modernism was about "interests" as well as faith. Its carriers, even when they were capitalist entrepreneurs, required state action to realize their plans.' The discussion of high modernist ideology spans pp. 4-6.
840. Bailey (1994, p. 51).
841. Gardner (2010, pp. 23–28).
842. Gardner (2010, p. 26).
843. Gardner (2010). Gardner quotes Tetlock (2005) on p. 26.
844. Gardner (2010, p. 26).
845. Gardner (2010, p. 27). Tetlock apparently named these expert mindsets in honour of Isaiah Berlin's fondness for the ancient Greek poet Archilochus' verses describing the qualities of the fox and the hedgehog. Gardner was using Tetlock (2005).
846. Desrochers and Geloso (2016a).
847. Sowell (1995, p. 2).
848. Sowell (1995, pp. 2–3).
849. Sowell (1995, pp. 4–5).
850. Sowell (1995, p. 67. See the discussion on pp. 67–70).
851. Sowell (1995, p. 67).

852. The terminology is borrowed from the Harvard historian of science and physicist Peter Galison, who has written about interdisciplinary work as carving out trading zones between disciplines, zones in which key researchers develop trading languages (pidgins). See Galison (1996) and Galison (1997, Chapter 9).
853. Jacobs (1992, p. xi).
854. Jacobs (1992).
855. Jacobs (1992, p. xii).
856. Taylor (2013, pp. 32–44) .
857. Taylor (2013, p. 34).
858. Taylor (2013, p. 34).
859. Jacobs (1992, p. 28).
860. Jacobs (1992, pp. 25–27).
861. Taylor (2013, p. 34).
862. Jacobs (1992). First mention of name on p. 28, but list of attributes on p. 23. See also Taylor (2013, Table on p. 35).
863. Jacobs (1992). First mention of name on p. 31, but list of attributes on p. 24. See also Taylor (2013, Table on p. 35).
864. Taylor (2013, pp. 35–37).
865. Taylor (2013, pp. 35–36).
866. Taylor (2013, p. 34).
867. Taylor (2013, pp. 35–37).
868. Taylor (2013, p. 37).
869. Taylor (2013, p. 36).

Chapter 7 Conclusion

870. Macaulay (1830).
871. O'Neill *et al.* (2018, p. 88).
872. Nordhaus (2018).
873. These frameworks are the Ends–Means Spectrum, the Planetary Boundaries biophysical framework, and the eHANPP (embodied human appropriation of net primary production). In: O'Neill *et al.* (2018, frameworks on p. 89).
874. Nordhaus (2018, para. 3).
875. Nordhaus (2018, para. 17).
876. Taylor has been adamant in his analysis of Jacobs' work that she never included capitalism in the Commercial syndrome: 'And the commercial syndrome is most certainly not '"capitalist": in the next toolkit in this chapter I will show capitalism to be more related to the Guardian syndrome, and furthermore...I will emphasize the importance of distinguishing between commerce and capitalism.' Taylor (2013, p. 40).
877. Nordhaus (2018, paras 8–9).
878. Simon (1996, Ch. 30).
879. Tupy (2018b).
880. Nordhaus (2018, para. 13).
881. His webpage can be seen at http://www.adamfrankscience.com/.

882. Frank (2018, p. 5).
883. Frank (2018). See pp. 12 and 16.
884. Frank (2018, p. 5, examples pp. 113–118).
885. Frank (2018, p. 9).
886. Frank (2018, p. 9).
887. Frank (2018, p. 9).
888. Link at https://www.mixcloud.com/TheJoeRoganExperience/1130-adam-frank/.
889. Frank (2018, Ch. 5, 169–202).
890. Nordhaus (2018, para. 16).
891. Nordhaus (2018, para. 18).
892. Price (2018, para. 20).
893. Price (2018, para. 20).
894. Simon (1996, Ch. 30).
895. Simon (1996, Ch. 30).

Bibliography

ACS (Undated). A greenhouse effect analogy. American Chemical Society website. URL https://www.acs.org/content/acs/en/climatescience/climatesciencenarratives/a-greenhouse-effect-analogy.html.

Adams P (2015). UN climate official: 'We should make every effort' to decrease world population. *Progressives Today*, April 6. URL http://www.progressivestoday.com/un-climate-official-we-should-make-every-effort-to-decrease-world-population-video/.

Adelman MA (1993). *The Economics of Petroleum Supply: Papers by M.A. Adelman, 1962–1993.* MIT Press.

Aitkenhead D (2016). Interview: James Lovelock: Before the end of this century, robots will have taken over. *The Guardian*, September 30. URL https://www.theguardian.com/environment/2016/sep/30/james-lovelock-interview-by-end-of-century-robots-will-have-taken-over.

Allitt P (2014). *A Climate of Crisis: America in the Age of Environmentalism*. Penguin.

Andersen H, Hepburn B (2016). Scientific method. In: EN Zalta (ed.), *The Stanford Encyclopedia of Philosophy,* URL https://plato.stanford.edu/archives/sum2016/entries/scientific-method/.

Anderson J (1803). On the comparative influence of agriculture and manufacture upon the morals and happiness of a people, and the improvement and stability of states (several parts). In: J Anderson (ed.), *Recreations in Agriculture, Natural History, Arts and Miscellaneous Literature, Volume 4,* S. Gosnell. URL https://books.google.ca/books?id=pmw0AAAAMAAJ.

Angus I, Butler S (2011). *Too Many People? Population, Immigration, and the Environmental Crisis*. Haymarket Books.

Anonymous (1879). Lord Derby on emigration and the land question. *The Malthusian*, 1(1), 5–6.

Anonymous (1887). Her Majesty's Jubilee – A scientific retrospect. *The Chemical News*, LV(1440), 299–300. URL http://books.google.ca/books?id=cJwEAAAAYAAJ.

Anonymous (1889). Statistics vs Malthus. *Westminster Review*, 131(3), 286–297. URL https://books.google.ca/books?id=S7WPjYl705kC&source=gbs_navlinks_s.

Anonymous (2000). David Brower (obituary). *The Telegraph*, November 8. URL https://www.telegraph.co.uk/news/obituaries/1373616/David-Brower.html.

Anonymous (2006). How gas price controls sparked '70s shortages. *Washington Times*, May 15. URL https://www.washingtontimes.com/news/2006/may/15/20060515-122820-6110r/.

Anonymous (2017a). Obituary: Douglas Ashmead, entrepreneur and business troubleshooter. *The Sunday Herald*, February 8. URL http://www.heraldscotland.com/opinion/obituaries/15079158.ObituaryDouglas_Ashmead__entrepreneur_and_business_troubleshooter/.

Anonymous (2017b). Pope Francis and population control. *The Catholic Journal*, March 29. URL https://www.catholicjournal.us/2017/03/29/pope-francis-population-control/.

Argus-Press (1970). Pollution prospect: A chilling one (Editorial). *Owosso Argus-Press*, January 20, 4. URL https://news.google.com/newspapers?id=jjgiAAAAIBAJ&sjid=9KsFAAAAIBAJ&pg=1371,2354081&hl=en.

Aristotle (NDa). *Meteorology Book II, Part 4*. (Approximately 350 BC), URL http://classics.mit.edu/Aristotle/meteorology.2.ii.html.

Aristotle (NDb). *Politics*. (Approximately 350 BC). Translated by Benjamin Jowett, URL http://classics.mit.edu/Aristotle/politics.html.

Armentano DT (1972). *The Myths of Antitrust: Economic Theory and Legal Cases*. Arlington House.

Ashmead D (1997). *Standing Room Only: Our Overcrowded Planet*. Robert Hale.

Astor M (2018). No children because of climate change? Some people are considering it. *New York Times*, February 5. URL https://www.nytimes.com/2018/02/05/climate/climate-change-children.html.

Atkinson E (1890/1889). *The Industrial Progress of the Nation: Consumption Limited, Production Unlimited*. G.P. Putnam's Sons. URL https://archive.org/details/industrialprogre00atki.

Ausubel J (1998). The environment for future business efficiency will win. *Pollution Prevention Review*, 8(1), 39–52. URL https://phe.rockefeller.edu/future_business/.

Ausubel J (2000). Where is energy going? *Industrial Physicist*, 6(1), 16–19. URL http://phe.rockefeller.edu/IndustrialPhysicistWhere/where.pdf.

Ausubel J (2007). Renewable and nuclear heresies. *International Journal of Nuclear Governance, Economy and Ecology*, 1(3), 229–243. URL https://phe.rockefeller.edu/docs/HeresiesFinal.pdf.

Ausubel J (2015). The return of nature. How technology liberates the environment. *The Breakthrough*, Spring. URL https://thebreakthrough.org/index.php/journal/past-issues/issue-5/the-return-of-nature.

Avery D (2000). *Saving the Planet with Pesticides and Plastics*. Hudson Institute.

Bacon RF, Hamor WA (1916). *The American Petroleum Industry, Volume I*. McGraw-Hill.

Bailey R (1994). *Eco-scam: The False Prophets of Ecological Apocalypse*. St Martins Press.

Bailey R (2015). *The End of Doom. Environmental Renewal in the Twenty-first Century*. Thomas Dunne Books, St Martin's Press.

Bailey R (2018a). High school students are very worried about overpopulation. They shouldn't be. *Reason.com*, January 18. URL https://reason.com/blog/2018/01/18/negative-population-growth-scaremongers.

Bailey R (2018b). Is degrowth the only way to save the world? *Hit and Run*, February 16. URL https://reason.com/blog/2018/02/16/is-degrowth-the-only-way-to-save-the-wor.

Ball P (2015). The trouble with scientists: How one psychologist is tackling human biases in science. *Nautilus*, May 14. URL http://nautil.us/issue/24/error/the-trouble-with-scientists.

Ball T (2014). *The Deliberate Corruption of Climate Science*. Stairway Press.

Ball T (2018). Population control? Sustainable development IS the proven solution. *Technocracy*, February 1. URL https://www.technocracy.news/index.php/2018/02/01/population-control-sustainable-development-proven-solution/.

Banta M (2015). Science's under-discussed problem with confirmation bias. *The Wilson Quarterly*, July 28. URL https://wilsonquarterly.com/stories/sciences-under-discussed-problem-with-confirmation-bias/.

Barber B (1952). *Science and the Social Order*. Free Press.

Barger H (1951). *The Transportation Industries, 1889–1946*. NBER.

Barnes B, Edge D (eds.) (1982). *Science in Context: Readings in the Sociology of Science*. MIT Press.

Barnett HJ, Morse C (1963). *Scarcity and Growth. The Economics of Natural Resource Availability*. Resources for the Future, Inc. by The Johns Hopkins Press.

Bashford A (2014). *Global Population. History, Geopolitics and Life on Earth*. Columbia University Press.

Bast J, Ferrara P (2018). The social benefits of fossil fuels. Policy brief, Heartland Institute. URL https://www.heartland.org/publications-resources/publications/the-social-benefits-of-fossil-fuels?mod=article_inline.

Bates M (1962/1955). *The Prevalence of People*. Charles Scribner's Sons.

Baudeau N (1910 (1771)). *Première Introduction à la Philosophie Économique*. Geunther. URL http://gallica.bnf.fr/ark:/12148/bpt6k80063h.r=+baudeau.langFR.

Bauer PT (1991). *The Development Frontier*. Harvard University Press.

Bauer PT (1998). Population growth: Disaster or blessing? *Independent Review*, 3(1), 67–76. URL http://www.independent.org/pdf/tir/tir_03_1_bauer.pdf.

BBC News (2009). Attenborough warns on population. *BBC News*, April 13. URL http://news.bbc.co.uk/2/hi/7996230.stm.

Beck RH, Kolankiewicz LJ (2000). The environmental movement's retreat from advocating US population stabilization (1970–1998): A first draft of history. *Journal of Policy History*, 12(1), 123–156. A slightly different version of the article is freely available at http://www.agoregon.org/files/RetreatfromStabilization.pdf.

Beckerman W (1974). *In Defence of Economic Growth*. Jonathan Cape.

Bell L (2012). Global warming alarmism: When science IS fiction. *Forbes*, May 29. URL https://www.forbes.com/sites/larrybell/2012/05/29/global-warming-alarmism-when-science-is-fiction/2/#431eec5217f7.

Ben-Ami D (2016). Beware greens in progressive clothing. *Spiked!*, March 2. URL http://www.spiked-online.com/newsite/article/beware-greens-in-progressive-clothing/18044#.Wp8RM23wayI.

Bernstam MS (1990). The wealth of nations and the environment. *Population and Development Review (Supplement: Resources, Environment, and Population: Present Knowledge, Future Options)*, 16, 333–373.

Blanco MI (2009). The economics of wind energy. *Renewable and Sustainable Energy Reviews*, 13, 1372–1382.

Blaug M (2000). Henry George: Rebel with a cause. *European Journal of the History of Economic Thought*, 7(2), 270–288.

Block B (2008). A look back at James Hansen's seminal testimony on climate, Part One. *Grist*, June 16. URL https://grist.org/article/a-climate-hero-the-early-years/.

Blomqvist L (2015a). It's time to scrap the ecological footprint. Earth Overshoot Day is fundamentally meaningless. *The Breakthrough*, August 13. URL https://thebreakthrough.org/index.php/issues/conservation/its-time-to-scrap-the-ecological-footprint.

Blomqvist L (2015b). Nature unbound. Decoupling for conservation. *Breakthrough Institute*, September 9. URL https://thebreakthrough.org/index.php/issues/decoupling/nature-unbound.

Blomqvist L (2016). Synthetic abundance: overcoming nature's scarcity. *The Breakthrough*, May 26. URL https://thebreakthrough.org/index.php/issues/conservation/synthetic-abundance.

Blomqvist L, Brook BW, Ellis EC, Kareiva PM, Nordhaus T, Shellenberger M (2013). Does the shoe fit? Real versus imagined ecological footprints. *PLOS Biology*, 11(11), e1001700. URL http://journals.plos.org/plosbiology/article?id=10.1371/journal.pbio.1001700.

Boehmer-Christiansen S (1997). A winning coalition of advocacy: climate research, bureaucracy and alternative' fuels: Who is driving climate change policy? *Energy Policy*, 25(4), 439–444.

Boisvert W (2014). The left vs. the climate. Why progressives should reject Naomi Klein's pastoral fantasy – and embrace our high-energy planet. *The Breakthrough*, September 18. URL https://thebreakthrough.org/index.php/programs/energy-and-climate/the-left-vs.-the-climate.

Bolin B (2007). *A History of the Science and Politics of Climate Change: The Role of the Intergovernmental Panel on Climate Change*. Cambridge University Press.

Bongaarts J (2002). Population: Ignoring its impact. *Scientific American*, 286(1), 67–69.

Bonniel MA (2016). En 1900 le pic de pollution à Paris est dû aux moteurs à crottin. *Le Figaro*, July 1. URL http://www.lefigaro.fr/histoire/archives/2016/07/01/26010--20160701ARTFIG00300-en-1900-le-pic-de-pollution-a-paris-est-du-aux-moteurs-a-crottin.php.

Bookchin M (1994). The population myth. In: *Which Way for the Ecology Movement?*, AK Press.

Booker C (2018). Global Warming. A Case Study in Groupthink. Report 28, Global Warming Policy Foundation. URL https://www.thegwpf.org/content/uploads/2018/02/Groupthink.pdf.

Botero G (1606). *The Greatness of Cities*. (Originally published in 1588 as *Delle Cause della Grandezza delle Città*), URL http://socserv2.socsci.mcmaster.ca/econ/ugcm/3ll3/botero/cities.

Boulding KE (1955). Man's march to 'The Summit'. *Population Bulletin*, August, 70. The encapsulation was originally presented to the Warner-Gren International Symposium on 'Man's Role in Changing the Face of the Earth,' Princeton (NJ), June 16–22, 1955.

Boulding KE (1966). The Economics of the coming Spaceship Earth. In: H Jarrett (ed.), *Environmental Quality in a Growing Economy,* Resources for the Future, Inc. by The Johns Hopkins Press.

Boulding KE (1970). Fun and games with the Gross National Product – The role of misleading indicators in social policy. In: HW Helfrich (ed.), *The Environmental Crisis: Man's Struggle to Live with Himself,* Yale University Press.

Bowden G (1985). The social construction of validity in estimates of US crude oil reserves. *Social Studies of Science*, 15(2), 207–240.

BP (2017). Statistical Review of World Energy 2017. Technical report, BP. URL https://www.bp.com/content/dam/bp/en/corporate/pdf/energy-economics/statistical-review-2017/bp-statistical-review-of-world-energy-2017-full-report.pdf.

Bradley Jr RL (2007). Resourceship: an Austrian theory of mineral resources. *Review of Austrian Economics*, 20(1), 63–90.

Bradley Jr RL (2008). John Holdren on global cooling (Part I in a Series on Obama's new science advisor, 'Dr. Doom'). *Master Resource*, December 30. URL https://www.masterresource.org/global-cooling-climate-change/john-holdren-on-global-cooling-part-i-in-a-series-on-obamas-new-science-advisor-dr-doom/.

Bradley Jr RL (2009). *Capitalism at Work: Business, Government and Energy*. M & M Scrivener Press.

Bradley Jr RL (2015). Global cooling: do not forget (false alarm was tied to coal burning too). *Master Resource*, December 3. URL https://www.masterresource.org/global-cooling-climate-change/global-cooling-revisited/.

Bradley Jr RL (2016). RFF: Going Malthusian in the 1970s (precursor to climate alarmism). *MasterResource.org*, January 26. URL https://www.masterresource.org/resources-for-the-future-rff/rff-going-malthusian-in-the-1970s/.

Bradley Jr RL (2017). Halloween thoughts from a Harvard man (Holdren can play himself tonight). *Master Resource*, October 31. URL https://www.masterresource.org/holdren-john/halloween-thoughts-obamas-science-advisor-will-holdren-halloween/.

Brander R (ND). Disgression: Exponential technology improvements – in coal! University of Calgary. URL http://www.cuug.ab.ca/branderr/eeepc/017_coal.html.

Brandt K (1945). The marriage of nutrition and agriculture. In: TW Schultz (ed.), *Food for the World,* University of Chicago Press.

Brandt K (1950). Review of *Road to Survival* by William Vogt. *Land Economics*, 26(1), 88–90.

Bray AJ (1991). The ice age cometh. *Policy Review*, 58, 82–84. URL http://www.unz.com/print/PolicyRev-1991q4--00082/?View=PDF.

Brook BW, Ellis EC, Perring MP, Mackay AW, Blomqvist L (2013). Does the terrestrial biosphere have planetary tipping points? *Trends in Ecology & Evolution*, 28(7), 396–401.

Brown H (1954). *The Challenge of Man's Future. An Inquiry Concerning the Condition of Man During the Years that Lie Ahead*. The Viking Press.

Bryce R (2010). *Power Hungry*. PublicAffairs.

Bryce R (2014). *Smaller Faster Lighter Denser Cheaper: How Innovation Keeps Proving the Catastrophists Wrong*. Perseus.

Bryson R (1968). All other factors being constant. A reconciliation of several theories of climate change. *Weatherwise*, 21(2), 56–62.

Bryson R (1976). Preface. In: *The Cooling,* (Lowell Ponte, op. cit), Prentice Hall.

BTI (2016). Frequently asked questions about population: Global population in the 21st century. *Breakthrough Institute*, March 9. URL https://thebreakthrough.org/index.php/issues/population/faqs-on-population.

Bühner M (2012). Why environmental regulation is not scaring off industry – On declining evidence for pollution haven theory. *Know the Flow*, October 8. URL https://www.ifu.com/knowtheflow/2012/why-environmental-regulation-is-not-scaring-off-the-industry-on-declining-pollution-haven-theory-evidence/.

Buonanduci M (2009). Dust bowl. In: CJ Cleveland (ed.), *Encyclopedia of the Earth*, URL http://www.eoearth.org/article/Dust_Bowl?topic=49465.

Burch GI, Pendell E (1947). *Human Breeding and Survival. Population Roads to Peace or War*. Penguin.

Butt N, de Oliveira PA, Costa MH (2011). Evidence that deforestation affects the onset of the rainy season in Rondonia, Brazil. *Journal of Geophysical Research: Atmospheres*, 116, D11120. URL https://agupubs.onlinelibrary.wiley.com/doi/full/10.1029/2010JD015174.

Cafaro P (2014). *How Many Is Too Many? The Progressive Argument for Reducing Immigration into the United States*. University of Chicago Press.

Cafaro P (2016). The environmental impact of immigration into the United States:. Expert report filed in Whitewater Draw Natural Resource Conservation District vs. DHS Secretary Jeh Johnson.

Canadian Party of Labour (1973). Abortion, population control, genocide: The scientific killers and who sent for them. A communist response to theories of overpopulation. Encyclopedia of Anti-Revisionism On-Line. The year of publication is putative, URL https://www.marxists.org/history/erol/ca.firstwave/cpl-abortion/section8.htm.

Cannan E (1922/1914). *Wealth: A Brief Explanation of the Causes of Economic Wealth*. P.S. King and Son. URL http://oll.libertyfund.org/titles/2063.

Caplan B (2007). Clark replies. *EconLog*, September 26. URL http://econlog.econlib.org/archives/2007/09/clark_replies.html.

Caradonna J, Borowy I, Green T, Victor PA, Cohen M, Gow A, Ignatyeva A, Schmelzer M, Vergragt P, Wangel J, Dempsey J, Orzanna R, Lorek S, Axmann J, Duncan R, Norgaard RB, Brown HS, Heinberg R (2015). A call to look past an ecomodernist manifesto: A degrowth critique. Resilience.org website. URL http://www.resilience.org/wp-content/uploads/articles/General/2015/05_May/A-Degrowth-Response-to-An-Ecomodernist-Manifesto.pdf.

Carlson AS (1956). *Economic Geography of Industrial Materials*. Reinhold Publishing Corporation.

Carter HD (1939). *If you Want to Invent*. Vanguard Press.

Carver L (2010). Where science meets politics – Controversy surrounding the relationship between population growth and climate change. *Consilience*, 4(1), 103–118.

Casey G, Galor O (2016). Population growth and carbon emissions. Working paper, Department of Economics, Brown University. URL https://www.brown.edu/academics/economics/sites/brown.edu.academics.economics/files/uploads/2016--8_paper_0.pdf.

Casey G, Galor O (2017a). Economic growth and reductions in carbon emissions. *VOX*, March 23. URL https://voxeu.org/article/economic-growth-and-reductions-carbon-emissions.

Casey G, Galor O (2017b). Is faster economic growth compatible with reductions in carbon emissions? The role of diminished population growth. *Environmental Research Letters*, 12(1), 014003. URL http://iopscience.iop.org/article/10.1088/1748--9326/12/1/014003.

Ceci SL, Williams WM (2018). Who decides what is acceptable speech on campus? Why restricting free speech is not the answer. *Perspectives on Psychological Science*, 13(3), 299–323. URL http://journals.sagepub.com/doi/pdf/10.1177/1745691618767324.

Chandler AD (1994/1990). *Scale and Scope. The Dynamics of Industrial Capitalism*. The Belknap Press of Harvard University Press.

Chandrasekhar S (1956/1954). *Hungry People and Empty Lands. An Essay on Population Problems and International Tensions*. George Allen & Unwin.

Chase A (1977). *The Legacy of Malthus*. Alfred A Knopf.

Chase S (1991). *Defending the Earth: A Dialogue between Murray Bookchin and Dave Foreman*. South End Press.

Chen HC (1911). *The Economic Principles of Confucius and his School*. PhD thesis, Department of Political Science, Columbia University. URL https://archive.org/details/economicprincipl00huan.

Chernow R (1998). *Titan. The Life of John D. Rockefeller Sr*. Random House.

Chertow MR (2001). The IPAT equation and its variants: Changing views of technology and environmental impact. *Journal of Industrial Ecology*, 4(4), 13–29.

Chu J (2017). Study: Technological progress alone won't stem resource use. Researchers find no evidence of an overall reduction in the world's consumption of materials. MIT News Office January 19. URL http://news.mit.edu/2017/technological-progress-alone-stem-consumption-materials-0119.

CIA (1974). A Study of Climatological Research as it Pertains to Intelligence Problems. Technical report, Central Intelligence Agency. URL http://www.climatemonitor.it/wp-content/uploads/2009/12/1974.pdf.

Clark C (1973). *The Myth of Over-Population*. Advocate Press.

Clark C (1975). *Population Growth: The Advantages*. R.L. Sassone.

Clark G (2007). *A Farewell to Alms. A Brief Economic History of the World*. Princeton University Press. URL https://press.princeton.edu/titles/8461.html.

Clark Jr WA (1974). *Energy for Survival: The Alternative to Extinction*. Anchor Books.

Clegg S (1841). *A Practical Treatise on the Manufacture and Distribution of Coal Gas; Its Introduction and Progressive Improvement*. John Weale. URL https://archive.org/details/practicaltreatis00clegrich.

Cohen AS (2016). Harvard's eugenics era. When academics embraced scientific racism, immigration restrictions, and the suppression of 'the unfit'. *Harvard Magazine*, March-April.

Cohen JE (1995). *How Many People can the Earth Support?* W.W. Norton & Company.

Cohen JE (2010). Population and climate change. *Proceedings of the American Philosophical Society*, 154(2), 158–182.

Collins HM, Pinch TJ (1982). *Frames of Meaning: The Social Construction of Extraordinary Science*. Routledge.

Conceivable Future (ND). The analysis. URL http://conceivablefuture.org/problems.
Conly S (2015). Here's why China's one-child policy was a good thing. *Boston Globe*, October 31. URL https://www.bostonglobe.com/opinion/2015/10/31/here-why-china-one-child-policy-was-good-thing/GY4XiQLeYfAZ8e8Y7yFycI/story.html.
Connelly M (2008). *Fatal Misconception. The Struggle to Control World Population*. Harvard University Press.
Cook RC (1951). *Human Fertility: The Modern Dilemma*. Sloane.
Copp N, Zanella A (1993). *Discovery, Innovation and Risk*. MIT Press.
Cosmides L, Tooby J (1997). Evolutionary psychology: A primer. Center for Evolutionary Psychology. URL https://www.cep.ucsb.edu/primer.html.
Cox J (2014). Contraception key in climate change fight: Gore and Gates. *Cnbc.com*, January 24. URL https://www.cnbc.com/2014/01/24/contraception-key-in-climate-change-fight-gore-and-gates.html.
Crist E, Mora C, Engelman R (2017). The interaction of human population, food production, and biodiversity protection. *Science*, 356(6355), 260–264.
Crory WG (1876). *East London Industries*. Longmans, Green, and Co. URL https://archive.org/details/eastlondonindus00crorgoog.
Crowards TM (1998). Safe minimum standards: costs and opportunities. *Ecological Economics*, 25(3), 303–314.
Cunfer G (2004). The dust bowl. In: *Encyclopedia of Economic and Business History*, Eh.Net. URL http://eh.net/encyclopedia/article/Cunfer.DustBowl.
Curran SR, de Sherbinin A (2004). Completing the picture: the challenges of bringing consumption into the population–environment equation. *Population and Environment*, 26(2), 107–131.
Curry J (2015). Unnatural consensus on climate change. *Financial Post*, December 29. URL http://business.financialpost.com/fp-comment/unnatural-consensus-on-climate-change.
Curry J (2017). Climate Models for the Layman. Briefing 24, Global Warming Policy Foundation. URL https://www.thegwpf.org/content/uploads/2017/02/Curry-2017.pdf.
Daily GC, Ehrlich PR (1992). Population, sustainability, and Earth's carrying capacity. *BioScience*, 42(10), 761–771.
Dando W (1980). *The Geography of Famine*. V. H. Winston and Sons.
Darwall R (2014). *The Age of Global Warming: A History*. Quartet Books.
Darwall R (2017a). The Anti-Development Bank. The World Bank's Regressive Energy Policies. Report 27, Global Warming Policy Foundation. URL https://www.thegwpf.org/content/uploads/2017/10/Darwall-WB-1.pdf.
Darwall R (2017b). Climate alarmists use the acid-rain playbook: The parallels between the two environmental frenzies are many, but the stakes are much higher now. *Wall Street Journal*, October 25. URL https://www.wsj.com/articles/climate-alarmists-use-the-acid-rain-playbook-1508969822.
Darwall R (2017c). *Green Tyranny: The Totalitarian Roots of the Climate Industrial Complex*. Encounter Books.
Daston LJ, Galison P (2007). *Objectivity*. MIT Press.
De Castro J (1946/1951). *The Geography of Hunger*. Little, Brown.

de Sherbinin A, Carr D, Cassels S, Jiang L (2007). Population and environment. *Annual Review of Environment and Resources*, 32, 345–373.

De Solla Price DJ (1965). Networks of scientific papers. *Science*, 149, 510–515.

De Steiguer JE (2006). *The Origins of Modern Environmental Thought*. The University of Arizona Press.

DeFries RS, Ellis EC, Chapin III FS, Matson PA, Turner II BL, Agrawal A, Crutzen PJ, Field C, Gleick P, Kareiva PM (2012). Planetary opportunities: A social contract for global change science to contribute to a sustainable future. *BioScience*, 62(6), 603–606.

Desrochers P (2008). Bringing inter-regional linkages back in: Industrial symbiosis, international trade and the emergence of the synthetic dyes industry in the late 19th century. *Progress in Industrial Ecology*, 5(5–6), 465–481.

Desrochers P (2009). Does the invisible hand have a green thumb? Incentives, linkages, and the creation of wealth out of industrial waste in Victorian England. *Geographical Journal*, 175(1), 3–16.

Desrochers P (2010). The environmental responsibility of business is to increase its profits (by creating value within the bounds of private property rights). *Industrial and Corporate Change*, 19(1), 161–204.

Desrochers P (2012). Freedom vs coercion in industrial ecology: A reply to Boons. *EconJournalWatch*, 9(2), 78–99. URL https://econjwatch.org/articles/freedom-versus-coercion-in-industrial-ecology-a-reply-to-boons.

Desrochers P (2015). Petrol power: An eco-revolution. *Spiked!*, July 20. URL http://www.spiked-online.com/newsite/article/petrol-power-an-eco-revolution/17207#.Voba_BUrLIU.

Desrochers P, Geloso V (2016a). Snatching the wrong conclusions from the jaws of defeat: A historical/resourceship perspective on Paul Sabin's *The Bet*: Paul Ehrlich, Julian Simon, and our gamble over Earth's future (Yale University Press, 2013). Part 2: The wager: protagonists and lessons. *New Perspectives on Political Economy*, 12(1–2), 5–41. URL http://www.cevroinstitut.cz/data/nppe-12.pdf.

Desrochers P, Geloso V (2016b). Snatching the wrong conclusions from the jaws of defeat: A historical/resourceship perspective on Paul Sabin's *The Bet*: Paul Ehrlich, Julian Simon, and our gamble over Earth's future (Yale University Press, 2013) Part 1: The missing history of thought: depletionism vs resourceship. *New Perspectives on Political Economy*, 12(1–2), 5–41. URL http://www.cevroinstitut.cz/data/nppe-12.pdf.

Desrochers P, Haight C (2014). Squandered profit opportunities? Some historical perspective on wasteful industrial behavior and the porter hypothesis. *Resources, Conservation and Recycling*, 92, 179–189.

Desrochers P, Hoffbauer C (2009). The post war intellectual roots of *The Population Bomb*. Fairfield Osborn's *Our Plundered Planet* and William Vogt's *Road to Survival* in retrospect. *Electronic Journal of Sustainable Development*, 1(3), 73–97. URL http://geog.utm.utoronto.ca/desrochers/The_Population_Bomb.pdf.

Desrochers P, Leppälä S (2010). Industrial symbiosis: Old wine in recycled bottles? Some perspective from the history of economic and geographical thought. *International Regional Science Review*, 33(3), 338–361.

Desrochers P, Reed A (2008). The Invisible Green Hand. Policy Primer 7, Mercatus Center, George Mason University.

Desrochers P, Shimizu H (2012a). Innovation and the Greening of Alberta's Oil Sands. Technical report, Montreal Economic Institute. URL http://www.iedm.org/41023-innovation-and-the-greening-of-albertas-oil-sands.

Desrochers P, Shimizu H (2012b). The locavore's dilemma: In praise of the 10,000-mile diet. *Public Affairs*. URL http://globavore.org/.

Desrochers P, Shimizu H (2016). Blowing hot air on the wrong target? A critique of the fossil fuel divestment movement in higher education. *Frontier Centre for Public Policy*, July.

Desrochers P, Szurmak J (2017). Long distance trade, locational dynamics and by-product development: insights from the history of the American cottonseed industry. *Sustainability*, 9(4), article 579. URL http://www.mdpi.com/2071-1050/9/4/579.

Deutsch L, Jansson A, Troell M, Ronnback P, Folke C, Kautsky N (2000). The ecological footprint: Communicating human dependence on nature's work. *Ecological Economics*, 32, 351–355.

Devas CS (1919/1907). *Political Economy*. Longmans, Green, & Co, 3rd edn. URL https://archive.org/details/politicalecon00deva.

Dobbin M (2014). Can you imagine? Toppling the fossil fuel empire. *The Tyee*, June 30. URL http://thetyee.ca/Opinion/2014/06/30/Toppling-Fossil-Fuel-Empire/.

Dobbs R, Oppenheim J, Thompson F, Brinkman M, Zornes M (2011). Resource Revolution: Meeting the World's Energy, Materials, Food, and Water Needs. McKinsey Global Institute, (November). URL https://www.mckinsey.com/business-functions/sustainability-and-resource-productivity/our-insights/resource-revolution.

Dodd G (1852). Penny wisdom. *Household Words*, 134(October 16), pp. 97–101. Quote on p. 99, URL https://archive.org/details/householdwordsa01dickgoog.

Draffkorn Kilmer A (1972). The Mesopotamian concept of overpopulation and its solution as reflected in the mythology. *Orientalia NS*, 41(2), 160–177. URL https://www.jstor.org/stable/43074504.

Dragos Aligica P (2007). *Prophecies of Doom and Scenarios of Progress. Herman Kahn, Julian Simon, and the Prospective Imagination*. Bloomsbury Publishing.

Driessen P, Skates C (2014). Google goes off the climate change deep end. *Townhall.com*, December 26. URL http://townhall.com/columnists/pauldriessen/2014/12/26/google-goes-off-the-climate-change-deep-end-n1935798/page/full.

Drysdale CR (1889). The Malthusian theory of population: A reply to Statistics versus Malthus. *Westminster Review*, 131(5), 561–573. URL https://books.google.ca/books?id=S7WPjYl705kC&source=gbs_navlinks_s.

Dryzek JS (2005). *The Politics of the Earth: Environmental Discourses*. Oxford University Press, 2nd edn.

East EM (1928/1923). *Mankind at the Crossroads*. Scribner.

Easterbrook G (2003). *The Progress Paradox: How Life Gets Better While People Feel Worse*. Random House.

Easterbrook G (2018). *It's Better than It Looks. Reasons for Optimism in an Age of Fear*. Public Affairs.

Editors of The Ecologist (1972). *A Blueprint for Survival.* Penguin. Excerpt available online at https://www.uow.edu.au/~sharonb/STS300/limits/writings/ecologistread.html.

Ehrlich AH, Ehrlich PR (2013). A confused statistician. *MAHB (Millennium Alliance for Humanity and the Biosphere)*, November 12. URL https://mahb.stanford.edu/blog/a-confused-statistician/.

Ehrlich PR (1968). *The Population Bomb.* Ballantine Books. Paul Ehrlich later acknowledged on numerous occasions the contribution of his wife in the writing of this book.

Ehrlich PR (1969). Eco-Catastrophe! *Ramparts Magazine*, September, 24–28. URL http://www.unz.com/print/Ramparts-1969sep-00024/?View=PDF.

Ehrlich PR, Ehrlich AH (1970). Population control and genocide. *New Democratic Coalition Newsletter.* Reprint in Holdren and Ehrlich, 1971.

Ehrlich PR, Ehrlich AH (1975/1974). *The End of Affluence.* Rivercity.

Ehrlich PR, Ehrlich AH (1996). *Betrayal of Science and Reason.* Island Press.

Ehrlich PR, Ehrlich AH (1997). Ehrlichs' fables. *Technology Review*, January 1. URL https://www.technologyreview.com/s/400001/ehrlichs-fables/.

Ehrlich PR, Ehrlich AH (2008). Too many people, too much consumption. *Yale Environment 360.* URL http://e360.yale.edu/features/too_many_people_too_much_consumption.

Ehrlich PR, Ehrlich AH, Holdren JP (1977). *Ecoscience: Population, Resources, and Environment.* W H Freeman & Co.

Ehrlich PR, Harte J (2015). Biophysical limits, women's rights and the climate encyclical. *Nature Climate Change*, 5, 904–905.

Ehrlich PR, Harte J (2018). Pessimism on the food front. *Sustainability*, 10(4), 1120.

Ehrlich PR, Holdren JP (1969). Population and panaceas: A technological perspective. *BioScience*, 19(12), 1065–1071. Reprinted in Holdren and Ehrlich (1971).

Ehrlich PR, Holdren JP (1970). Overpopulation and the potential for ecocide. Center for the Study of Democratic Institutions. Reprinted in Holdren and Ehrlich (1971).

Ehrlich PR, Holdren JP (1971). Impact of population growth. *Science*, 171(3977), 1212–1217.

Ellis EC (2012). The planet of no return. Human resilience on an artificial Earth. *The Breakthrough*, Winter. URL https://thebreakthrough.org/index.php/journal/past-issues/issue-2/the-planet-of-no-return.

Ellis EC, Kaplan JO, Fuller DQ, Vavrus S, Goldewijk KK, Verburg PH (2013). Used planet: A global history. *Proceedings of the National Academy of Sciences*, 110(20), 7978–7985. URL http://www.pnas.org/content/110/20/7978.

Engels F (1844). *Outlines of a Critique of Political Economy.* URL http://www.marxists.org/archive/marx/works/1844/df-jahrbucher/outlines.htm.

EPP (1965). Report of the Environmental Pollution Panel (Restoring the Quality of our Environment) of the President's Science Advisory Committee. Technical report, President's Science Advisory Committee. URL https://dge.carnegiescience.edu/labs/caldeiralab/Caldeira%20downloads/PSAC,%201965,%20Restoring%20the%20Quality%20of%20Our%20Environment.pdf.

Epstein A (2011). Vindicating capitalism: The real history of the Standard Oil Company. Originally published in 2008, this was made freely available on the web in five parts Part I: The fallacious textbook story https://www.masterresource.org/epstein-alex/vindicating-capitalism-standard-oil-i/, Part II: The phenom https://www.masterresource.org/epstein-alex/vindicating-capitalism-standard-oil-ii/, Part III: The missing context of Standard's rise to supremacy, https://www.masterresource.org/epstein-alex/vindicating-capitalism-standard-oil-iii/, Part IV: Pioneering in big business, https://www.masterresource.org/epstein-alex/the-real-history-of-the-standard-oil-company-part-iv-pioneering-in-big-business/, Part V: Lessons, https://www.masterresource.org/epstein-alex/capitalism-vindicated-standard-oil-part-v/.

Epstein A (2014). *The Moral Case for Fossil Fuels*. Penguin.

Eschenbach W (2010). Ecological footprints – A good idea gone bad. *Watts Up with That?*, August 26. URL https://wattsupwiththat.com/2010/08/26/ecological-footprints-a-good-idea-gone-bad/.

Estall RC, Buchanan RO (1973). *Industrial Activity and Economic Geography. A Study of the Forces behind the Geographical Location of Productive Activity in Manufacturing Industry*. Hutchinson University Library.

Everett A (1823). *New Ideas on Population: with Remarks on the Theories of Malthus and Godwin*. Oliver Everett. URL https://archive.org/details/newideasonpopula00ever.

Fernbach PM, Rogers T, Fox CR, Sloman SA (2013). Political extremism is supported by an illusion of understanding. *Psychological Science*, 24, 939–946.

Ferrill MJ (2011). *Rainfall follows the plow*. University of Nebraska-Lincoln. URL http://plainshumanities.unl.edu/encyclopedia/doc/egp.ii.049.

Fiala N (2008). Measuring sustainability: Why the ecological footprint is bad economics and bad environmental science. *Ecological Economics*, 67(4), 519–525.

Fieldner AC (1925). Significant progress in research on fuels. *Annals of the American Academy of Political and Social Science*, 119, 13–23.

Findlay A (1917). *The Treasures of Coal Tar*. D. Van Nostrand. URL https://archive.org/details/treasurescoalta00findgoog.

Fitter A (2013). Are ecosystem services replaceable by technology? *Environmental and Resource Economics*, 55(4), 513–524.

Fleck L (1981). *Genesis and Development of a Scientific Fact*. University of Chicago Press, rev. edn. Trans. Fred Bradley and Thaddeus J. Trenn.

Fleck L (1981/1935). Epistemological conclusions from the established history of a concept. In: F Bradley, TJ Trenn (eds.), *Genesis and Development of a Scientific Fact*, University of Chicago Press, rev. edn.

Floud R, Fogel RW, Harris B, Hong SC (2011). Cambridge University Press and National Bureau of Economic Research.

Fong B (2017). The climate crisis? It's capitalism, stupid. *New York Times*, November 20. URL https://www.nytimes.com/2017/11/20/opinion/climate-capitalism-crisis.html.

Foster P (2015). The man who shaped the climate agenda in Paris, Maurice Strong, leaves a complicated legacy. *National Post*, November 29. URL http://nationalpost.com/opinion/peter-foster-the-man-who-shaped-the-climate-agenda-in-paris-maurice-strong-leaves-a-complicated-legacy.

Frank A (2018). *Light of the Stars: Alien Worlds and the Fate of the Earth*. W.W. Norton & Company.

Fumento M (1993). *Science Under Siege*. William Morrow & Co.

Furedi F (2010). A depletionist view of history and humanity (Review of David Willets' *The Pinch*). *Spiked!*, February 26.

Galison P (1996). Introduction: the context of disunity. In: P Galison, DJ Stump (eds.), *The Disunity of Science: Boundaries, Contexts, and Power,* Stanford University Press.

Galison P (1997). *Image and Logic: A Material Culture of Microphysics*. University of Chicago Press.

Gardner D (2010). *Future Babble: Why Expert Predictions Fail – and Why We believe Them Anyway*. McLelland & Stewart.

Garfield E (1955). Citation indexes for science: A new dimension in documentation through association of ideas. *Science*, 122(3159), 108–111.

George H (1879). *Progress and Poverty. An Inquiry into the Cause of Industrial Depressions and of Increase of Want with Increase of Wealth: The Remedy*. Doubleday, Page & Co. URL http://econlib.org/library/YPDBooks/George/grgPP.html.

Giere RN, Bickle J, Mauldin RF (2006). *Understanding Scientific Reasoning*. Thomson Higher Education, 5th edn.

Gimenez ME (1973). Befolkningsproblemet: Marx kontra Malthus. *Den Ny Verden*, December, 74–88. ('The population issue: Marx vs Malthus', *Journal of the Institute of Development Research*; Copenhagen, Denmark). Non-paginated English translation available at https://www.colorado.edu/Sociology/gimenez/work/popissue.html.

Goddard S (2013). 1970s global cooling scare. *Real Science*. URL https://stevengoddard.wordpress.com/1970s-ice-age-scare/.

Godwin W (1820). Of Population. An Enquiry concerning the Power of Increase in the Numbers of Mankind, being an Answer to Mr. Malthus's essay on that subject. URL http://oll.libertyfund.org/titles/godwin-of-population-an-enquiry-concerning-the-power-of-increase-in-the-numbers-of-mankind.

Goklany I (2007). The Improving State of the World: Why We're Living Longer, Healthier, More Comfortable Lives on a Cleaner Planet. Technical report, Cato Institute.

Goklany I (2012). Global Warming Policies Might be Bad for your Health. Report 8, Global Warming Policy Foundation. URL https://www.thegwpf.org/images/stories/gwpf-reports/goklany-public_health.pdf.

Goklany I (2014). Unhealthy Exaggeration. The WHO Report on Climate Change. Briefing 13, Global Warming Policy Foundation. URL https://www.thegwpf.org/content/uploads/2014/11/WHO-2.pdf.

Goklany I (2015). Carbon Dioxide. The Good News. Report 18, Global Warming Policy Foundation. URL https://www.thegwpf.org/content/uploads/2015/10/benefits1.pdf.

Goklany I, Morris J (2011). The decline in deaths from extreme weather, 1900–2010. Policy Study 393, Reason Foundation. URL http://reason.org/news/show/decline-deaths-extreme-weather.

Gonnard R (1923). *Histoire des Doctrines de la Population*. Nouvelle Librairie Nationale.

Goodman S, Greenland S (2007). Why most published research findings are false: Problems in the analysis. *PLoS Medicine*, 4(4), 773. URL https://www.ncbi.nlm.nih.gov/pmc/articles/PMC1855693/.

Gordon P, Richardson HW (1998). Farmland preservation and ecological footprints: A critique. *Planning & Markets*, 1(1). URL http://www-pam.usc.edu/volume1/v1i1a2print.html.

Gore A (1992). *Earth in the Balance: Ecology and the Human Spirit*. Houghton Mifflin.

Graham T (2008). Ted Turner pushes one-child policy in PBS interview. *NewsBusters.org*, April 5. URL https://www.newsbusters.org/blogs/nb/tim-graham/2008/04/05/ted-turner-pushes-one-child-policy-pbs-interview.

Greeley WB (1925). The relation of geography to timber supply. *Economic Geography*, 1(1), 1–14.

Grieger A (2012). Only one earth: Stockholm and the beginning of modern environmental diplomacy. *Arcadia*, 10.

Grigg D (1979). Ester Boserup's theory of agrarian change: A critical review. *Progress in Human Geography*, 3(1), 64–84.

Grimshaw R (1889). Industrial applications of cottonseed oil. *Journal of the Franklin Institute*, 127(3), 191–203.

Grossman R (2012). The importance of human population to sustainability. *Environment, Development and Sustainability*, 14, 973–977.

Haas W, Krausmann F, Wiedenhofer D, Hein M (2015). How circular is the global economy? An assessment of material flows, waste production, and recycling in the European Union and the world in 2005. *Journal of Industrial Ecology*, 19(5), 765–777. URL http://onlinelibrary.wiley.com/doi/10.1111/jiec.12244/epdf.

Haberman C (2015). The unrealized horrors of population explosion. *New York Times*, May 31. URL https://www.nytimes.com/2015/06/01/us/the-unrealized-horrors-of-population-explosion.html.

Hajkowicz S (2015). *Global Megatrends: Seven Patterns of Change Shaping Our Future*. Commonwealth Scientific and Industrial Research Organisation.

Hanania J, Stenhouse K, Donev J (2015). Energy Education. URL http://energyeducation.ca/encyclopedia/McKelvey_box.

Hansen J (2009). Coal-fired power stations are death factories. Close them. *The Guardian*, February 15. URL https://www.theguardian.com/commentisfree/2009/feb/15/james-hansen-power-plants-coal.

Hansen J, Sato M, Kharecha P, Beerling D, Berner R, Masson-Delmotte V, Pagani M, Raymo M, Royer DL, Zachos JC (2008). Target atmospheric CO2: Where should humanity aim? *Open Atmospheric Science Journal*, 2, 217–231. URL http://benthamopen.com/ABSTRACT/TOASCJ-2-217.

Hanson EP (1949). *New Worlds Emerging*. Duell, Sloan and Pearce.

Hanson EP (2003). Tropical adaptation – a re-evaluation. In: JR Mather (ed.), *Seventy-Five Years of Geography at The University of Delaware,* Reprint of paper presented at the 1951 Meetings of the Association of American Geographers, Chicago, Illinois.

Hardin G (1968). The tragedy of the commons. *Science*, 162(3859), 1243–1248. URL http://science.sciencemag.org/content/162/3859/1243.

Hardin G (1974). Lifeboat ethics: The case against helping the poor. *Psychology Today*, September. URL http://www.garretthardinsociety.org/articles/art_lifeboat_ethics_case_against_helping_poor.html.

Hart M (2015). *Hubris. The Troubling Science, Economics and Politics of Climate Change*. Compleat Desktops Publishing.

Harte J, Harte ME (2008). Cool the Earth, Save the Economy. Solving the climate crisis is easy. Cool the Earth. URL http://www.cooltheearth.us/downloadtracker.php?file=Cool_the_Earth_Save_the_Economy.pdf.

Hartmann B (1999). *Reproductive Rights and Wrongs: The Global Politics of Population Control*. South End, rev. edn.

Hastorf AH, Cantril H (1954). They saw a game: A case study. *Journal of Abnormal Psychology*, 49, 129–134.

Hawke DF (1988). *Nuts and Bolts of the Past: A History of American Technology, 1776–1860*. Harper & Row.

Heffernan O (2009). Planetary boundaries. *Climate Feedback (Nature Climate Change)*, September 23. URL http://blogs.nature.com/climatefeedback/2009/09/planetary_boundaries_1.html.

Heilbroner R (1974). *An Inquiry into the Human Prospect*. W.W. Norton & Company.

Hickman L (2010). Maurice Strong on climate 'conspiracy', Bilberberg and population control. *The Guardian*, June 23. URL https://www.theguardian.com/environment/blog/2010/jun/22/maurice-strong-interview-global-government.

Higgs K (2014). *Collision Course. Endless Growth on a Finite Planet*. MIT Press.

Hillaby J (1952). British scientists told of dilemma. *New York Times*, September 4.

Hoff DS (2012). *The State and the Stork: The Population Debate and Policy Making in US History*. University of Chicago Press.

Hoff DS, Robertson T (2016). Malthus today. In: RJ Mayhew (ed.), *New Perspectives on Malthus*, Cambridge University Press.

Holden C, Levy DM (1993). Birth control and the amelioration controversy. *History of Political Economy*, 25(2), 283–311.

Holdren JA, Ehrlich AH, Ehrlich PR (1973). *Human Ecology: Problems and Solutions*. W.H. Freeman and Company.

Holdren JP (2002). Energy: Asking the wrong question. *Scientific American*, 286(1), 65–67.

Holdren JP, Ehrlich PR (1971a). *Global Ecology. Readings Toward a Rational Strategy for Man*. Harcourt Brace Jovanovich.

Holdren JP, Ehrlich PR (1971b). Resource realities. In: JP Holdren, PR Ehrlich (eds.), *Global Ecology: Readings Towards a Rational Strategy for Man*, Harcourt Brace Jovanovich.

Holdren JP, Ehrlich PR, Ehrlich AH, Harte J (1980). Bad news: is it true? *Science NS*, 210(4476), 1296–1301.

Huber PW, Mills MP (2005). *The Bottomless Well. The Twilight of Fuel, the Virtue of Waste, and Why We Will Never Run Out of Energy*. Basic Books.

Huffington Post (2014). Hope on Earth: A conversation. *HuffPost Live*, May 21. URL https://www.newsbusters.org/blogs/nb/sean-long/2014/05/22/alarmist-paul-ehrlich-predicts-need-eat-bodies-your-dead.

Hughes G (2017). The Bottomless Pit. The Economics of Carbon Capture and Storage. Report, Global Warming Policy Foundation. URL https://www.thegwpf.org/content/uploads/2017/07/CCS-Hughes2017.pdf.

Hume D (1742/1777). Of the populousness of ancient nations. In: *Political Discourses*, Kincaid and Donaldson. URL http://www.econlib.org/library/LFBooks/Hume/hmMPL34.html.

Hutchinson EP (1967). *The Population Debate. The Development of Conflicting Theory up to 1900*. Houghton Mifflin.

Huxley A (1958). *Brave New World Revisited*. Harper & Brothers. URL https://www.huxley.net/bnw-revisited/.

Hynes HP (1993). Taking Population out of the Equation: Reformulating I=PAT. Institute for Women and Technology. URL http://www.readingfromtheleft.com/PDF/IPAT-Hynes.pdf.

Idso CD (2013). The positive externalities of carbon dioxide: Estimating the monetary benefits of rising atmospheric CO_2 concentrations on global food production. *Centre for the Study of Carbon Dioxide and Global Change*, October 21. URL http://web.uvic.ca/~kooten/Agriculture/CO2FoodBenefit%282013%29.pdf.

Inman M (2010). Mining the truth on coal supplies. A view that the world's leading electricity fuel – and major contributor to climate change – is running out. *National Geographic News*, September 9. URL https://news.nationalgeographic.com/news/2010/09/100908-energy-peak-coal/.

Ioannidis JPA (2005). Why most published research findings are false. *PLoS Medicine*, 2(8), 696–701. URL https://www.ncbi.nlm.nih.gov/pmc/articles/PMC1182327/pdf/pmed.0020124.pdf.

Ioannidis JPA, Munafo MR, Fusar-Poli P, Nosek BA, David SP (2014). Publication and other reporting biases in cognitive sciences: Detection, prevalence, and prevention. *Trends in Cognitive Sciences*, 18, 235–241.

IPCC (2017). Working Group 1: The Scientific Basis. Assessment report, Intergovernmental Panel on Climate Change. URL https://www.ipcc.ch/ipccreports/tar/wg1/042.htm.

Isaacson E (1912). *The Malthusian Limit. A Theory of a Possible Static Condition for the Human Race*. Methuen & Co. URL https://archive.org/details/malthusianlimitt00isaa.

Jacks GV, Whyte RO (1939). *The Rape of the Earth. A World Survey of Soil Erosion*. Faber and Faber Ltd.

Jacobs J (1969). *The Economy of Cities*. Random House.

Jacobs J (1992). *Systems of Survival: A Dialogue on the Moral Foundations of Commerce and Politics*. Random House.

Jacobs M (2012). Green Growth: Economic Theory and Political Discourse. Working paper CCCEP 108/GRI 92, Centre for Climate Change Economics and Policy/Grantham Research Institute on Climate Change and the Environment. URL http://www.lse.ac.uk/GranthamInstitute/wp-content/uploads/2012/10/WP92-green-growth-economic-theory-political-discourse.pdf.

Jacques PJ, Dunlap RE, Freeman M (2008). The organisation of denial: Conservative think tanks and environmental scepticism. *Environmental Politics*, 17(3), 349–385.

Janis IL (1972). *Victims of Groupthink: A Psychological Study of Foreign-policy Decisions and Fiascoes*. Houghton Mifflin. The book was revised and published in 1982 as *Groupthink: Psychological Studies of Policy Decisions and Fiascoes*.

Jarrett H (2011). *Environmental Quality in a Growing Economy*. Resources for the Future, Inc. by the Johns Hopkins Press.

Jevons WS (1866/1865). *The Coal Question. An Inquiry Concerning the Progress of the Nation, and the Probable Exhaustion of Our Coal-Mines*. MacMillan and Co. URL http://www.econlib.org/library/YPDBooks/Jevons/jvnCQ.html.

Johnson S (2010). *Where Good Ideas Come From: The Natural History of Innovation*. Riverhead Books.

Jones R (1859). *Literary Remains, Consisting of Lectures and Tracts on Political Economy of the Late Rev. Richard Jones*. J. Murray. URL https://archive.org/details/literaryremainsc00jone.

Jørgensen AE, Vigsøe D, Kristoffersen A, Rubin O (2002). Assessing the ecological footprint: A look at the WWF's Living Planet Report 2002. *Environmental Assessment Institute*. URL https://www.dors.dk/files/media/graphics/Synkron-Library/Publikationer/IMV/2002/ecological_footprint.pdf.

Kahn H, Brown WM, Martel L (1976). *The Next 200 Years: A Scenario for America and the World*. Morrow.

Kanter J (2009). Scientist: Warming could cut population to 1 billion. *New York Times*, March 13. URL http://dotearth.blogs.nytimes.com/2009/03/13/scientist-warming-could-cut-population-to-1-billion/?_r=0.

Kasun J (1999/1988). *The War Against Population: The Economics and Ideology of Population Control*. Ignatius, rev. edn.

Kauppi PE, Ausubel JH, Fang J, Mather AS, Sedjo RA, Waggoner PE (2006). Returning forests analyzed with the forest identity. *Proceedings of the National Academy of Sciences*, 103(46), 17574–17579. URL http://www.pnas.org/content/103/46/17574.full.

Kauppi PE, Sandström V, Lipponen A (2018). Forest resources of nations in relation to human well-being. *PLoS ONE*, 13(5).

Kay W (2018). *From Malthus to Mifepristone: A Primer on the Population Control Movement*. Amazon Digital Services LLC.

Kaysen C (1972). The computer that printed out W*O*L*F. *Foreign Affairs*, 50(4), 660–668. URL https://www.foreignaffairs.com/articles/1972-07-01/computer-printed-out-wolf.

Keir M (1926). *The Epic of Industry*. Yale University Press.

Kelley AC (1999). The Population Debate in Historical Perspective: Revisionism Revisited. Working Paper 99–09, Duke University Economics. URL https://papers.ssrn.com/sol3/papers.cfm?abstract_id=182633.

Kelley MB (1949). Population and food supply: The current scare. *The Scientific Monthly*, 68(1), 17–26. URL https://archive.org/details/in.ernet.dli.2015.534670.

Kershaw JBC (1928). *The Recovery and Use of Industrial and Other Waste*. Ernest Benn Limited.

Klein N (2014). *This Changes Everything: Capitalism vs the Climate*. Simon & Schuster.

Knappenberger PC, Michaels PJ (2014). Current wisdom: Record global temperature – Conflicting reports, contrasting implications. *Cato at Liberty*, December 10. URL http://www.cato.org/blog/current-wisdom-record-global-temperature-conflicting-reports-contrasting-implications.

Kneese AV (1970). Economic responsibility for the by-products of production. *Annals of the American Academy of Political and Social Science*, 389, 56–62. Special issue: Society and Its Physical Environment.

Knight LU (ND). Voluntary Human Extinction Movement website. URL http://www.vhemt.org/.

Knorr-Cetina K (1999). *Epistemic Cultures: How the Sciences Make Knowledge*. Harvard University Press.

Koningstein R, Fork D (2014). What it would really take to reverse climate change. *IEEE Spectrum*, November 18. URL http://spectrum.ieee.org/energy/renewables/what-it-would-really-take-to-reverse-climate-change.

Kropotkin P (1912/1898). *Fields, Factories and Workshops: or Industry Combined with Agriculture and Brain Work with Manual Work*. Thomas Nelson & Sons. URL http://theanarchistlibrary.org/library/petr-kropotkin-fields-factories-and-workshops-or-industry-combined-with-agriculture-and-brain-w.

Kruger J, Dunning D (1999). Unskilled and unaware of it: How difficulties in recognizing one's own incompetence lead to inflated self-assessments. *Journal of Personality and Social Psychology*, 77(6), 1121–1134.

Kuhn TS (1962). *The Structure of Scientific Revolutions*. University of Chicago Press.

Kunda Z (1990). The case for motivated reasoning. *Psychological Bulletin*, 108(3), 480–498.

Laframboise D (2009). Global disaster is so 1976. *NoFrakkingConsensus*, December 20. URL https://nofrakkingconsensus.com/2009/12/20/global-disaster-is-so-1976/.

Laframboise D (2011). An IPCC history lesson. *No Frakking Consensus*, February 15. URL https://nofrakkingconsensus.com/2011/02/15/an-ipcc-history-lesson/.

Laframboise D (2013). The scare story of 1881. *NoFrakkingConsensus.com*, May 10. URL https://nofrakkingconsensus.com/2013/05/10/the-scare-story-of-1881/.

Lalasz B (2013). Debate: What good are planetary boundaries? *Cool Green Science*, March 25. URL https://blog.nature.org/science/2013/03/25/debate-what-good-are-planetary-boundaries/.

Lamborn LL (1904). *Cottonseed Products. A Manual of the Treatment of Cottonseed for its Products and their Utilization in the Arts*. D. Van Nostrand Company. URL https://archive.org/details/cottonseedprodu00lambgoog.

Landsberg HH (1964). *Natural Resources for US Growth: A Look Ahead to the Year 2000*. Resources for the Future, Inc. by The Johns Hopkins Press.

Lane R (2015). *The Nature of Growth: The Postwar History of the Economy, Energy and the Environment*. PhD thesis, Department of International Relations, University of Sussex. URL http://sro.sussex.ac.uk/59597/.

Lardner D (1840). *The Steam Engine Familiarly Explained and Illustrated; with an Historical Sketch of its Invention and Progressive Improvement; its Applications to Navigation and Railways*. Taylor and Walton. URL https://books.google.ca/books?id=avcCyVp0T3sC.

Latour B (2017). The Anthropocene and the destruction of the globe. In: *Facing Gaia: Eight Lectures on the New Climatic Regime*, Polity Press.

Latour B, Woolgar S (1979). *Laboratory Life: The Social Construction of Scientific Facts*. Sage Publications.

Le Prestre Vauban S (1707). *Projet d'une Dixme Royale*. URL http://gallica.bnf.fr/ark:/12148/bpt6k105092d.

Le Roy Ladurie E (1971). *Times of Feast, Times of Famine: A History of Climate since the Year 1000*. Doubleday & Company. Revised and updated from 1967 French edition, translated by Barbara Bray.

Leffler WL (2008). *Petroleum Refining in Nontechnical Language*. PennWell, 4th edn.

Lenin VI (1901). *The Agrarian Question and the 'Critics of Marx'*, Vol. 2–3. Zarya.

Lewin B (2017). *Searching for the Catastrophe Signal. The Origins of the Intergovernmental Panel on Climate Change*. GWPF Books.

Lindzen R (2016). Global Warming and the Irrelevance of Science. Essay 4, Global Warming Policy Foundation. URL https://www.thegwpf.org/content/uploads/2016/04/Lindzen.pdf.

Lloyd HD (1881). The story of a great monopoly. *The Atlantic*, March. URL https://www.theatlantic.com/magazine/archive/1881/03/the-story-of-a-great-monopoly/306019/.

Lomborg B (2001). *The Skeptical Environmentalist. Measuring the Real State of the World*. Cambridge University Press.

Lomborg B (2014). How green policies hurt the poor. Cold? Hungry? Short of cash? You can always eat carbon credits. *The Spectator*, April 5. URL http://www.spectator.co.uk/2014/04/let-them-eat-carbon-credits/.

Lord CG, Ross L, Lepper MR (1979). Biased assimilation and attitude polarization: The effects of prior theories on subsequently considered evidence. *Journal of Personality and Social Psychology*, 37(11), 2098–2209.

Lox F (1992). *Packaging and Ecology*. Pira International.

Luker K (1984). *Abortion and the Politics of Motherhood*. University of California Press.

Lunge G (1887). *Coal Tar and Ammonia*. Gurney and Jackson. URL https://archive.org/details/coaltarandammon00lunggoog.

Luten DB (1980). Ecological optimism in the social sciences: The question of limits to growth. *American Behavioral Scientist*, 24(1), 125–151.

Macaulay TB (1830). Review of Sir Thomas More; or, Colloquies on the Progress and Prospects of Society by Robert Southey, Esq., LL.D., Poet Laureate. 2 volumes. London: 1829. *Edinburgh Review*, January. URL http://www.econlib.org/library/Essays/macS1.html.

Machiavelli N (1517). *Discourses on the First Decade of Titus Livius by Niccolo Machiavelli: Citizen and Secretary of Florence*. Published posthumously in 1531, translated from the Italian by Ninian Hill Thomson, URL http://www.online-literature.com/machiavelli/titus-livius/66/.

Machlup F (1962). The supply of inventors and inventions. In: National Bureau of Economic Research (ed.), *The Rate and Direction of Inventive Activity: Economic and Social Factors*, Princeton University Press. URL http://papers.nber.org/books/univ62-1.

Maddox J (1972). *The Doomsday Syndrome*. McGraw-Hill.

Magee CL, Devezas TC (2017). A simple extension of dematerialization theory: Incorporation of technical progress and the rebound effect. *Technological Forecasting & Social Change*, 117, 196–205.

Malin JC (1949). Review of *Road to Survival*. *Pacific Historical Review*, 18(2), 243–245.

Malthus TR (1826). *An Essay on the Principle of Population, or a View of Its Past and Present Effects on Human Happiness; with an Inquiry into Our Prospects Respecting the Future Removal or Mitigation of the Evils Which It Occasions*. John Murray. 6th edn. URL http://www.econlib.org/library/Malthus/malPlong.html.

Manitou Foundation (2017). Short Biography. MauriceStrong.net. URL https://www.mauricestrong.net/index.php/short-biography-mainmenu-6.

Mann C (2013). What if we never run out of oil? New technology and a little-known energy source suggest that fossil fuels may not be finite. This would be a miracle – and a nightmare. *The Atlantic*, May. URL https://www.theatlantic.com/magazine/archive/2013/05/what-if-we-never-run-out-of-oil/309294/.

Mann C (2018a). The book that incited a worldwide fear of overpopulation. *Smithsonian Magazine*, January. URL https://www.smithsonianmag.com/innovation/book-incited-worldwide-fear-overpopulation-180967499/.

Mann C (2018b). Can Planet Earth feed 10 billion people? Humanity has 30 years to find out. *The Atlantic*, March. URL https://www.theatlantic.com/magazine/archive/2018/03/charles-mann-can-planet-earth-feed-10-billion-people/550928/.

Mann C (2018c). *The Wizard and the Prophet: Two Remarkable Scientists and Their Dueling Visions to Shape Tomorrow's World*. Alfred A. Knopf.

Marshall A (1890). *Principles of Economics*, Vol. 1. MacMillan and Co. URL https://books.google.ca/books?id=bykoAAAAYAAJ&source=gbs_navlinks_s.

Martine G (2009). Population dynamics and policies in the context of global climate change. In: JM Guzmán, G Martine, G McGranahan, D Schensul, C Tacoli (eds.), *Population Dynamics and Climate Change*, United Nations Population Fund and International Institute for Environment and Development. URL http://citeseerx.ist.psu.edu/viewdoc/download?rep=rep1&type=pdf&doi=10.1.1.175.8928.

Marx K (1906/1894). *Capital*, Vol. 3. Charles H. Kerr & Company. URL http://www.archive.org/details/capitalcritiqueo03marx.

Mather KF (1944). *Enough and to Spare. Mother Earth can Nourish Every Man in Freedom*. Harper & Brothers.

McCollough J, Check Jr HF (2010). The Baleen whales' saving grace: The introduction of petroleum based products in the market and its impact on the whaling industry. 2(10), 3142–3157. URL http://www.mdpi.com/2071-1050/2/10/3142.

McDonald C (2015). How many Earths do we need? *BBC News*, June 16. URL http://www.bbc.com/news/magazine-33133712.

McGee JS (1958). Predatory price cutting: The Standard Oil (N. J.) case. *Journal of Law and Economics*, 1(1), 137–169.

McKibben B (1998a). *Maybe One. A Personal and Environmental Argument for Single-Child Families*. Simon & Schuster.

McKibben B (1998b). A special moment in history. The fate of our planet will be determined in the next few decades, through our technological, lifestyle, and population choices. *The Atlantic*, May. URL https://www.theatlantic.com/magazine/archive/1998/05/a-special-moment-in-history/377106/.

McKie R (2012). Stephen Emmott: Overpopulation is at the root of all the planet's troubles. *The Guardian*, July 15. URL https://www.theguardian.com/technology/2012/jul/15/overpopulation-root-planet-problems-emmott.

Meadows DH (1995). Who Causes Environmental Problems? Retrieved from the Donella Meadows Archives January 12. URL http://donellameadows.org/archives/who-causes-environmental-problems/.

Meadows DH, Meadows DL, Randers J, Behrens III WW (1972). *Limits to Growth. A Report for The Club of Rome's Project on the Predicament of Mankind*. Universe Books. URL http://www.donellameadows.org/wp-content/userfiles/Limits-to-Growth-digital-scan-version.pdf.

Meek R (ed.) (1971/1953). *Marx and Engels on the Population Bomb*. Ramparts Press, 2nd edn.

Meldola R (1905). *Coal and What We Get from It. A Romance of Applied Science*. Society for Promoting Christian Knowledge. URL https://archive.org/details/coalandwhatwege00meldgoog.

Mencken HL (1918). *In Defense of Women*. Alfred P. Knopf. URL http://onlinebooks.library.upenn.edu/webbin/gutbook/lookup?num=1270.

Merton RK (1968/1957). *Social Theory and Social Structure*. The Free Press/Simon & Schuster.

Miall S (1931). *A History of the British Chemical Industry*. Ernest Benn Limited.

Mill JS (1869). *On Liberty*. Longman, Roberts, & Green, 4th edn. URL http://www.econlib.org/library/Mill/mlLbty5.html.

Mill JS (1920/1848). *Principles of Political Economy with some of their Applications to Social Philosophy*. Longmans, Green and Co., Ashley edn. URL http://oll.libertyfund.org/titles/mill-principles-of-political-economy-ashley-ed.

Mock B (2013). How the Sierra Club learned to love immigration: A racist fringe of the nation's oldest and largest environmental group lost its battle over immigration. An inside look at the power struggle. *Colorlines*. URL https://www.colorlines.com/articles/how-sierra-club-learned-love-immigration.

Montague GH (1903). The later history of the Standard Oil Company. *The Quarterly Journal of Economics*, 17(2), 293–325.

Montague GH (1904). *The Rise and Progress of the Standard Oil Company*. Harper and Brothers. https://archive.org/details/riseprogressofst00montuoft or https://socialsciences.mcmaster.ca/econ/ugcm/3ll3/montague/standardoil.pdf.

Moore S, White KH (2016). *Fueling Freedom: Exposing the Mad War on Energy*. Regnery Publishing.

Mora C (2014). Revisiting the environmental and socioeconomic effects of population growth: a fundamental but fading issue in modern scientific, public, and political circles. *Ecology and Society*, 19(1). URL https://www.ecologyandsociety.org/vol19/iss1/art38/.

Moran A (ed.) (2015). *Climate Change: The Facts*. Stockade Books and Institute of Public Affairs. URL http://www.nipccreport.org/.

Morris E (2007). From horse power to horsepower. *Access*, 30, 2–9. URL http://www.uctc.net/access/30/Access%2030%20-%2002%20-%20Horse%20Power.pdf.

Morriss AP, Bogart WT, Meiners RE, Dorchak A (2011). *The False Promise of Green Energy*. Cato Institute.

Murtaugh PA, Schlax MG (2009). Reproduction and the carbon legacies of individuals. *Global Environmental Change*, 19(1), 14–20. URL https://www.biologicaldiversity.org/programs/population_and_sustainability/pdfs/OSUCarbonStudy.pdf.

Myers N, Simon JL (1994). *Scarcity or Abundance? A Debate on the Environment*. W.W. Norton & Company. URL http://www.juliansimon.com/writings/Norton/.

NASA/Goddard Space Flight Center (2016). Carbon dioxide fertilization greening Earth, study finds. URL www.sciencedaily.com/releases/2016/04/160426162610.htm.

Negative Population Growth (2017). National survey reveals US students' concerns about population and environment issues. Press release, December 19. URL http://www.npg.org/library/press-releases/pr-12192017.html.

New York Times (1959). Experts discuss monsters of sea. *New York Times*, 28 April.

Nisbet R (1980). *History of the Idea of Progress*. Basic Books.

Nitti FS (1894). *Population and the Social System*. S. Sonnenschein. URL https://archive.org/details/populationandso00nittgoog.

Norberg J (2016). *Progress. Ten Reasons to Look Forward to the Future*. OneWorld.

Nordhaus T (2018). The Earth's carrying capacity for human life is not fixed. *Aeon*, July 5. URL https://aeon.co/ideas/the-earths-carrying-capacity-for-human-life-is-not-fixed.

Nordhaus T, Blomqvist L, Shellenberger M (2012a). Beyond planetary boundaries. *The Breakthrough*, June 22. URL https://thebreakthrough.org/index.php/programs/conservation-and-development/beyond-planetary-boundaries.

Nordhaus T, Blomqvist L, Shellenberger M (2012b). The planetary boundaries hypothesis. A review of the evidence. *The Breakthrough Institute*. URL https://thebreakthrough.org/blog/Planetary%20Boundaries%20web.pdf.

Nosek B (2017). Letter from the executive director. Center for Open Science. URL https://cos.io/about/brief-history-cos-2013-2017/.

Nuccitelli D (2015). Scientists warned the president about global warming 50 years ago today. *The Guardian*, November 5. URL https://www.theguardian.com/environment/climate-consensus-97-per-cent/2015/nov/05/scientists-warned-the-president-about-global-warming-50-years-ago-today.

O'Barney GO (1980). Global 2000 Report to the President: Entering the Twenty-First Century, Volume 1. Technical report, Seven Locks Press. URL https://www.cartercenter.org/resources/pdfs/pdf-archive/global2000reporttothepresident--enteringthe21stcentury-01011991.pdf.

O'Fallon BD, Fehren-Schmit L (2011). Native Americans experienced a strong population bottleneck coincident with European contact. *Proceedings of the National Academy of Sciences*, 108(51), 20444–20448.

Ogden CK (1917). *Uncontrolled Breeding: Or, Fecundity Versus Civilization; a Contribution to the Study of Over-population as the Cause of War and the Chief Obstacle to the Emancipation of Women*. Critic and Guide Co. (Written as 'Adelyne More'), URL https://archive.org/details/uncontrolledbre00moregoog.

Olson S (1971). *The Depletion Myth: A History of Railroad Use of Timber*. Harvard University Press.

O'Neill BC, Dalton M, Fuch R, Jiang L, Pachauri S, Zigova K (2010). Global demographic trends and future carbon emissions. *Proceedings of the National Economy of Sciences*, 107(41), 17521–17526. URL http://www.pnas.org/content/107/41/17521.

O'Neill DW, Fanning AL, Lamb WF, Steinberger JK (2018). A good life for all within planetary boundaries. *Nature Sustainability*, 1 February, 88–95. URL https://www.nature.com/articles/s41893--018--0021--4.pdf.

Oosthoek KJ (1998). The role of wood in world history. *Environmental History Resources*, October 18. URL http://www.eh-resources.org/wood.html.

Oransky I (2015). Unlike a rolling stone: Is science really better than journalism at self-correction? *The Conversation*, April 12. URL https://mashable.com/2015/04/12/science-self-correction/#SUNf62PlXaqT.

Ortes G (1775). *Riflessioni sulla popolazione delle nazioni per rapporto all'economia nazionale (Reflections on the Population of Nations in Relation to National Economy)*. URL https://books.google.ca/books?id=xlVmAAAAcAAJ.

Osborn Jr HF (1948). *Our Plundered Planet*. Little, Brown. URL http://chla.library.cornell.edu/cgi/t/text/text-idx?c=chla;idno=2932687.

Pachauri RK (2015). IPCC resignation letter, February 24. URL http://www.ipcc.ch/pdf/ar5/150224_Patchy_letter.pdf.

Paddock W, Paddock P (1967). *Famine 1975!* Little, Brown.

Patzek T, Croft GD (2010). A global coal production forecast with multi-Hubbert cycle analysis. *Energy*, 35(8), 3109–3122. URL https://www.sciencedirect.com/science/article/pii/S0360544210000617.

Paunio M (2018). Kicking Away the Energy Ladder. Briefing 30, Global Warming Policy Foundation.

PBS (2008). Ted Turner on Charlie Rose. Charlie Rose Show, April 1, 2008. URL http://www.tedturner.com/2008/04/ted-turner-on-charlie-rose-pbs-part-3/.

Pearce F (2010). *Peoplequake. Mass Migration, Ageing Nations and the Coming Population Crash*. Eden Project Books.

Pearce F (2014). It's not overpopulation that causes climate change, it's overconsumption. *The Guardian*, September 19. URL https://www.theguardian.com/commentisfree/2014/sep/19/not-overpopulation-that-causes-climate-change-but-overconsumption.

Perelman M (1979). Marx, Malthus and the concept of natural resource scarcity. *Antipode*, 11(2), 80–91.

Peron J (1995). Exploding population myths. *Fraser Institute Critical Issues Bulletin*, October. URL https://www.fraserinstitute.org/sites/default/files/ExplodingPopulationMyths.pdf.

Perry GP (1908). *Wealth from Waste or Gathering Up the Fragments*. Fleming H. Revell Company.

Peterson TC, Connolley WM, Fleck J (2008). The myth of the 1970s global cooling scientific consensus. *Bulletin of the American Meteorological Society*, 89, 1325–37.

Petroni S (2009). Policy review: Thoughts on addressing population and climate change in a just and ethical manner. *Population and Environment*, 30(6), 275–289.

Petroski H (1992). *The Evolution of Useful Things*. Random House.

Petschel-Held G, Schellnhuber HJ, Bruckner T, Tóth FL, Hasselmann K (1999). The tolerable windows approach: theoretical and methodological foundations. *Climatic Change*, 41(3–4), 303–331.

Pett J (2012). The cartoon seen 'round the world'. *Lexington Herald Leader*, March 18. URL https://www.kentucky.com/opinion/op-ed/article44162106.html.

Petty W (1888/1682). *Essays on Mankind and Political Arithmetic*. Cassell & Company. URL http://www.archive.org/details/essaysonmankindp00pettuoft.

Phillips L (2015). *Austerity Ecology and the Collapse-Porn Addicts. A Defence of Growth, Progress, Industry and Stuff*. Zero Books.

Pinker S (2018a). Enlightenment environmentalism. The case for ecomodernism. *The Breakthrough*, Winter. URL https://thebreakthrough.org/index.php/journal/no.-8-winter-2018/enlightenment-environmentalism.

Pinker S (2018b). The Enlightenment is working. *Wall Street Journal*, February 9. URL https://www.wsj.com/articles/the-enlightenment-is-working-1518191343.

Pinker S (2018c). *Enlightenment Now: The Case for Reason, Science, Humanism, and Progress*. Viking Press.

Plato (Approximately 360 BC). *Critias*. Translated by Benjamin Jowett, URL http://classics.mit.edu/Plato/critias.html.

Plato (Approximately 380 BC). *The Republic*. Translated by Benjamin Jowett, URL http://classics.mit.edu/Plato/republic.html.

Plautz J (2014). The climate-change solution no one will talk about. *The Atlantic*, November 1. URL https://www.theatlantic.com/health/archive/2014/11/the-climate-change-solution-no-one-will-talk-about/382197/.

Playfair L (1852). On the chemical principles involved in the manufactures of the exhibition as indicating the necessity of industrial instruction. In: *Lectures on the Results of the Great Exhibition of 1851*, Society for the Encouragement of Arts, Manufactures and Commerce. URL https://books.google.ca/books?id=fw4LAAAAIAAJ.

Plimer I (2015). The science and politics of climate change. In: A Moran (ed.), *Climate Change: The Facts*, Stockade Books and Institute of Public Affairs.

PMC (2011). Global population's annual growth. Population Media Center, May 2. URL https://www.populationmedia.org/2011/05/02/global-populations-annual-growth/.

Podesta J, Wirth T (2018). Women's rights issues are climate change issues. *Washington Post*, January 23. URL https://www.washingtonpost.com/opinions/womens-rights-issues-are-climate-change-issues/2018/01/22/c59b9b00-f65a-11e7-b34a-b85626af34ef_story.html.

Polimeni J, Mayumi K, Giampietro M, Alcott B (2008). *Jevons' Paradox: The Myth of Resource Efficiency*. Earthscan. URL https://uberty.org/wp-content/uploads/2015/08/John_M._Polimeni_Kozo_Mayumi_Mario_Giampietro.pdf.

Ponte L (1976). *The Cooling*. Prentice-Hall.

Popper K (1959). *The Logic of Scientific Discovery*. Routledge.

PopularTechnologynet (2013). 1970s global cooling alarmism. *PopularTechnology.net*, February 28. URL http://www.populartechnology.net/2013/02/the-1970s-global-cooling-alarmism.html.

Population Matters (2018). Climate change and children – a growing concern? *Population Matters Newswatch*, February 7. URL https://www.populationmatters.org/climate-change-and-children-a-growing-concern/.

Porritt J (2015). The hypocrisy at the heart of today's food security debate. *Sustainable Food Trust*, July 24. URL https://sustainablefoodtrust.org/articles/overpopulation-food-security-debate/.

Porter E (1995). *Are We Running Out of Oil?* American Petroleum Institute. URL https://www.scribd.com/document/354879536/API-DP-081--1995.

PRB (2014). Making the Connection: Population Dynamics and Climate Compatible Development Recommendations from an Expert Working Group. Technical report, Population Reference Bureau. URL http://www.prb.org/pdf15/population-climate-full-paper.pdf.

Preston SH (1996). The effect of population growth on environmental quality. *Population Research and Policy Review*, 15(2), 95–108.

Price ED (1886). The utilisation of waste materials. In: *Hazell's Annual Encyclopedia*, Hazell, Watson and Viney. URL http://books.google.ca/books?id=dv0BAAAAYAAJ&source=gbs_book_other_versions_r&cad=1_1.

Price RG (2018). My Krauthammer conversion. *C2C Journal*, July 7. URL http://www.c2cjournal.ca/2018/07/my-krauthammer-conversion/.

Priest T (2014). Hubbert's peak. The great debate over the end of oil. *Historical Studies in the Natural Sciences*, 44(1), 37–79.

Proudhon PJ (1886/1848). *The Malthusians*. International Publishing Company. URL https://theanarchistlibrary.org/library/pierre-joseph-proudhon-the-malthusians.

Prystupa M (2015). China ends one-child policy. Is the Earth's climate doomed? *National Observer*, October 31. URL https://www.nationalobserver.com/2015/10/31/news/china-ends-one-child-policy-earths-climate-doomed.

PWFS (1967). The World's Food Problem. Volume 1: Report of the Panel on the World Food Supply. Technical report, President's Science Advisory Committee.

Reed LW (1980). Witch-hunting for robber barons: The Standard Oil story. *The Freeman*, March. URL https://fee.org/articles/witch-hunting-for-robber-barons-the-standard-oil-story/.

Rees J (1985). *Natural Resources: Allocation, Economics and Policy*. Methuen & Co. Ltd.

Rees WE (2002). Footprint: Our impact on Earth is getting heavier. *Nature*, 420, 267–268. URL https://www.nature.com/articles/420267b.

Reiter P (2008). Global warming and malaria: knowing the horse before hitching the cart. *Malaria Journal*, 7(Suppl 1), S3.

Relman DA, Hamburg MA, Choffnes ER, Mack A (2008). *Global Climate Change and Extreme Weather Events: Understanding the Contributions to Infectious Disease Emergence: Workshop Summary*. National Academies Press. URL https://www.ncbi.nlm.nih.gov/books/NBK45737/.

Reuters (2009). China says population controls help fight climate change. *Reuters*, December 11. URL https://uk.reuters.com/article/us-climate-copenhagen-china-population/china-says-population-controls-help-fight-climate-change-idUKTRE5BA1ME20091211.

Revkin AC (2015). Can humanity's 'great acceleration' be managed and, if so, how? *New York Times Dot Earth*, January 15. URL https://dotearth.blogs.nytimes.com/2015/01/15/can-humanitys-great-acceleration-be-managed-and-if-so-how/.

Ridley M (2002). The profits of doom. *The Spectator*, 23 February. URL http://archive.spectator.co.uk/article/23rd-february-2002/10/the-profits-of-doom.

Ridley M (2010). *The Rational Optimist*. Harper.

Rieder TN (2016). *Toward a Small Family Ethic. How Overpopulation and Climate Change Are Affecting the Morality of Procreation*. Springer.

Ripple WJ, Wolf C, Newsome TM, Galetti M, Alamgir M, Crist E, Mahmoud MI, Laurance WF (2017). World scientists' warning to humanity: a second notice. *BioScience*, 67(12), 1026–1028. URL https://academic.oup.com/bioscience/article/67/12/1026/4605229.

Ritchie H (2017). What the history of London's air pollution can tell us about the future of today's growing megacities. Our World in Data. URL https://ourworldindata.org/london-air-pollution.

Ritchie H, Roser M (2018a). Renewables. Our World in Data. URL https://ourworldindata.org/renewables.

Ritchie H, Roser M (2018b). Water access, resources & sanitation. Our World in Data. URL https://ourworldindata.org/water-access-resources-sanitation.

Robert TM (1798). *An Essay on the Principle of Population as It Affects the Future Improvement of Society, with Remarks on the Speculations of Mr. Godwin, M. Condorcet, and Other Writers*. URL http://www.econlib.org/library/Malthus/malPop.html.

Roberts R (2018). John Ioannidis on statistical significance, economics and replication. EconTalk Podcast. The Library of Economics and Liberty. URL http://www.econtalk.org/john-ioannidis-on-statistical-significance-economics-and-replication/?highlight=%5B%22john%22,%22ioannidis%22%5D.

Robertson TS (2012). *The Malthusian Moment: Global Population Growth and the Birth of American Environmentalism*. Rutgers University Press.

Robinson FS (2009). *The Case for Rational Optimism*. Transaction Publishers.

Rockefeller Commission (1972). Population and the American Future. Technical report, Commission on Population Growth and the American Future. Non-paginated version available at http://www.population-security.org/rockefeller/001_population_growth_and_the_american_future.htm.

Rockström J, Steffen W, Noone K, Persson A, Chapin FS, Lambin E, Lenton TM, Scheffer M, Folke C, Schellnhuber HJ, Nykvist B, de Wit CA, Hughes T, van der Leeuw S, Rodhe H, Sörlin S, Snyder PK, Costanza R, Svedin U, Falkenmark M, Karlberg L, Corell RW, Fabry VJ, Hansen J, Walker B, Liverman D, Richardson K, Crutzen P, , Foley J (2009a). Planetary boundaries: exploring the safe operating space for humanity. *Ecology and Society*, 14(2), Article 32. URL http://www.ecologyandsociety.org/vol14/iss2/art32/.

Rockström J, Steffen W, Noone K, Persson A, Chapin FS, Lambin EF, Lenton TM, Scheffer M, Folke C, Schellnhuber HJ, Nykvist B, de Wit CA, Hughes T, van der Leeuw S, Rodhe H, Sörlin S, Snyder PK, Costanza R, Svedin U, Falkenmark M, Karlberg L, Corell RW, Fabry VJ, Hansen J, Walker B, Liverman D, Richardson K, Crutzen P, Foley JA (2009b). A safe operating space for humanity. *Nature*, 461, 472–475. URL https://www.nature.com/articles/461472a.

Røpke I (2004). Analysis: The early history of modern ecological economics. *Ecological Economics*, 50, 293–314. URL https://www.researchgate.net/publication/222564668_The_Early_History_of_Modern_Ecological_Economics.

Roser M (2015). Energy production & changing energy sources. Our World in Data. URL http://ourworldindata.org/data/resources-energy/energy-production-and-changing-energy-sources/.

Roser M (2017). Life expectancy. Our World in Data. URL https://ourworldindata.org/life-expectancy.

Roser M, Ortiz-Ospina E (2017/2013). World population growth. Our World in Data. URL https://ourworldindata.org/world-population-growth.

Roser M, Ortiz-Ospina E (2018). Global extreme poverty. Our World in Data. URL https://ourworldindata.org/extreme-poverty.

Roser M, Ritchie H (2017). Food per person. Our World in Data. URL https://ourworldindata.org/food-per-person.

Roser M, Ritchie H (2018a). Indoor air pollution. Our World in Data. URL https://ourworldindata.org/indoor-air-pollution.

Roser M, Ritchie H (2018b). Yields and land use in agriculture. Our World in Data. URL https://ourworldindata.org/yields-and-land-use-in-agriculture.

Rosling H (2013). Viewpoint: Five ways the world is doing better than you think. *BBC News Magazine*, November 6. URL http://www.bbc.com/news/magazine-24835822.

Rosling H, Rosling O, Rönnlund AR (2018). *Factfulness. Ten Reasons We're Wrong About the World – and Why Things Are Better Than You Think*. Flatiron Books.

Ross L, Ward A (1996). Naive realism in everyday life: implications for social conflict and misunderstanding. In: ESR Brown Terrance, E Turiel (eds.), *Values and Knowledge*, Erlbaum.

Royal Society (2012). People and the Planet. Technical report, The Royal Society. URL https://royalsociety.org/topics-policy/projects/people-planet/.

Ruddiman WF (2003). The anthropogenic greenhouse era began thousands of years ago. *Climatic Change*, 61(3), 261–293. URL http://stephenschneider.stanford.edu/Publications/PDF_Papers/Ruddiman2003.pdf.

Ryan JA (1911). *Theories of population*. Robert Appleton Company. URL http://www.newadvent.org/cathen/12276a.htm.

Sabin P (2013). *The Bet*. Yale University Press.

Sady W (2017). Ludwik Fleck. In: EN Zalta (ed.), *The Stanford Encyclopedia of Philosophy*, URL https://plato.stanford.edu/archives/fall2017/entries/fleck/.

Saether A (1993). Otto Diederich Lütken – 40 years before Malthus? *Population Studies*, 47(3), 511–517.

Saint Jerome (1893). The perpetual virginity of blessed Mary. In: P Schaff, H Wace (eds.), *A Select Library of Nicene and Post-Nicene Fathers of the Christian Church: St. Jerome: Letters and select works*, Christian Literature Company. URL https://books.google.ca/books?id=NQUNAAAAIAAJ.

Saito K (2016). Why ecosocialism needs Marx. *Monthly Review*, November 1. URL https://monthlyreview.org/2016/11/01/why-ecosocialism-needs-marx/.

Sanger M (1922). *The Pivot of Civilization*. Project Gutenberg. URL https://www.gutenberg.org/files/1689/1689-h/1689-h.htm.

Satterthwaite D (2006). *Barbara Ward and the Origins of Sustainable Development*. International Institute for Environment and Development. URL http://pubs.iied.org/pdfs/11500IIED.pdf.

Satterthwaite D (2009). The implications of population growth and urbanization for climate change. *Environment & Urbanization*, 21(2), 545–567. URL http://journals.sagepub.com/doi/abs/10.1177/0956247809344361.

Sax K (1955). *Standing Room Only*. Beacon Press.

Say JB (1821). *Letters to Mr. Malthus, and A Catechism of Political Economy (translated from the French by John Richter)*. Sherwood, Neely and Jones. URL http://oll.libertyfund.org/titles/say-letters-to-mr-malthus-and-a-catechism-of-political-economy.

Sayre NF (2008). The genesis, history, and limits of carrying capacity. *Annals of the Association of American Geographers*, 98(1), 120–134.

Scherer FM (2011). Standard Oil as a technological innovator. *Review of Industrial Organization*, 38(3), 225–233. Non-gated version available at https://research.hks.harvard.edu/publications/getFile.aspx?Id=644.

Schnaiberg A (1980). *The Environment: From Surplus to Scarcity*. Oxford University Press.

Schneider SH, Mesirow LE (1977). *The Genesis Strategy. Climate and Global Survival*. Plenum Books.

Schumpeter JA (1954). *History of Economic Analysis*. Oxford University Press.

Scientific American (2009). Earth Talk: Does population growth impact climate change? Does the rate at which people are reproducing need to be controlled to save the environment? *Scientific American*, July 29. URL http://www.scientificamerican.com/article/population-growth-climate-change/.

Scott JC (1998). *Seeing Like a State: How Certain Schemes to Improve the Human Condition Have Failed*. Yale University Press.

Scovronicka N, Budolfson MB, Dennig F, Fleurbaey M, Siebert A, Socolow RH, Spears D, Wagner F (2017). Impact of population growth and population ethics on climate change mitigation policy. *Proceedings of the National Academy of Sciences*, 114(46), 12338–12343. URL http://www.pnas.org/content/114/46/12338.

Shelesnyak MC (ed.) (1969). *Growth of Population: Consequences and Control*. Gordon and Breach.

Shelford VA (1919). Fortunes in wastes and fortunes in fish. *The Scientific Monthly*, 9(7), 97–124. URL https://archive.org/details/scientificmonthl09ameruoft.

Simon JL (1977). *The Economics of Population Growth*. Princeton University Press.

Simon JL (1981). *The Ultimate Resource*. Princeton University Press.

Simon JL (ed.) (1990). *Population Matters: People, Resources, Environment, and Immigration*. Transaction Publishers.

Simon JL (1994). The art of forecasting: A wager. *Cato Journal*, 14(1), 159–161. URL http://object.cato.org/sites/cato.org/files/serials/files/cato-journal/1994/5/cj14n1--14.pdf.

Simon JL (1995). *The State of Humanity*. Basil Blackwell. URL http://old.positivepress.com/pn/essays/stateof1.php3.

Simon JL (1996). *The Ultimate Resource 2*. Princeton University Press. URL http://www.juliansimon.com/writings/Ultimate_Resource/.

Simon JL (ed.) (1998). *The Economics of Population: Classic Writings*. Transaction Publishers.

Simon JL (1999a). *The Hoodwinking of a Nation*. URL http://www.juliansimon.com/writings/Truth_Shortage/.

Simon JL (1999b). *Hoodwinking the Nation*. Transaction Publishers. The online Simon archive version of this work we are using elsewhere in this book has a different title and differs slightly in terms of content.

Simon JL (2001). Global confusion, 1980: A hard look at the Global 2000 report. *The Public Interest*, 65(3), 3–20. URL https://www.nationalaffairs.com/storage/app/uploads/public/58e/1a4/d02/58e1a4d0260b1901870571.pdf.

Simon JL, Kahn H (1984). *The Resourceful Earth: A Response to Global 2000*. Basil Blackwell.

Smil V (1998). Future of oil: trends and surprises. *OPEC Review*, 22(4), 253–276.

Smil V (2001). *Enriching the Earth. Fritz Haber, Carl Bosch, and the Transformation of World Food Production*. MIT Press.

Smil V (2006). Energy at the Crossroads. Background notes for a presentation at the Global Science Forum Conference on Scientific Challenges for Energy Research, Paris, May 17–18, 2006. URL http://phad.cc.umanitoba.ca/~vsmil/pdf_pubs/oecd.pdf.

Smil V (2008). *Global Catastrophes and Trends: The Next Fifty Years*. MIT Press.

Smil V (2014a). *Energy in World History*. Westview Press.

Smil V (2014b). A global transition to renewable energy will take many decades. *Scientific American*, January 1, 52–57.

Smil V (2014c). How green is Europe? *The American*, September 30. URL http://www.vaclavsmil.com/wp-content/uploads/smil-article-how-green-is-europe-20140930.pdf.

Smil V (2017). *Energy and Society: A History*. MIT Press.

Smith JR, Phillips MO, Smith TR (1961). *Industrial and Commercial Geography*. Henry Holt and Company, 4th edn.

Smith N (2018). The population bomb has been defused. The Earth and humanity will survive as fertility rates fall almost everywhere. *Bloomberg Views*, March 18. URL https://www.bloomberg.com/view/articles/2018-03-16/decline-in-world-fertility-rates-lowers-risks-of-mass-starvation.

Sowell T (1995). *The Vision of the Anointed: Self-Congratulation as a Basis for Social Policy*. Basic Books.

Spencer H (1857). Progress: Its law and cause. *The Westminster Review*, April.

Spencer H (1891). Progress: Its law and cause. In: *Essays: Scientific, Political and Speculative, Vol. 1*, Williams and Norgate. Non-paginated version available at http://oll.libertyfund.org/titles/spencer-essays-scientific-political-and-speculative-3-vols-1891.

Spengler JJ (1933). Population doctrines in the United States. I. Anti-Malthusianism. *Journal of Political Economy*, 41(4), 433–467.

Spengler JJ (1966). The economist and the population question. *The American Economic Review*, 56(1/2), 1–24.

Spengler JJ (1966/1942). *French Predecessors of Malthus. A Study in Eighteenth-century Wage and Population Theory*. Routledge.

Spitz PH (1988). *Petrochemicals. The Rise of an Industry*. John Wiley & Sons.

Stanberry L (2017). Gloria Steinem: Feminist unicorn and self-professed hope-aholic. *Factory 29*, May 9. URL http://www.refinery29.com/2017/05/153643/gloria-steinem-exclusive-interview-create-cultivate-conference.

Stangeland CE (1904). Pre-Malthusian theories of population: A study in economic theory. *Studies in History, Economics and Public Law*, 21(3), 395–746. URL https://archive.org/details/premalthusiandoc00stanrich.

Steffen W, Richardson K, Rockström J, Cornell SE, Fetzer I, Bennett EM, Biggs R, Carpenter SR, de Vries W, de Wit CA, Folke C, Gerten D, Heinke J, Mace GM, Persson LM, Ramanathan V, Reyers B, Sörlin S (2015). Planetary boundaries: guiding human development on a changing planet. *Science*, 347(6223), 1259855. Supporting and promotional material is available at http://www.stockholmresilience.org/research/research-news/2015-01-15-planetary-boundaries---an-update.html.

Steffen W, Rockström J, Costanza R (2011). How defining planetary boundaries can transform our approach to growth. *Solutions*, 2(3), 59–65.

Sterman JD, Siegel L, Rooney JN (2018). Does replacing coal with wood lower CO_2 emissions? Dynamic lifecycle analysis of wood bioenergy. *Environmental Research Letters*, 13(1), 015007. URL http://iopscience.iop.org/article/10.1088/1748-9326/aaa512/meta.

Steven G, Greenland S (2007). Assessing the unreliability of the medical literature: A response to Why most published research findings are false. URL http://www.bepress.com/jhubiostat/paper135.

Stott P (2007). Global warming is not a crisis. *ABC News*, March 9. URL https://abcnews.go.com/International/story?id=2938762&page=1.

Strong M (1972). Opening Statement by Maurice Strong, Secretary-General of the Conference. United Nations Conference on the Human Environment. URL https://www.mauricestrong.net/index.php/speeches-remarks3/103-stockholm.

Strong M (2009). IUCN Environmental Dialogue. URL https://www.mauricestrong.net/index.php/conference-report.

Sulston J, Rumsby M, Green N (2013). People and the planet. *Environmental and Resource Economics*, 55(4), 469–474. URL https://link.springer.com/article/10.1007/s10640-013-9681-8.

Sutton WR (1984). *Herman Frasch: German immigrant chemist, Standard Oil, petroleum; Ohio, Louisiana*. PhD thesis. URL https://digitalcommons.lsu.edu/cgi/viewcontent.cgi?article=4970&context=gradschool_disstheses.

Symes J (1886). The plain truth about Malthusianism. *The Malthusian*, 8(6), 46–47.

Taber CS, Lodge M (2006). Motivated skepticism in the evaluation of political beliefs. *American Journal of Political Science*, 50(3), 755–769.

Talbot FA (1920). *Millions from Waste*. J.B. Lippincott Company.

Tarbell IM (1904). *The History of the Standard Oil Company*. McClure, Phillips & Company. URL https://archive.org/details/cu31924096224799.

Taylor PJ (2013). *Extraordinary Cities: Millennia of Moral Syndromes, World-Systems and City/State Relations*. Edward Elgar.

Tertullian (Quintus Septimius Florens Tertullianus) (Approximately 203 AD). *On the Soul*. URL http://www.newadvent.org/fathers/0310.htm.

Tetlock P (2005). *Expert Political Judgment*. Princeton University Press.

Thornton S (2017). Karl Popper. In: EN Zalta (ed.), *The Stanford Encyclopedia of Philosophy*, URL https://plato.stanford.edu/archives/sum2017/entries/popper/.

Tinbergen J, Dolman AJ, van Ettinger J (1976). *RIO: Reshaping the International Order. A Report to the Club of Rome*. New American Library.

Tobias MC (2013). The Ehrlich factor: A brief history of the fate of humanity, with Dr Paul R. Ehrlich. *Forbes*, January 16. URL https://www.forbes.com/sites/michaeltobias/2013/01/16/the-ehrlich-factor-a-brief-history-of-the-fate-of-humanity-with-dr-paul-r-ehrlich/#6755fcf32a1e.

Tobin KA (2004). *Politics and Population Control: A Documentary History*. Greenwood Publishing Group.

Toynbee A (1913/1884). *Lectures on the Industrial Revolution of the Eighteenth Century in England; Popular Addresses, Notes and Other Fragments, Together with a Reminiscence*. Longmans, Green. URL https://archive.org/details/lecturesonindust00toynuoft.

Tupy ML (2018a). Julian Simon Was Right: A Half-Century of Population Growth, Increasing Prosperity, and Falling Commodity Prices. Economic Development Bulletin 29, Cato Institute. URL https://www.cato.org/publications/economic-development-bulletin/julian-simon-was-right-half-century-population-growth.

Tupy ML (2018b). What are the exceptions to human progress? *HumanProgress.org*, February 2. URL http://humanprogress.org/blog/what-are-the-exceptions-to-human-progress.

UN (ND). Timothy E. Wirth (USA). United Nations Foundation webpage. URL http://www.unfoundation.org/who-we-are/board/timothy-e-wirth.html.

UN (1973/1953). The Determinants and Consequences of Population Trends. New Summary of Findings on Interaction of Demographic, Economic and Social Factors. Volume 1. Population Studies 50, United Nations Department of Economic and Social Affairs. Authored anonymously by economist Joseph Spengler.

UN (2001). World Population Monitoring 2001. Population, Environment and Development. Technical report, United Nations Department of Economic and Social Affairs, Population Division. URL http://www.un.org/en/development/desa/population/publications/environment/population-monitoring.shtml.

UN (ND). Views and Policies Concerning Population Growth and Fertility among Governments in Intermediate-Fertility Countries. Technical report, Department of Economic and Social Affairs, United Nations Population Division. URL http://www.un.org/esa/population/publications/completingfertility/RevisedPOPDIVPPSpaper.PDF.

UNEP (ND). Maurice F. Strong. United Nations Environment Programme webpage. URL http://web.unep.org/exhibit/UNEP-Executive-directors/maurice-f-strong.

UNEP (2016). Global Material Flows and Resource Productivity. Assessment Report for the UNEP International Resource Panel. Technical report, United Nations Environment Program International Resource Panel. URL http://www.resourcepanel.org/reports/global-material-flows-and-resource-productivity.

UNEP IRP (2011). Decoupling Natural Resource use and Environmental Impacts from Economic Growth. Technical report, UNEP International Resource Panel. URL https://sustainabledevelopment.un.org/index.php?page=view&type=400&nr=151&menu=1515.

UNEP IRP (2016). Global Material Flows and Resource Productivity. Assessment report, United Nations Environment Program International Resource Panel.

United States Congress (1973). Energy Reorganization Act of 1973. Hearings First Session, on H.R. 11510, Ninety-third Congress. URL https://babel.hathitrust.org/cgi/pt?id=mdp.39015001314395;view=1up;seq=3.

USBC (1907). Report of the Commissioner of Corporations on the Petroleum Industry. Washington. Technical report, US Bureau of Corporations. URL https://catalog.hathitrust.org/Record/100437904.

USGARP (1975). Understanding Climatic Change. Technical report, United States Committee for the Global Atmospheric Research Program. URL https://archive.org/details/understandingcli00unit.

USIC (1899). *An Inside View of Trusts.* United States Industrial Commission. URL https://archive.org/details/cu31924030065977.

Vallin P (1983). French Roman Catholics and Malthusianism before 1870. In: J Dupâquier, A Fauve-Chamoux, E Grebenik (eds.), *Malthus, Past and Present,* Academic Press.

van den Bergh J, Verbruggen H (1999). Spatial sustainability, trade and indicators: an evaluation of the ecological footprint. *Ecological Economics*, 29(1), 61–72.

Various (1998). Bicentennial Symposium on Malthus's Essay on Population. *Organization and Environment* 11 (4).

Vinck D (2010). *The Sociology of Scientific Work*. Edward Elgar.

Vogt W (1948). *Road to Survival.* William Sloane Associates, Inc.

von Storch H, Stehr N (2006). Anthropogenic climate change: a reason for concern since the 18th century and earlier. *Geografiska Annaler Series A: Physical Geography*, 88(2), 107–113. URL http://www.hvonstorch.de/klima/pdf/geografiske-annaler-2006.pdf.

Voosen P (2018). Meet Vaclav Smil, the man who has quietly shaped how the world thinks about energy. *Science*, March 21. URL http://www.sciencemag.org/news/2018/03/meet-vaclav-smil-man-who-has-quietly-shaped-how-world-thinks-about-energy.

Wackernagel M, Rees W (1996). *Our Ecological Footprint*. New Society Press.

Waggoner PE, Ausubel JH (2002). A framework for sustainability science: A renovated IPAT identity. *Proceedings of the National Academy of Sciences*, 99(12), 7860–7865. URL http://www.pnas.org/content/pnas/99/12/7860.full.pdf.

Walker G (2007). Newsmaker of the year: Rajendra Pachauri. *Nature*, 450(7173), 1150–1155. URL http://www.nature.com/news/2007/071219/full/4501150a.html.

Ward B (1973). Only one Earth. *UNESCO Courier*, January, pp. 8–10. URL http://unesdoc.unesco.org/images/0007/000748/074879eo.pdf.

Ward B, Dubos R (1972). *Only One Earth: The Care and Maintenance of a Small Planet*. W.W. Norton & Company.

Ward JD, Sutton PC, Werner AD, Costanza R, Mohr SH, Simmons CT (2016). Is decoupling GDP growth from environmental impact possible? *PLOS One*, 11(10), e0164733. URL http://journals.plos.org/plosone/article?id=10.1371/journal.pone.0164733.

Waterfield B (2013). EU policy on climate change is right even if science was wrong, says commissioner. *The Daily Telegraph*, September 16. URL https://www.telegraph.co.uk/news/earth/environment/climatechange/10313261/EU-policy-on-climate-change-is-right-even-if-science-was-wrong-says-commissioner.html.

Watts A (2013). The 1970s global cooling compilation – Looks much like today: A compilation of news articles on the global cooling scare of the 1970s. *WattsUpWithThat?*, March 1. URL https://wattsupwiththat.com/2013/03/01/global-cooling-compilation/.

Watts A (2014). A brief history of climate panic and crisis... both warming and cooling. *WattsUpWithThat?*, July 29. URL https://wattsupwiththat.com/2014/07/29/a-brief-history-of-climate-panic-and-crisis-both-warming-and-cooling/.

Wayland F (1870/1838). *Elements of Political Economy*. Gould and Lincoln. URL http://www.franciswayland.org/wayland.pdf.

Weart S (2018). *The Discovery of Global Warming*. American Institute of Physics. URL https://history.aip.org/climate/index.htm.

Weissman S (1971). Prologue. In: RL Meek (ed.), *Marx and Engels on the Population Bomb*, The Ramparts Press, 2nd edn.

Welch S, Miewald R (1983). *Scarce Natural Resources. The Challenge to Public Policy-making*. Sage Publications.

Wernick A (2018). Biodiversity loss has an enormous impact on humans. *Living on Earth*, April 21. URL https://www.pri.org/stories/2018-04-21/biodiversity-loss-has-enormous-impact-humans-according-un-report.

Whitaker JR (1940). World view of destruction and conservation of natural resources. *Annals of the Association of American Geographers*, 30(3), 143–162.

Whitehead AN (1917). *The Organization of Thought*. Williams and Norgate. URL https://archive.org/details/organisationofth00whit.

Whitehouse D (2015). 2014 global temperature stalls another year. *Global Warming Policy Foundation*, January 16. URL http://www.thegwpf.com/2014-global-temperature-stalls-another-year/.

Whyte MK, Feng W, Cai Y (2015). Challenging myths about China's one-child policy. *The China Journal*, 74, 144–159. URL https://scholar.harvard.edu/files/martinwhyte/files/challenging_myths_published_version.pdf.

Wiedmann T, Barrett J (2010). A review of the ecological footprint indicator – Perceptions and methods. *Sustainability*, 2(6), 1645–1693. URL http://www.mdpi.com/2071-1050/2/6/1645.

Williams M (2003). *Deforesting the Earth. From Prehistory to Global Crisis*. University of Chicago Press.

Williamson HF, Daum AR (1959). *The American Petroleum Industry. The Age of Illumination 1859–1899*. Northwestern University Press.

Wilson R (2013). Limiting population growth is not the answer to global warming. 'Elephant in the room' has weak relationship to greater carbon emissions. *The Breakthrough*, October 28. URL https://thebreakthrough.org/index.php/programs/energy-and-climate/limiting-population-growth-is-not-the-answer-to-global-warming.

Wolfe AB (1928). The population problem since the World War: A survey of literature and research. *Journal of Political Economy*, 36(5), 529–559.

Wright CD (1904). Science and economics. *Science*, 20(352), 897–909.

Wrigley EA (1969). *Population and History*. World University Library.

Wrigley EA (1988). *Continuity, Chance and Change*. Cambridge University Press.

Wrigley T (2011). Opening Pandora's Box: A new look at the Industrial Revolution. *VOX*, July 22. URL https://voxeu.org/article/industrial-revolution-energy-revolution.

WWF (2016). Ecological footprint. WWF webpage. URL http://wwf.panda.org/about_our_earth/all_publications/ecological_footprint2/.

Wyatt S, Milojevic S, Park HW, Leydesdorff L (2017). Intellectual and practical contributions of scientometrics to STS. In: U Felt, R Fouché, CA Miller, L Smith-Doerr (eds.), *The Handbook of Science and Technology Studies*, MIT Press.

Wynes S, Nicholas KA (2017). The climate mitigation gap: Education and government recommendations miss the most effective individual actions. *Environmental Research Letters*, 12(7), 091001.

Yandle B, Bhattarai M, Vijayaraghavan M (2002). The Environmental Kuznets Curve: A Primer. Research Study 02–1. URL https://www.perc.org/wp-content/uploads/2018/05/environmental-kuznets-curve-primer.pdf.

Zaichun SP, Myneni RB, Huang M, Zeng Z, Canadell JG, Ciais P, Sitch S, Friedlingstein P, Arneth A, Cao C, Cheng L, Kato E, Koven C, Li Y, Lian X, Liu Y, Liu R, Mao J, Pan Y, Peng S, nuelas JP, Poulter B, Pugh TAM, Stocker BD, Viovy N, Wang X, Wang Y, Xiao Z, Yang H, Zaehle S, Zeng N (2016). Greening of the Earth and its drivers. *Nature Climate Change*, 6, 791–795.

Zaretsky R (2016). Donald Trump and the myth of mobocracy: How the dubious ideas of a 19th century Frenchman reverberate in 2016. *The Atlantic*, July 27. URL https://www.theatlantic.com/international/archive/2016/07/trump-le-bon-mob/493118/.

Zimmermann EW (1933). *World Resources and Industries. A Functional Appraisal of the Availability of Agricultural and Industrial Resources*. Harper & Brothers.

Zubrin R (2012a). *Merchants of Despair. Radical Environmentalists, Criminal Pseudo-Scientists, and the Fatal Cult of Antihumanism*. New Atlantis. URL https://www.thenewatlantis.com/publications/merchants-of-despair.

Zubrin R (2012b). The population control holocaust. *The New Atlantis*, Spring. URL https://www.thenewatlantis.com/publications/the-population-control-holocaust.

Zubrin R (2014). The carbon-benefit deniers. *National Review Online*, September 26. URL http://www.nationalreview.com/energy-week/388902/carbon-benefit-deniers-robert-zubrin.

Index

About the GWPF

The Global Warming Policy Foundation is an all-party and non-party think tank and a registered educational charity which, while openminded on the contested science of global warming, is deeply concerned about the costs and other implications of many of the policies currently being advocated.

Our main focus is to analyse global warming policies and their economic and other implications. Our aim is to provide the most robust and reliable economic analysis and advice. Above all we seek to inform the media, politicians and the public, in a newsworthy way, on the subject in general and on the misinformation to which they are all too frequently being subjected at the present time.

The key to the success of the GWPF is the trust and credibility that we have earned in the eyes of a growing number of policy makers, journalists and the interested public. The GWPF is funded overwhelmingly by voluntary donations from a number of private individuals and charitable trusts. In order to make clear its complete independence, it does not accept gifts from either energy companies or anyone with a significant interest in an energy company.

Views expressed in the publications of the Global Warming Policy Foundation are those of the authors, not those of the GWPF, its trustees, its Academic Advisory Council members or its directors.

Made in the USA
Middletown, DE
23 December 2018